PEST AND PARASITES

CONTROL AND ELIMINATION STRATEGIES

ENV BOOKS SERIES

PEST AND PARASITES

CONTROL AND ELIMINATION STRATEGIES

Editor

Dr. Pawan Kumar 'Bharti'

Society for Environment, Health
Awareness of Nutrition & Toxicology (SEHAT)
B-225/5D, Top Floor, Subhash Gali, Road No. 7, Block B
Ashok Nagar, Shahdara
Delhi-110093
(India)

DPH

DISCOVERY PUBLISHING HOUSE PVT. LTD.
INDIA

Published by:
Namit Wasan
DISCOVERY PUBLISHING HOUSE PVT. LTD.
4383/4B, Ansari Road, Darya Ganj
New Delhi-110 002 (India)
Phone : +91-11-23279245; 23253475; 43596065
E-mail : discoverybooksindia@gmail.com
discoverypublishinghouse@gmail.com
namitwasan9@gmail.com
web : www.discoverypublishinggroup.com

***First Edition:* 2019**

ISBN: 978-93-86841-99-5

Pest and Parasites: ***Control and Elimination Strategies***

Printed at:
Infinity Imaging Systems
Delhi

PREFACE

Parasites are plants or animals that live on or in a host getting their nutrients from that host. A host is an organism that supports a parasite. Sometimes the host is harmed by the parasite, and sometimes the relationship is neutral. But the host never benefits from the arrangement. When the parasite does have a negative impact on the host, it doesn't often kill the host directly, but the stressors that come with having parasites can kill.

A parasite is an organism that lives on or in a host and gets its food from or at the expense of its host. Parasites can cause disease in humans. Some parasitic diseases are easily treated and some are not. The burden of these diseases often rests on communities in the tropics and subtropics, but parasitic infections also affect people in developed countries.

Parasites are classified based on their interactions with their hosts and on their life cycles. An obligate parasite is totally dependent on the host to complete its life cycle, while a facultative parasite is not. A direct parasite has only one host while an indirect parasite has multiple hosts. For indirect parasites, there will always be a definitive host and an intermediate host.

The present book updates the subject content of pest control, ecto-parasites, phytoparasitic nematods, parasitic infection of fish, integrated pest management, pin work control of few plants, pest control of rodents and ectoparasites of farm animals.

Thanks are due to publisher and contributors from various institutions and universities.

The book will be helpful for the researchers, academia working in the field of pest control, ecto-parasites, phytoparasitic nematods, parasitic infection of fish, integrated pest management, pin work control of few plants, pest control of rodents and ectoparasites of farm animals.

Editors
(envbooks@gmail.com)

CONTENTS

Preface

1. Parasite and Parasitism : *An Introduction* 1
2. Biorationale Strategies for Management of Phytoparasitic Nematodes Associated with Banana 21
   Nimisha A. M., Nisha M. S., and Esakkimuthu M.
3. Integrated Pest Management for Rodent in Buildings 48
   Abd El-Aleem Saad Soliman Desoky
4. Global Scenario of Tomato Pin Worm, Tuta Absoluta (Meyrick) and their Management 54
   V.K. Mishra, N.N. Singh and Varucha Misra
5. Ecto-Parasites of Farm Animals: *Alleviation and Control Measures* 61
   Abd El-Aleem Saad Soliman Desoky
6. Field Release and Evaluation Techniques of Bio Control Agents in Integrated Pest Management 136
   D. Sudha Rani, Ch. Chiranjeevi, T. Madhumathi and S. Krishnam Raju
7. New Trends in Control of Parasitic Infections in Marine Fish 160
   Hussien A.M. Osman and Mona S. Zaki

Index 191

Pest and Parasites : *Control & Elimination Strategies* **Pages 1–20**
***Edited by:* Dr. Pawan Kr. 'Bharti'**
ISBN: 978-93-86841-99-5
***Edition:* 2019**
***Published by:* Discovery Publishing House Pvt. Ltd., New Delhi (India)**

1 Parasite and Parasitism
An Introduction

Definitions

1. An organism that lives on or in an organism of another species, known as the host, from the body of which it obtains nutriment.
2. A person who receives support, advantage, or the like, from another or others without giving any useful or proper return, as one who lives on the hospitality of others.
3. In ancient Greece, a person who received free meals in return for amusing or impudent conversation, flattering remarks, etc.
4. Parasites are plants or animals that live on or in a host getting their nutrients from that host. A host is an organism that supports a parasite. Sometimes the host is harmed by the parasite, and sometimes the relationship is neutral. But the host never benefits from the arrangement. When the parasite does have a negative impact on the host, it doesn't often kill the host directly, but the stressors that come with having parasites can kill.

Parasite

A parasite is an organism that lives on or in a host and gets its food from or at the expense of its host. Parasites can cause disease in humans. Some parasitic diseases are easily treated and some are not. The burden of these diseases often rests on communities in the tropics and subtropics, but parasitic infections also affect people in developed countries.

Ectoparasites are parasites that live outside the body. In animals, they live on the skin and can cause itching and rashes. Endoparasites are parasites that live inside the body. For instance, they may live in the blood system, muscles, liver, brain, or digestive systems of animals.

Parasites are not one-size-fits-all. There are several main categories of parasites that can affect animals and plants. Probably the most-studied parasites are the ones that affect humans. Broadly grouped, they include protozoa, helminths, and arthropods. More familiar, less mysterious names are lice, ticks, mites, bed bugs, flukes, and tapeworms.

Protozoa

Protozoa are microscopic, one-celled organisms that can be free-living or parasitic in nature. They are able to multiply in humans, which contributes to their survival and also permits serious infections to develop from just a single organism. Transmission of protozoa that live in a human's intestine to another human typically occurs through a fecal-oral route (for example, contaminated food or water or person-to-person contact). Protozoa that live in the blood or tissue of humans are transmitted to other humans by an arthropod vector (for example, through the bite of a mosquito or sand fly).

Entamoeba Histolytica

The protozoa that are infectious to humans can be classified into four groups based on their mode of movement:

Sarcodina – the ameba, e.g., Entamoeba

Mastigophora – the flagellates, e.g., Giardia, Leishmania

Ciliophora – the ciliates, e.g., Balantidium

Sporozoa – organisms whose adult stage is not motile e.g., Plasmodium, Cryptosporidium

Protozoa are single-celled organisms. They are usually found in food and water that is contaminated by animal waste. Amoebic dysentery and giardia are examples of protozoa infections that invade the digestive system.

In the case of giardia, the symptoms can include diarrhea, stomach cramps, weight loss, and dehydration. Some people have fewer symptoms, but severe infections cause dramatic symptoms.

Other protozoa are spread by a vector, an organism that transmits diseases, like a mosquito, and infect the blood or tissue. Malaria and African sleeping sickness are two protozoa parasites that might be familiar to you. When an infected mosquito taps into your bloodstream to gather blood, they leave the parasites behind.

One particularly interesting protozoa parasite is Toxoplasma gondii. It often infects cats, rodents, and people. Scientists have estimated that 1/3 to 1/2 of all people have the parasite. Humans get it from eating infected sheep, pigs, cows, and from exposure to infected cat feces.

What makes this parasite surprising is that it affects behavior. Infected rodents lose their fear of cat urine, which raises their chances of getting eaten by cats. That passes the parasite to cats.

In most people with Toxoplasma gondii, there are few symptoms of an infection, or perhaps they will have a short stint with flu-like symptoms. But in some people, it is thought to cause schizophrenia, suicides, and reduced reaction time.

Helminth, Arthropod, and Plant Parasites

Helminths are large, multicellular organisms that are generally visible to the naked eye in their adult stages. Like protozoa, helminths can be either free-living or parasitic in nature. In their adult form, helminths cannot multiply in humans. There are three main groups of helminths (derived from the Greek word for worms) that are human parasites:

Flatworms (platyhelminths) – these include the trematodes (flukes) and cestodes (tapeworms).

Thorny-headed worms (acanthocephalins) – the adult forms of these worms reside in the gastrointestinal tract. The acanthocephala are thought to be intermediate between the cestodes and nematodes.

Roundworms (nematodes) – the adult forms of these worms can reside in the gastrointestinal tract, blood, lymphatic system or subcutaneous tissues. Alternatively, the immature (larval) states can cause disease through their infection of various body tissues. Some consider the helminths to also include the segmented worms (annelids)—the only ones important medically are the leeches. Of note, these organisms are not typically considered parasites.

Helminth parasites might be what most people picture parasites would look like. It includes the worm-like parasites, such as roundworms, tapeworms, and flukes. They are passed to people from contaminated water and food; they can burrow into bare feet if they are in the soil, and they can be passed by way of a vector.

The helminth that causes schistosomiasis is transmitted to humans by burrowing into skin while swimming in water that is infested with Schistosoma. Liver flukes, which are fairly common in some regions of the world, infect people when they eat raw or undercooked freshwater fish (think: sushi). They are flatworms that live in the liver's bile ducts.

Arthropods are invertebrate animals with jointed appendages, segmented bodies, and exoskeletons such as crustaceans, insects and arachnids. Not all arthropods are parasites themselves, but they can be temporary hosts.

Some of our most dreaded parasitic diseases are passed along by arthropods:

- Mosquitoes carry malaria and yellow fever.
- Sandflies carry leishmaniasis.
- Fleas that live on some rodents carry plague.
- Mites transmit scabies.
- Let's not forget ticks, which can give us Lyme disease and Rocky Mountain spotted fever.

Ectoparasites

Although the term ectoparasites can broadly include blood-sucking arthropods such as mosquitoes (because they are dependent on a blood meal from a human host for their survival), this term is generally used more narrowly to refer to organisms such as ticks, fleas, lice, and mites that attach or burrow into the skin and remain there for relatively long periods of time (e.g., weeks to months). Arthropods are important in causing diseases in their own right, but are even more important as vectors, or transmitters, of many different pathogens that in turn cause tremendous morbidity and mortality from the diseases they cause.

Parasitic Infections

Parasitic infections cause a tremendous burden of disease in both the tropics and subtropics as well as in more temperate climates. Of all parasitic diseases, malaria causes the most deaths globally. Malaria kills approximately 660,000 people each year, most of them young children in sub-Saharan Africa.

The Neglected Tropical Diseases (NTDs), which have suffered from a lack of attention by the public health community, include parasitic diseases such as lymphatic filariasis, onchocerciasis, and Guinea worm disease. The NTDs affect more than 1 billion people—one-sixth of the world's population—largely in rural areas of low-income countries. These diseases extract a large toll on endemic populations, including lost ability to attend school or work, retardation of growth in children, impairment of cognitive skills and development in young children, and the serious economic burden placed on entire countries.

However, parasitic infections also affect persons living in developed countries, including the United States.

Diseases

Parasites are living things that use other living things - like your body - for food and a place to live. You can get them from contaminated food or water, a bug bite, or sexual contact. Some parasitic diseases are easily treated and some are not.

Parasites range in size from tiny, one-celled organisms called protozoa to worms that can be seen with the naked eye. Some parasitic diseases occur in the United States. Contaminated water supplies can lead to Giardia infections. Cats can transmit toxoplasmosis, which is dangerous for pregnant women. Others, like malaria, are common in other parts of the world.

If you are traveling, it's important to drink only water you know is safe. Prevention is especially important. There are no vaccines for parasitic diseases. Some medicines are available to treat parasitic infections.

Diagnosis of Parasitic Diseases

Many kinds of lab tests are available to diagnose parasitic diseases. The kind of test(s) your health care provider will order will be based on your signs and symptoms, any other medical conditions you may have, and your travel history. Diagnosis may be difficult, so your health care provider may order more than one kind of test.

What kinds of tests are used to diagnose parasitic diseases?

See below for a list of some commonly used tests your health care provider may order.

1. **A fecal (stool) exam, also called an ova and parasite test (O&P)**

   This test is used to find parasites that cause diarrhea, loose or watery stools, cramping, flatulence (gas) and other abdominal illness. CDC recommends that three or more stool samples, collected on separate days, be examined. This test looks for ova (eggs) or the parasite.

   Your health care provider may instruct you to put your stool specimens into special containers with preservative fluid. Specimens not collected in a preservative fluid should be refrigerated, but not frozen, until delivered to the lab or the health care provider's office.

   Your health care provider may request that the lab use special stains or that special test be performed to look for parasites not routinely screened for.

2. **Endoscopy/Colonoscopy**

   Endoscopy is used to find parasites that cause diarrhea, loose or watery stools, cramping, flatulence (gas) and other abdominal illness. This test is used when stool exams do not reveal the cause of your diarrhea. This test is a procedure in which a tube is inserted into the mouth (endoscopy) or rectum (colonoscopy) so that the doctor, usually a gastroenterologist, can examine the intestine. This test looks for the parasite or other abnormalities that may be causing your signs and symptoms.

3. **Blood tests**

   Some, but not all, parasitic infections can be detected by testing your blood. Blood tests look for a specific parasite infection; there is no blood test that will look for all parasitic infections. There are two general kinds of blood tests that your doctor may order:

A. Serology

This test is used to look for antibodies or for parasite antigens produced when the body is infected with a parasite and the immune system is trying to fight off the invader.

This test is done by your health care provider taking a blood sample and sending it to a lab.

B. Blood smear

This test is used to look for parasites that are found in the blood. By looking at a blood smear under a microscope, parasitic diseases such as filariasis, malaria, or babesiosis, can be diagnosed.

This test is done by placing a drop of blood on a microscope slide. The slide is then stained and examined under a microscope.

X-ray, Magnetic Resonance Imaging (MRI) scan, Computerized Axial Tomography scan (CAT).

These tests are used to look for some parasitic diseases that may cause lesions in the organs.

Parasitism

In biology/ecology, parasitism is a non-mutual symbiotic relationship between species, where one species, the parasite, benefits at the expense of the other, the host. Traditionally parasite (in biological usage) referred primarily to organisms visible to the naked eye, or macroparasites (such as helminths). Parasites can be microparasites, which are typically smaller, such as protozoa, viruses, and bacteria. Examples of parasites include the plants mistletoe and cuscuta, and animals such as hookworms.

Unlike predators, parasites typically do not kill their host, are generally much smaller than their host, and will often live in or on their host for an extended period. Both are special cases of consumer-resource interactions. Parasites show a high degree of specialization, and reproduce at a faster rate than their hosts. Classic examples of parasitism include interactions between vertebrate hosts and tapeworms, flukes, the Plasmodium species, and fleas. Parasitism differs from the parasitoid relationship in that parasitoids generally kill their hosts.

Parasites reduce host biological fitness by general or specialized pathology, such as parasitic castration and impairment of secondary sex characteristics, to the modification of host behavior. Parasites increase their own fitness by exploiting hosts for resources necessary for their survival, e.g. food, water, heat, habitat, and transmission[clarification needed]. Although parasitism applies unambiguously to many cases, it is part of a continuum of types of interactions between species, rather than an exclusive category. In many cases, it is difficult to demonstrate harm to the host. In others, there may be no apparent specialization on the part of the parasite, or the interaction between the organisms may remain short-lived.

First used in English 1539, the word parasite comes from the Medieval French parasite, from the Latin parasitus, the latinisation of the Greek παράσιτος (parasitos), "one who eats at the table of another" and that from παρά (para), "beside, by" + σῖτος (sitos), "wheat". Coined in English in 1611, the word parasitism comes from the Greek παρά (para) + σιτισμός (sitismos) "feeding, fattening". In its original sense, it was not strictly pejorative in nature; being a parasitos was an accepted lifestyle, whereby a person could live off the hospitality of others, and in return provide "flattery, simple services, and a willingness to endure humiliation".

Types of Parasites

Parasites are classified based on their interactions with their hosts and on their life cycles. An obligate parasite is totally dependent on the host to complete its life cycle, while a facultative parasite is not. A direct parasite has only one host while an indirect parasite has multiple hosts. For indirect parasites, there will always be a definitive host and an intermediate host.

Human head lice (Pediculus humanus capitis) are ectoparasites.

Parasites that live on the outside of the host, either on the skin or the outgrowths of the skin, are called ectoparasites (e.g. lice, fleas, and some mites).

Those that live inside the host are called endoparasites (including all parasitic worms). Endoparasites can exist in one of two forms: intercellular parasites (inhabiting spaces in the host's body) or intracellular parasites (inhabiting cells in the host's body). Intracellular parasites, such as protozoa, bacteria or viruses, tend to rely on a third organism, which is generally known as the carrier or vector. The vector does the job of transmitting them to the host. An example of this interaction is the transmission of malaria, caused by a protozoan of the genus Plasmodium, to humans by the bite of an anopheline mosquito.

Those parasites living in an intermediate position, being half-ectoparasites and half-endoparasites, are called mesoparasites.

Schistosoma mansoni is an endoparasite that lives in human blood vessels.

An epiparasite is one that feeds on another parasite. This relationship is also sometimes referred to as hyperparasitism, exemplified by a protozoan (the hyperparasite) living in the digestive tract of a flea living on a dog.

Social parasites take advantage of interactions between members of social organisms such as ants, termites, and bumblebees. Examples include Phengaris arion, a butterfly whose larvae employ mimicry to parasitize certain species of ants, Bombus bohemicus, a bumblebee who invades the hives of other species of bee and takes over reproduction, their young raised by host workers, and Melipona scutellaris, a eusocial bee where virgin queens escape killer workers and invade another colony without a queen. An extreme example of social parasitism is the ant species of Tetramorium inquilinum of the Alps, which spend their whole lives on the back of Tetramorium host ants. With tiny and deprecated bodies they have evolved for one single task: holding on to their host. If they fall off, they most likely would not have the strength to climb back on top of another ant, and eventually they will die.

In kleptoparasitism (from the Greek κλέπτης (kleptes), thief), parasites appropriate food gathered by the host. An example is the brood parasitism practiced by cowbirds, whydahs, cuckoos, and black-headed ducks which do not build nests of their own and leave their eggs in nests of other species. The host behaves as a "babysitter" as they raise the young as their own. If the host removes the cuckoo's eggs, some cuckoos will return and attack the nest to compel host birds to remain subject to this parasitism.

Intraspecific social parasitism may also occur. One example of this is parasitic nursing, where some individuals take milk from unrelated females. In wedge-capped capuchins, higher ranking females sometimes take milk from low ranking females without any reciprocation. The high ranking females benefit at the expense of the low ranking females.

Parasitism can take the form of isolated cheating or exploitation among more generalized mutualistic interactions. For example, broad classes of plants and fungi exchange carbon and nutrients in common mutualistic mycorrhizal relationships; however, some plant species known as myco-heterotrophs "cheat" by taking carbon from a fungus rather than donating it.

An adelpho-parasite (from the Greek αδελφός (adelphos), brother) is a parasite in which the host species is closely related to the parasite, often being a member of the same family or genus. An example of this is the citrus blackfly parasitoid, Encarsia perplexa, unmated females of which may lay haploid eggs in the fully developed larvae of their own species. These result in the production of male offspring. The marine worm Bonellia viridis has a similar reproductive strategy, although the larvae are planktonic.

Autoinfection is the infection of a primary host with a parasite, particularly a helminth, in such a way that the complete life cycle of the parasite happens in a single organism, without the involvement of another host. Therefore, the primary host is at the same time the secondary host of the parasite. Some of the organisms where autoinfection occurs are Strongyloides stercoralis, Enterobius vermicularis, Taenia solium, and Hymenolepis nana. Strongyloidiasis for example involves premature transformation of noninfective larvae in infective larvae, which can then penetrate the intestinal mucosa (internal autoinfection) or the skin of the perineal area (external autoinfection). Infection can be maintained by repeated migratory cycles for the remainder of the person's life.

Animal Defenses

Skin

The first line of defense against invading parasites is the skin. Skin is made up of layers of dead cells and acts as a physical barrier to invading organisms. These dead cells contain the protein keratin, which makes skin tough and waterproof. Most microorganisms needs a moist environment to survive. By keeping the skin dry, it prevents invading organisms from colonizing. Furthermore, human skin also secretes sebum, which is toxic to most microorganisms.

Mouth

The mouth contains saliva, which prevents foreign organisms from getting into the body orally. Furthermore, the mouth also contains lysozyme, an enzyme found in tears and the saliva. This enzyme breaks down cell walls of invading microorganisms.

Stomach

Should the organism pass the mouth, the stomach is the next line of defense. The stomach contains hydrochloric acid and gastric acids, which makes its pH level around 2. In this environment, the acidity of the stomach helps kill most microorganisms that try to invade the body through the gastric intestinal tract.

Eyes

Parasites can also invade the body through the eyes. The lashes on the eyelid prevents invading microorganisms from entering the eye in the first place. Even if the microorganism does get into the eye, tears contain the enzyme lysozyme, which will kill most invading microorganisms.

Immune System

Should the parasite enter the body, the immune system is a vertebrate's major defense against parasitic invasion. The immune system is made up of different families of molecules. These include serum proteins and pattern recognition receptors (PRRs). PRRs are intracellular and cellular receptors that activate dendritic cells, which in turn activate the adaptive immune system's lymphocytes. Lymphocytes such as the T cells and antibody producing B cells with variable receptors that recognize parasites.

Insect Defenses

Insects often adapt their nests to aid in parasite defense. For example, one of the key reasons the Polistes canadensis nests across multiple combs rather than building a single comb like much of the rest of its genus is as a defense mechanism against the infestation of tineid moths. The tineid moth lays its eggs within the wasps' nests and then these eggs hatch into larvae that can burrow from cell to cell and prey on wasp pupae. Adult wasps attempt to remove and kill moth eggs and larvae by chewing down the edges of cells, coating the cells with an oral secretion that gives the nest a dark brownish appearance.

Plant Defenses

In response to parasitic attack, plants undergo a series of metabolic and biochemical reaction pathways that will enact defensive responses. For example, parasitic invasion causes an increase in the jasmonic acid-insensitivel (JA) and NahG (SA) pathway. These pathways produce chemicals that induce defensive responses, such as the production of chemicals or defensive molecules to fight off the attack. Different biochemical pathways are activated by different parasites. In general, there are two types of responses that can be activated by the pathways. Plants can either initiate a specific or non-specific response. Specific responses involve gene-gene recognition of the plant and parasite. This can be mediated by the ability of the plant's cell receptors recognizing and binding molecules that are located on the cell surface of parasites. Once the plant's receptors recognizes the parasite, the plant localizes the defensive compounds to that area creating a hypersensitive response. This form of defense mechanism localizes the area of attack and keeps the parasite from spreading. Furthermore, a specific response against parasitic attack prevents the plants from wasting its energy by increasing defenses where it's not need. However, specific defensive responses only target specific parasites. If the plant lacks the ability to recognize a parasite, specific defense responses won't be activated. Nonspecific defensive responses work against all parasites. These responses are active over time and are systematic, meaning that the responses are not confined to an area of the plant, but rather spread throughout the entirety of the organism. However, nonspecific responses are energy costly, since the plant has to ensure that the genes producing the nonspecific responses are always expressed.

Evolutionary Aspects

Parasitism has arisen independently many times. Depending on the definition used, as many as half of all animals have at least one parasitic phase in their life cycles, and is frequent in plants and fungi. Almost all free-living animals are host to one or more parasitic taxa.

Parasites evolve in response to their hosts' defences, sometimes in a manner specific to a particular host taxon and specializing to the point where they infect only a single species. Such narrow host specificity can be costly over evolutionary time, however, if the host species becomes extinct. Therefore, many parasites can infect a variety of more or less closely related host species, with different success rates.

In turn, host defenses coevolve in response to attacks by parasites. Theoretically, parasites may have an advantage in this evolutionary arms race because their generation time commonly is shorter. Hosts reproduce less quickly than parasites, and therefore have fewer chances to adapt than their parasites do over a given span of time.

Long-term coevolution sometimes leads to a relatively stable relationship tending to commensalism or mutualism, as, all else being equal, it is in the evolutionary interest of the parasite that its host thrives. A parasite may evolve to become less harmful for its host or a host may evolve to cope with the unavoidable presence of a parasite—to the point that the parasite's absence causes the host harm. For example, although animals infected with parasitic worms are often clearly harmed, and therefore parasitized, such infections may also reduce the prevalence and effects of autoimmune disorders in animal hosts, including humans. In a more extreme example, some nematode worms cannot reproduce, or even survive, without infection by Wolbachia bacteria.

Competition between parasites tends to favor faster reproducing and therefore more virulent parasites. Parasites whose life cycle involves the death of the host, to exit the present host and sometimes to enter the next, evolve to be more virulent or even alter the behavior or other properties of the host to make it more vulnerable to predators. Parasites that reproduce largely to the offspring of the previous host tend to become less virulent or mutualist, so that its hosts reproduce more effectively.

The presumption of a shared evolutionary history between parasites and hosts can sometimes elucidate how host taxa are related. For instance, there has been dispute about whether flamingos are more closely related to the storks and their relatives, or to ducks, geese and their relatives. The fact that flamingos share parasites with ducks and geese is evidence these groups may be more closely related to each other than either is to storks.

Parasitism is part of one explanation for the evolution of secondary sex characteristics seen in breeding males throughout the animal world, such as the plumage of male peacocks and manes of male lions. According to this theory, female hosts select males for breeding based on such characteristics because they indicate resistance to parasites and other disease.

Co-speciation

In rare cases, a parasite may even undergo co-speciation with its host. One particularly remarkable example of co-speciation exists between the simian foamy virus (SFV) and its primate hosts. In one study, the phylogenies of SFV polymerase and the mitochondrial cytochrome oxidase subunit II from African and Asian primates were compared. Surprisingly, the phylogenetic trees were very congruent in branching order and divergence times. Thus, the simian foamy viruses may have co-speciated with Old World primates for at least 30 million years.

Evolutionary events like host switch, host shift, the duplication or extinction of parasite species (without similar events on the host phylogeny) often erode topographical similarities between host and parasite phylogenies.

ECOLOGY

Quantitative Ecology

A single parasite species usually has an aggregated distribution across host individuals, which means that most hosts harbor few parasites, while a few hosts carry the vast majority of parasite individuals. This poses considerable problems for students of parasite ecology: the use of parametric statistics should be avoided. Log-transformation of data before the application of parametric test, or the use of non-parametric statistics is recommended by several authors. However, this can give rise to further problems.Therefore, modern day quantitative parasitology is based on more advanced biostatistical methods.

Diversity Ecology

Hosts represent discrete habitat patches that can be occupied by parasites. A hierarchical set of terminology has come into use to describe parasite assemblages at different host scales.

Infrapopulation: All the parasites of one species in a single individual host.

Metapopulation: All the parasites of one species in a host population.

Infracommunity: All the parasites of all species in a single individual host.

Component community: All the parasites of all species in a host population.

Compound community: All the parasites of all species in all host species in an ecosystem.

The diversity ecology of parasites differs markedly from that of free-living organisms. For free-living organisms, diversity ecology features many strong conceptual frameworks including Robert MacArthur and E. O. Wilson's theory of island biogeography, Jared Diamond's assembly rules and, more recently, null models such as Stephen Hubbell's unified neutral theory of biodiversity and biogeography. Frameworks are not so well-developed for parasites and in many ways they do not fit the free-living models. For example, island biogeography is predicated on fixed spatial relationships between habitat patches ("sinks"), usually with reference to a mainland ("source"). Parasites inhabit hosts, which represent mobile habitat patches with dynamic spatial relationships. There is no true "mainland" other than the sum of hosts (host population), so parasite component communities in host populations are metacommunities.

Nonetheless, different types of parasite assemblages have been recognized in host individuals and populations, and many of the patterns observed for free-living organisms are also pervasive among parasite assemblages. The most prominent of these is the interactive-isolationist continuum. This proposes that parasite assemblages occur along a cline from interactive communities, where niches are saturated and interspecific competition is high, to isolationist communities, where there are many vacant niches and interspecific interaction is not as important as stochastic factors in providing structure to the community. Whether this is so, or whether community patterns simply reflect the sum of underlying species distributions (no real "structure" to the community), has not yet been established.

Adaptation

Parasites infect hosts that exist within their same geographical area (sympatric) more effectively. This phenomenon supports the "Red Queen hypothesis—which states that interactions between species (such as host and parasites) lead to constant natural selection for adaptation and counter adaptation." The parasites track the locally common host phenotypes, therefore the parasites are less infective to allopatric (from different geographical region) hosts.

Experiments published in 2000 discuss the analysis of two different snail populations from two different sources—Lake Ianthe and Lake Poerua in New Zealand. The populations were exposed to two pure parasites (digenetic trematode) taken from the same lakes. In the experiment, the snails were infected by their sympatric parasites, allopatric parasites and mixed sources of parasites. The results suggest that the parasites were more highly effective in infecting their sympatric snails than their allopatric snails. Though the allopatric snails were still infected by the parasites, the infectivity was much less when compared to the sympatric snails. Hence, the parasites were found to have adapted to infecting local populations of snails.

Transmission

Parasites have a variety of methods to infect hosts. For example, the Acanthamoeba enters the body when the environment is not hostile, and Strongyloides stercoralis enters the body when a host steps on infected ground while barefoot. Many parasites enter the food of their hosts and wait to be eaten. Plasmodium malariae uses a mosquito host to transmit malaria, and Loa loa parasites use deer flies to enter hosts.

Parasites inhabit living organisms and therefore face problems that free-living organisms do not. Hosts, the only habitats in which parasites can survive, actively try to avoid, repel, and destroy parasites. Parasites employ numerous strategies for getting from one host to another, a process sometimes referred to as parasite transmission or colonization.

Some endoparasites infect their host by penetrating its external surface, while others must be ingested. Once inside the host, adult endoparasites need to shed offspring into the external environment to infect other hosts. Many adult endoparasites reside in the host's gastrointestinal tract, where offspring can be shed along with host excreta. Adult stages of tapeworms, thorny-headed worms and most flukes use this method.

Among protozoan endoparasites, such as the malarial parasites and trypanosomes, infective stages in the host's blood are transported to new hosts by biting-insects, or vectors.

Larval stages of endoparasites often infect sites in the host other than the blood or gastrointestinal tract. In many such cases, larval endoparasites require their host to be consumed by the next host in the parasite's life cycle in order to survive and reproduce. Alternatively, larval endoparasites may shed free-living transmission stages that migrate through the host's tissue into the external environment, where they actively search for or await ingestion by other hosts. The foregoing strategies are used, variously, by larval stages of tapeworms, thorny-headed worms, flukes and parasitic roundworms.

Some ectoparasites, such as monogenean worms, rely on direct contact between hosts. Ectoparasitic arthropods may rely on host-host contact (e.g. many lice), shed eggs that survive off the host (e.g. fleas), or wait in the external environment for an encounter with a host (e.g. ticks). Some aquatic leeches locate hosts by sensing movement and only attach when certain temperature and chemical cues are present.

Some parasites modify host behavior in order to increase the transmission between hosts, often in relation to predator and prey (parasite increased trophic transmission). For example, in California salt marshes, the fluke Euhaplorchis californiensis reduces the ability of its killifish host to avoid predators. This parasite matures in egrets, which are more likely to feed on infected killifish than on uninfected fish. Another example is the protozoan Toxoplasma gondii, a parasite that matures in cats but can be carried by many other mammals. Uninfected rats avoid cat odors, but rats infected with T. gondii are drawn to this scent, which may increase transmission to feline hosts.

Roles in Ecosystems

Modifying the behavior of infected hosts, to make transmission to other hosts more likely to occur, is one way parasites can affect the structure of ecosystems. For example, in the case of Euhaplorchis californiensis (discussed above) it is plausible that the local predator and prey species might be different if this parasite were absent from the system.

Although parasites are often omitted in depictions of food webs, they usually occupy the top position. Parasites can function like keystone species, reducing the dominance of superior competitors and allowing competing species to co-exist.

Many parasites require multiple hosts of the different species to complete their life cycles and rely on predator-prey or other stable ecological interactions to get from one host to another. In this sense, the parasites in an ecosystem reflect the health of that system.

Significance

Although parasites are generally considered to be harmful, the eradication of all parasites would not necessarily be beneficial. Parasites account for as much as or more than half of life's diversity; they perform an important ecological role (by weakening prey) that ecosystems would take some time to adapt to; and without parasites organisms may eventually tend to asexual reproduction, diminishing the diversity of sexually dimorphic traits. Parasites provide an opportunity for the transfer of genetic material between species. On rare, but significant, occasions this may facilitate evolutionary changes that would not otherwise occur, or that would otherwise take even longer.

Ectoparasites are organisms which inhabit the skin or outgrowths of the skin of another organism (the host) for various periods, and may be detrimental to the latter.

Various ectoparasites cause significant infestations in many kinds of domestic animals including livestock, pets, laboratory animals, poultry, fish and bees. Many of these ectoparasites (e.g. most lice) are host specific , while others (e.g. man y ticks) parasitize a wider range of hosts. Several ectoparasites currently associated with domestic animals have been acquired by the introduction of either host or parasite into new regions, as animals have become domesticated throughout the world. For example, cattle, goats, and other important domestic livestock species have been introduce d into much of Africa , where they may now fall victim to the ravage s of native tsetse flies (Glossina spp.) an d ticks, as well as pathogen s transmitted by these parasites. Relatively rapid intercontinental transportation of these animals has compounded the problem.

T h e vast majority of ectoparasites are invertebrates. Most invertebrate ectoparasites are arthropods; insects and arachnids typically parasitize terrestrial domestic animals, while crustaceans are associated with fish.

Many ectoparasites are known to be vectors of pathogens, which the parasites typically transmit to hosts while feeding or (occasionally) defaecating. However, ectoparasites - especially in large aggregations - ma y also debilitate domestic animals in other ways, by causing the following disorders:

- anaemia
- detrimental immune reactions (hypersensitivity, anaphylaxis, etc.)
- irritability
- dermatitis
- skin necrosis
- low weight gains (particularly important in livestock)
- secondary infection
- focal haemorrhages

- blockage of orifices (ears, etc.)
- inoculation of toxins
- exsanguination (occasionally).

Subdermally-located parasitic larval stages of certain flies cause a condition termed 'myiasis', which may lead to significant tissue damage and secondary infection (11, 50, 100).

Nevertheless, ectoparasite infestations of many domestic animals are minor and seem to cause little harm to the host.

This introductory chapter will briefly outline the main characteristics, higher-level classification and economic importance of the principal metazoan ectoparasites affecting domestic animals. Less coverage is given to ectoparasites associated with laboratory animals, an d for further details o n this subject, readers are referred to a previous review (28). However, more information is provide d on ectoparasites of bees and fish, as these area s are not dealt with elsewhere in this volume , and also on those of birds, not fully covered elsewhere. This chapter attempts to follow a natural (phylogenetic) classification for the ectoparasites discussed. Table I is a taxonomic compilation of the principal ectoparasites of various domestic animals and the main pathogen s transmitted by these parasites. Both in Table I and throughout this brief overview, the various taxa of ectoparasites are considered o n an evolutionary scale by sequentially addressing flukes, leeches, arthropods and finally vertebrates.

Alphabatic List of Parasite

A

Acanthamoeba Infection

Acanthamoeba Keratitis Infection

African Sleeping Sickness (African trypanosomiasis)

Alveolar Echinococcosis (Echinococcosis, Hydatid Disease)

Amebiasis (Entamoeba histolytica Infection)

American Trypanosomiasis (Chagas Disease)

Ancylostomiasis (Hookworm)

Angiostrongyliasis (Angiostrongylus Infection)

Anisakiasis (Anisakis Infection, Pseudoterranova Infection)

Ascariasis (Ascaris Infection, Intestinal Roundworms)

B

Babesiosis (Babesia Infection)

Balantidiasis (Balantidium Infection)

Balamuthia

Baylisascariasis (Baylisascaris Infection, Raccoon Roundworm)
Bed Bugs
Bilharzia (Schistosomiasis)
Blastocystis hominis Infection
Body Lice Infestation (Pediculosis)

C

Capillariasis (Capillaria Infection)
Cercarial Dermatitis (Swimmer's Itch)
Chagas Disease (American Trypanosomiasis)
Chilomastix mesnili Infection (Nonpathogenic [Harmless] Intestinal Protozoa)
Clonorchiasis (Clonorchis Infection)
CLM (Cutaneous Larva Migrans, Ancylostomiasis, Hookworm)
"Crabs" (Pubic Lice)
Cryptosporidiosis (Cryptosporidium Infection)
Cutaneous Larva Migrans (CLM, Ancylostomiasis, Hookworm)
Cyclosporiasis (Cyclospora Infection)
Cysticercosis (Neurocysticercosis)
Cystoisospora Infection (Cystoisosporiasis) formerly Isospora Infection

D

Dientamoeba fragilis Infection
Diphyllobothriasis (Diphyllobothrium Infection)
Dipylidium caninum Infection (dog or cat tapeworm infection)
Dirofilariasis (Dirofilaria Infection)
DPDx
Dracunculiasis (Guinea Worm Disease)
Drinking Water
Dog tapeworm (Dipylidium caninum Infection)

E

Echinococcosis (Cystic, Alveolar Hydatid Disease)
Elephantiasis (Filariasis, Lymphatic Filariasis)
Endolimax nana Infection (Nonpathogenic [Harmless] Intestinal Protozoa)
Entamoeba coli Infection (Nonpathogenic [Harmless] Intestinal Protozoa)
Entamoeba dispar Infection (Nonpathogenic [Harmless] Intestinal Protozoa)
Entamoeba hartmanni Infection (Nonpathogenic [Harmless] Intestinal Protozoa)

Entamoeba histolytica Infection (Amebiasis)
Entamoeba polecki
Enterobiasis (Pinworm Infection)

F

Fascioliasis (Fasciola Infection)
Fasciolopsiasis (Fasciolopsis Infection)
Filariasis (Lymphatic Filariasis, Elephantiasis)
Foodborne Diseases

G

Giardiasis (Giardia Infection)
Gnathostomiasis (Gnathostoma Infection)
Guinea Worm Disease (Dracunculiasis)

H

Head Lice Infestation (Pediculosis)
Heterophyiasis (Heterophyes Infection)
Hookworm Infection, Human
Hookworm Infection, Zoonotic (Ancylostomiasis, Cutaneous Larva Migrans [CLM])
Hydatid Disease (Cystic, Alveolar Echinococcosis)
Hymenolepiasis (Hymenolepis Infection)

I

Intestinal Roundworms (Ascariasis, Ascaris Infection)
Iodamoeba buetschlii Infection (Nonpathogenic [Harmless] Intestinal Protozoa)
Isospora Infection (see Cystoisospora Infection)

K

Kala-azar (Leishmaniasis, Leishmania Infection)
Keratitis (Acanthamoeba Infection)

L

Leishmaniasis (Kala-azar, Leishmania Infection)
Lice Infestation (Body, Head, or Pubic Lice, Pediculosis, Pthiriasis)
Loiasis (Loa loa Infection)
Lymphatic filariasis (Filariasis, Elephantiasis)

M

Malaria (Plasmodium Infection)
Microsporidiosis (Microsporidia Infection)

Mite Infestation (Scabies)

Myiasis

N

Naegleria Infection

Neurocysticercosis (Cysticercosis)

Neglected Parasitic Infections in the U.S.

Neglected Tropical Diseases

Nonpathogenic (Harmless) Intestinal Protozoa

O

Ocular Larva Migrans (Toxocariasis, Toxocara Infection, Visceral Larva Migrans)

Onchocerciasis (River Blindness)

Opisthorchiasis (Opisthorchis Infection)

P

Paragonimiasis (Paragonimus Infection)

Pediculosis (Head or Body Lice Infestation)

Pthiriasis (Pubic Lice Infestation)

Pinworm Infection (Enterobiasis)

Plasmodium Infection (Malaria)

Pneumocystis jirovecii Pneumonia

Pseudoterranova Infection (Anisakiasis, Anisakis Infection)

Pubic Lice Infestation ("Crabs," Pthiriasis)

R

Raccoon Roundworm Infection (Baylisascariasis, Baylisascaris Infection)

Recreational Water

River Blindness (Onchocerciasis)

S

Sappinia

Sarcocystosis (Sarcocystosis Infection)

Scabies

Schistosomiasis (Bilharzia)

Sleeping Sickness (Trypanosomiasis, African; African Sleeping Sickness)

Soil-transmitted Helminths

Strongyloidiasis (Strongyloides Infection)

Swimmer's Itch (Cercarial Dermatitis)

Swimming Pools

T

Taeniasis (Taenia Infection, Tapeworm Infection)

Tapeworm Infection (Taeniasis, Taenia Infection)

Toxocariasis (Toxocara Infection, Ocular Larva Migrans, Visceral Larva Migrans)

Toxoplasmosis (Toxoplasma Infection)

Trichinellosis (Trichinosis)

Trichinosis (Trichinellosis)

Trichomoniasis (Trichomonas Infection)

Trichuriasis (Whipworm Infection, Trichuris Infection)

Trypanosomiasis, African (African Sleeping Sickness, Sleeping Sickness)

Trypanosomiasis, American (Chagas Disease)

V

Visceral Larva Migrans (Toxocariasis, Toxocara Infection, Ocular Larva Migrans)

W

Waterborne Diseases

Whipworm Infection (Trichuriasis, Trichuris Infection)

Z

Zoonotic Diseases (Diseases spread from animals to people)

Zoonotic Hookworm Infection (Ancylostomiasis, Cutaneous Larva Migrans [CLM])

REFERENCES

https://en.wikipedia.org/wiki/Parasitism

https://medlineplus.gov/parasiticdiseases.html

http://study.com/academy/lesson/what-is-a-parasite-definition-types-examples.html

https://www.cdc.gov/parasites/az/

https://www.cdc.gov/parasites/

http://study.com/academy/lesson/what-is-a-parasite-definition-types-examples.html

https://www.cdc.gov/parasites/references_resources/diagnosis.html

http://www.dictionary.com/browse/parasite

Pest and Parasites : *Control & Elimination Strategies* Pages 21–47
***Edited by:* Dr. Pawan Kr. 'Bharti'**
ISBN: 978-93-86841-99-5
***Edition:* 2019**
***Published by:* Discovery Publishing House Pvt. Ltd., New Delhi (India)**

2

Biorationale Strategies for Management of Phytoparasitic Nematodes Associated with Banana

[1]Nimisha A. M., [2]Nisha M. S. and Esakkimuthu M.

ABSTRACT

Banana (Musaspp) is one of the most important fruit crop in the tropic as well as subtropics. Phytoparasitic nematodes are one of the major factors negatively affecting the banana production throughout the world. Important plant parasitic nematodes associated with banana are, root knot nematode, Meloidogyne incognita (Kofoid and White), reniform nematode, Rotylenchulusreniformis Linford and Oliveira, spiral nematode, Helicotylenchusdihystera (Cobb) Sher, Cystnematode, Heteroderaoryzicola, burrowing nematode, Radopholussimilis (Cobb), lance nematode, Hoplolaimusindicus, lesion nematode, Pratylenchussp., ring nematode, Criconema spp and dagger nematode, Xiphinema spp. The comparative effect of biofumigation, mulching, bioagents and organic manures for the management of nematodes in the rhizosphere of banana was studied and the results revealed that all the biorationale methods were having significant effect on reducing plant parasitic nematodes in the rhizosphere of banana.

Keywords: Banana, biofumigation, biorationale, Phytoparasitic nematodes, rhizosphere

INTRODUCTION

Banana (*Musa* spp) is one of the most important fruit crop in the tropic as well as subtropics. It has been grown in 107 countries and the fourth most important food crop after rice, wheat and maize in the world. India is the largest producer of banana followed by China, Philippines and Indonesia. In India banana is grown in an area of 8.8 lakh ha with a production of 300 lakh t annum^{-1} with a productivity of 34.1t ha^{-1} (NHB, 2017). It contributes 22 per cent to global production. In India, Tamil Nadu is the largest producer of banana followed by Maharashtra and Karnataka. Phytoparasitic nematodes are one of the major factors negatively affecting the banana production throughout the world. More than 151 nematode species of 51 genera have

[1] Kerala Agricultural University, COA, Vellayani
[2] Kerala Agricultural University, RARS, Pilicode

been documented worldwide (Gowen and Queneherve, 1990). The nematode of major concern in banana production throughout the world is burrowing nematode, *Radopholus similis* (Cobb.) Thorne which cause yield loss of 30 to 60 per cent. Other nematode species *viz.*, lesion nematode, *Pratylenchus coffeae* (Zimmermann.), spiral nematode, *Helicotylenchus multicinctus* (Cobb.) and root-knot nematode, *Meloidogyne incognita* (Kofoid and White.) co-habit with *R. similis* resulting substantial yield loss. Besides direct damage, they serve as predisposing agents in development of disease complexes with fungi and bacteria. Infection by burrowing nematode causes toppling of banana at harvesting stage. The major symptoms include reduced root system with dark and necrotic lesions on roots and rhizomes so that tree falls under weight of fruit or in wind. Banana is one of the major fruit crop cultivated throughout Kerala. Kerala has a productivity of 8.8 t ha^{-1} with a production of 5.45 lakh t $annum^{-1}$ from an area of 61936 ha (FIB, 2017). The major nematode pests of banana in Kerala are *R. similis* and *Heterodera oryzicola* Rao and Jayaprakash. Incidentally, the first report of occurrence of *R. similis* on banana from India was made from Kerala (Nair *et al.*, 1966) where the entire crop was damaged and lost due to its attack. Infestation of cyst nematode, *H. oryzicola* on banana c.v. Nendran was observed for the first time from India was also made from Kerala (Charles and Venkitesan, 1984). Since then nematode has become a potential pest in the banana ecosystem of Kerala. The suitability of a host for plant parasitic nematodes is expressed as the ability of the nematode to multiply on the plant. Information on distribution and reproduction of nematodes in different varieties of banana is important for sustainable production because use of resistant cultivars is considered one of the best and environmentally safe alternatives among the non-chemical methods of nematode management. Commonly used red labelled nematicides *viz.*, phorate and carbofuran have been banned in Kerala. Nowadays organic farming is gaining momentum and Kerala will be converted to a fully organic state in the near future. In the context of safe to eat concept bio intensive management strategy giving emphasis to non-chemical methods have to be undertaken. Therefore, understanding the diversity, community behaviour and population dynamics of the nematodes associated with banana is essential to evolve an eco-friendly management strategy.

Nematode Association in Banana

International level: Plant parasitic nematodes are the major pest of banana throughout the world. A survey lead by Eissa *et al.* (2003) revealed the presence of eight genera of nematodes in the banana orchards grown in four Nile Delta and four Upper Egypt Governorates. The major nematodes obtained from banana roots were *Meloidogyne* sp. and *Helicotylenchus* sp. Kamira *et al.* (2003) reported that *H. multicinctus* (89 per cent), *Meloidogyne* sp. (54 per cent) and *R. similis* (30 per cent) were the most widely distributed nematodes in the rhizosphere of banana in eastern and western Democratic Republic of Congo. *R. similis* was the major plant parasitic nematode associated with banana in Belize (Ramclam and Araya, 2006). It accounts 56-84 per cent of the overall nematode population present in the rhizosphere of banana. *H. multicinctus, Meloidogyne* sp. and *Pratylenchus goodeyi* Sher and Allen were the most abundant plant parasitic nematodes associated with banana in Crete, Greece (Tzortzakakis, 2008). In conventional system of banana cultivation, *R. similis* was the principal phytoparasitic nematode obtained and the population of free living nematodes were low and plant parasites were very high. In organic cultivation of banana, *H. multicinctus* and *Meloidogyne* sp. were the most abundant plant parasitic nematodes recorded. The populations of free-living nematodes were very high in organic production system which includes the beneficial *Mononchus* sp. and Dorylaimids (Rodriguez *et al.*, 2012). In a survey lead by Chitamba *et al.* (2013) in Rusitu Valley, Zimbabwe disclosed that *Meloidogyne* sp., *R. similis, Pratylenchus* sp. and *Helicotylenchus* sp. were the major phyto parasitic nematodes present in the root zone of banana. Study conducted by Zhao *et al.* (2013) in Hainan province, China revealed that *Meloidogyne* sp., *Rotylenchulus* sp., *Pratylenchus* sp., *Ditylenchus* sp., *Helicotylenchus* sp., *Tylenchorhynchus* sp., and *Aphelenchus* sp. were the nematodes associated with banana. *Meloidogyne* sp. and *Rotylenchulus* sp. were the most widely distributed plant parasitic nematodes. Kasapoglu *et al.* (2015) in Turkey revealed that *Helicotylenchus dihystera* (Cobb) Sher, *H. multicinctus, M. incognita* and *Meloidogyne javanica* Treub were the major nematodes present in the rhizosphere of banana. Ozarslandan and Dincer (2015) reported that *Helicotylenchus* sp. was the predominant nematode affecting banana in Turkey in terms of both the percentage of infected area and population density. *H. multicinctus, H. dihystera, M. incognita, M. javanica, Meloidogyne* sp., *Paratylenchus* sp., *P. coffeae, R. similis* and *Rotylenchulus reniformis* Linford and Oliveira were the major nematodes present in the rhizosphere of banana at Bahia state of Brazil (Oliveira *et al.*, 2015). According to Posadas *et al.* (2016) *Helicotylenchus* sp., *M.incognita, M. arenaria, Criconema* sp., *H. multicinctus* and *R. similis* were the major plant parasitic nematodes associated with rhizosphere of banana in Veracruz, Mexico.

National level*:* Banana is one of the major fruit crop in India. Khan (1999) reported that *R. similis* was the widely distributed plant parasitic nematode in banana plantations of the north eastern states (Assam, Bihar, Nagaland, West Bengal and eastern region of Uttar Pradesh). Kumar (2002) identified several plant parasitic nematodes from the banana field of Tamil Nadu *viz., R. similis, M. incognita, P. coffeae, H. multicinctus, Hoplolaimus indicus* Sher, *Tylenchorhynchus martini* Fielding, and *Criconemoides* sp. Later, Cannayane *et al.* (2007) reported the presence of eight plant parasitic nematodes associated with banana in Tamil Nadu *viz., P. coffeae, R. similis, M. incognita, H. multicinctus, H. oryzicola,*

Hoplolaimus sp. and *Xiphinema* sp. Sundararaju (2009) reported that banana cultivar Nendran was highly susceptible to nematode infestation and highest population was recorded during flowering stage followed by harvesting stage. Kaur *et al.* (2010) identified seven plant parasitic nematode species from the rhizosphere of banana 'Grand Naine' from Patiala district of Punjab *viz., M. incognita, M. javanica* Treub, *Helicotyenchus chambus, R. reniformis, P. coffeae* and a free living nematode *Thornenema* sp. Kalaiarasan *et al.* (2010) reported *R. similis, P. coffeae, H. multicinctus, M. incognita, Tylenchorhynchus* sp. and *R. reniformis* from Andhra Pradesh. Gantait *et al.* (2010a) reported that there were 46 species of soil and plant parasitic nematodes associated with banana at West Bengal. They classified them under five different trophic groups of nematodes *viz.*, plant feeders (17 species), omnivores (16 spp.), predators (8 spp.), bacteria feeders (3 spp.) and hyphal feeders (2 spp.). Occurrence of seventeen species of plant parasitic nematodes associated with banana *viz., P. coffeae, Pratylenchus brachyurus, P. similis, M. incognita, M. javanica, H. indicus, R. reniformis, H. multicinctus, H. abunaamai, H incisus, H. gratus, H. dihystera, Tylenchorhynchus nudus, T. mashhoodi, T. coffeae, Hirschmanniella mucronata* and *Criconemoides* sp. (Khan and Hasan, 2011). A random survey was conducted at Nadia and North 24-Parganas district of West Bengal and Vellayani areas of Thiruvanathapuram, Kerala. The occurrence of three different trophic group of nematodes *viz.* phytoparasitic nematodes (17 species), predatory nematodes (*Mylonchulus, Iotonchus* and *Ironus*) and large number of saprozoic nematodes were identified from the rhizosphere of banana. *Pratylenchus crenatus* and *P. coffeae* were the major nematode pests of banana at Haringhata block of Nadia district. *R similis, H. multicinctus,* and *P. coffeae* were recorded as the major nematode pests of banana at Vellayani, Kerala. *H. multicinctus* was the most abundant nematode among them. Root knot nematodes were very low in banana cultivar Ney Poovan (AB) and CO-I (AAB). The population of *P. coffeae* was found to be very less in Ney Poovan (AB), Karpooravelli (ABB), Booditha (CT), Gross Michel (AAA) and Red Banana (AAA) (Roy *et al.*, 2014). The major nematode pests of banana in Kerala are *R. similis* and *H. oryzicola*. The first report of occurrence of *R. similis* on banana from India was made from Kerala (Nair *et al.*, 1966) where entire crop was damaged and lost due to its attack. Infestation of cyst nematode, *H. oryzicola* on banana cv. Nendran was observed for the first time from India was also made from Kerala (Charles and Venkitesan, 1984).

Symptoms of Damage and Yield Loss caused by Nematodes

According to Nair *et al.* (1966) reported the infestation of *R. similis for the first time from India and they observed symptoms like yellowing of leaves, necrosis of rhizome, brown lesions on roots. Overall effect they observed was a weak, shallow root system with a lot of dead areas and the entire crop was lost due to its attack.* Bannon (1977) reported that *R. similis* was a serious pest of banana worldwide and it alone recorded a yield loss of 12.5 t ha^{-1}. Tiwari *et al.* (2000) reported *R. similis* as the major nematode pest of banana causing a yield loss of 30.76 to 41 per cent. Jonathan and Rajendran (2000) reported an avoidable yield loss of 30.9 per cent in banana cv. Poovan due to *M. incognita* using carbofuran 3G at 4kg a.i ha^{-1} as check. Phytoparasitic nematodes were recognized as major constraints to banana production in Kenya, causing up to 85 per cent yield loss in banana (Musabyiman *et al.,* 2000).

Association of Nematodes with other Microorganisms

The direct damage, nematodes serve as predisposing agents in development of disease complexes with fungi, bacteria and viruses. Interactions between *Meloidogyne* spp. and fusarium wilt pathogens has been studied and documented in tomatoes (Abawi and Barker, 1984); alfalfa; chickpeas (Kumar *et al.,* 1988; Maheswari *et al.,*1997); beans (France and Abawi, 1994); cotton (De Vay *et al.,* 1997); banana (Jonathan and Rajendran,1998); peas (Siddiqui and Mahmood, 1999) and lentils (De *et al.,* 2001). Pathak and Keshari (2004) reported that high wilting was observed in cauliflower plants inoculated with both *M. incognita* and *Fusarium oxysporum* Schlecht especially when nematode was present fourteen days prior to fungus. *M. incognita* and *F. oxysporum* together cause disease complex in cabbage in Karnataka (Rajinikanth, 2011).

Community Analysis of Nematodes Associated with Banana

Community analysis of nematodes collected from Puri district, Orissa, revealed that 20 plant parasitic nematodes were present in the rhizosphere of banana. Highest frequency and importance and prominence values was recorded by *Tylenchorhynchus mashhoodi* (86.6 per cent) followed by *M. incognita* (71.1 per cent). *H. mucronata* and *Hemicycliophora demani* were newly reported from banana. The banana cultivars Patkapura, Mendhi and Kathia were found to be resistant to nematodes, while the local banana cv. Champa was the least resistant followed by Robusta, Bantala and Dwarf Cavendish (Ray and Parija., 1987). Analysis of soil and root samples collected from Manipur recorded the occurrence of twenty genera of saprophytic and plant parasitic nematodes associated with banana. *Helicotylenchus* was the most frequently occurred species with an absolute frequency (95 per cent), relative density (41.4 per cent), prominence value (403.5) and importance value (539.9) followed by *Tylenchorhynchus,* which recorded corresponding values of 75 per cent, 37.4 per cent, 323.8 and 436.2, respectively (Anandi *et al.,* 2000). Results of the survey conducted in banana plantations in Coimbatore, Tamil Nadu revealed the occurrence of eight genera of plant parasitic nematodes *viz., H. multicinctus, Hoplolaimus* sp. *Meloidogyne* sp., *P coffeae, R. similis, Rotylenchulus* sp., *Tylenchorhynchus* sp. *Xiphinema* sp. and *H. multicinctus* recorded the highest absolute frequency, relative frequency, absolute density, relative density, prominence value, importance value and relative biomass and lower in *Xiphinema* sp. and *Hoplolaimus* sp. (Rajendran *et al.*, 2002). Sundararaju (2006) reported that there were 13 genera of plant parasitic nematodes associated with different cultivars of banana grown in West Godavari, East Godavari, Guntur and Nellore districts of Andhra Pradesh. *M. incognita* was the chief nematode species having the highest prominence value, followed by *P. coffeae* and *H. multicinctus*. In a survey guided by Sudheer *et al.* (2008) in Andhra Pradesh revealed that *M. incognita* was most abundant nematode associated with banana. Community analysis of the nematodes showed that *Helicotylenchus* sp. was the predominant species with highest prominence value (7.65) followed by *M. incognita* (7.33). Lowest prominence value was recorded by *R. reniformis* (3.53). Gantait *et al.* (2010b) reported that there were 14 nematode species associated with banana in West Bengal in which 8 species from order Dorylaimida and 6 species from order Tylenchida. *R. reniformis* was the predominant species among Tylenchids.

Community Analysis of Nematodes Associated with Other Crops

According to Ramana and Dasgupta. (1998) conducted a survey on ginger in Darjeeling district of West Bengal; they discovered the presence of eight genera and ten species of plant parasitic nematodes. *R. reniformis*, *P. coffeae* and *H. multicinctus* were the most prominent nematodes in that area. Nandwana *et al.* (2005) conducted a survey of nematodes in sugarcane ecosystem in Bundi district of Rajasthan. Community analysis revealed that highest prominence value (1163.4) and an absolute frequency of 94 per cent were recorded by *Helicotylenchus* spp followed by *Tylenchorhynchus* spp and *Pratylenchus* spp. Senthamizh *et al.* (2005) reported that eleven species of plant parasitic nematodes were found associated with groundnut in Erode district of Tamil Nadu. Among which *P. brachyurus* and *R. reniformis* were present in more than 50 per cent of the samples collected. Community analysis of soil samples collected from lentil revealed the presence of five species of plant parasites in which largest absolute frequency (85.71), density (231.42) and prominence value (21.42) were recorded by *T. mashhoodi* (Ali *et al.*, 2006). Community analysis of soil samples collected from Chittoor district of Andhra Pradesh revealed that *M. incognita* was the predominant nematode with highest absolute and relative frequencies, relative density and prominence value (Naidu *et al.*, 2007). Patel *et al.* (2008) conducted a survey in onion, garlic, wheat, brinjal, castor, cotton, coconut and flowering plants in Junagadh district of Gujarat and Diu, a Union Territory and community behaviour of nematodes were studied. They described five plant parasitic nematodes *viz.*, *R. reniformis*, *Helicotylenchus* sp., *Tylenchorhynchus* sp., *Meloidogyne* sp. and *Pratylenchus* sp. from these host plants. In Junagadh district *Helicotylenchus* sp. were recorded with highest absolute frequency (40.91) followed by *Tylenchorhynchus* sp. (36.36). While in Diu, *Meloidogyne* sp. recorded the highest frequency (70.00) followed by *Pratylenchus* sp. Community analysis of nematodes in village Khawas of Barmer district, Rajasthan in pearl millet and gram crops showed that *Tylenchorhynchus* sp. was the predominant plant parasitic nematode with prominence value (46.81) followed by a saprophytic nematode *Acrobeles* sp.(18.92) (Kadela, 2008).Community analysis conducted by Maina (2011) in Nyandarua and Embu Agro-ecological Zones of Kenya revealed that lesion nematodes were having highest frequency in soil (87 per cent) followed by *Helicotylenchus* spp. (82 per cent) and *Tylenchorhynchus* spp. (67 per cent) in cabbage. *Helicotylenchus* sp., *M. incognita, Tylenchorhynchus* sp. and *R. reniformis* were the major plant parasitic nematodes present in the rhizosphere of pineapple in which *Helicotylenchus* sp. was the predominant species followed by *M. incognita* (Devi, 2007). *Helicotylenchus* sp. and *Meloidogyne* sp. were the most frequently occurring plant parasitic nematodes in the rhizosphere of cardamom grown in Cardamom Research Station, Pampadumpara. (Sreeja, 2011). Narayana (2012) reported that nematodes present in the rhizosphere of cardamom in Kerala described at three trophic groups *viz.*, plant parasites (*Helicotylenchus* sp. and *Meloidogyne* sp.), fungal feeders (Aphelenchids and Enoplids), bacterial feeders (Rhabditids), omnivorous (Dorylaimids) and predators (Mononchids). Community analysis conducted by Cyriac (2013) in nematode infested cardamom plantations of Idukki district, Kerala revealed that *H. pseudorobustus* was the most frequently occurring plant parasitic nematode with an absolute frequency of 100 per cent followed by *R. reniformis.* A survey conducted by Varghese (2015) in cabbage growing areas *viz.*, Idukki, Kollam and Thiruvananthapuram districts of Kerala revealed the presence of *M. incognita, R. reniformis, Helicotylenchus* sp., *Tylenchorhynchus* sp. *R. similis* and *Xiphinema* sp. The highest prominence value was recorded by *Helicotylenchus* sp.

Influence of different Seasons on Plant Parasitic Nematode Population

Research evidenced that, Varghese and Nair (1968) reported that nematode population in the rhizosphere of banana was higher in the rainy season and low in summer. A large number of free living nematode species were also found to be associated with banana during rainy season in Kerala. Saeed and Ashrafi (1971) recorded an average number of 1,500 nematodes 100 ml soil^{-1} from a banana plantation but after 6 inch of rain over 12 days, it had declined to 300 nematodes 100 ml soil^{-1}. The numbers of free living nematodes were also declined from 2,300 to 1,100 nematodes 100 ml soil^{-1}.The population dynamics of *R. similis* was related to development stage of the banana and to climatic conditions. Climatic factors favourable for the build-up of nematode population in soil were mean soil temperature between 23 and 25°C, and a water tension level close to zero (Hugon *et al.*, 1984). A survey conducted by Choudhary and Phukan (1990) revealed that maximum number of phytoparasitic nematodes occurred in March and minimum in December in the rhizosphere of banana.The investigation on the population fluctuations of *H. multicinctus* in rhizosphere of banana revealed that there were three peaks during the year (March, June-July and October-November). Lowest population was recorded in December. A positive correlation was observed between nematode population and monthly rainfall. But heavy rainfall resulted reduction in number of nematodes in soil. There was no such effect for temperature in nematode population in soil (Nath *et al.*, 1998). *M. incognita* population dynamics in banana was closely correlated with the average monthly temperature and rainfall (LiXunDong *et al.*, 1998.). Kumar (2002) reported that the lowest and highest nematode population for *R. similis* was recorded in May (45) and November (72), May (13.5) and January (30.5) for *M. incognita,* May (18.5) and September (41.0) for *P. coffeae,* January (15.5) and March (27.0) for *H. multicinctus,* July (17.5) and February (29.5) for *H. indicus,* July (11.5) and October (21.5) for *T. martini,* and June (7.0) and December (14.5) for *Criconemoides* sp. The population of *R. similis* was found to be increasing from November to April and then decreasing trend was observed from May to October. The maximum *R. similis* population was recorded in April (86 nematodes g root^{-1}) and the minimum was in July (20 nematodes g root^{-1}). The population of *P. coffeae* was maximum from October to December and the minimum from May to August. Higher population of *P. coffeae* was observed during rainy season (October to December) (Sundararaju, 2002). Correlation coefficient analysis of *R. similis, H. multicinctus* and *M. incognita* revealed that minimum air temperature (0.45) and rain (0.76) were significantly and positively correlated with population of nematodes in the rhizosphere of banana (Shreenivasa *et al.*, 2002).Li Shu Qing *et al.* (2003) reported that fluctuation in population of *M. incognita* in soil was closely correlated with the temperature and rainfall. *M. incognita* finished its post infection development within 34 days when average daily temperature was below 13.5°C. The optimum temperature for the development of eggs was 20-30°C.The population of *P. coffeae* in the roots of the banana was found to be reduced during the winter months of the year and maintained nearly constant during the wettest months when the field was almost continuously flooded (Bergh *et al.*, 2005). In a survey conducted by Gantait *et al.* (2010c) revealed the presence of eight nematodes belongs to order Dorylaimida associated with banana in Paschim, Medinipur district of West Bengal. Among the nematodes, five species *viz., Dorylaimus innovatus, Prodorylaimus sukuli, Aporcelaimellus subhasi, Oriverutus lobatus* and *Paractinolaimus aruprus* were found throughout the year. The remaining 3 species *viz., Laimydorus siddiqii, Thonus garhwaliensis* and *Promumtazium elongatum* were found during some months of the year and their number were very low. Maximum number of Dorylaimids recorded during monsoon and in the spring and minimum number recorded during winter and summer season. Gantait *et al.* (2011) reported that there are fourteen species of plant parasitic nematodes discovered from the rhizosphere of banana in West Bengal. A bimodal pattern of population fluctuation was exhibited by the nematodes with maximum population during August or September and minimum during March. An increasing trend in nematode populations observed after rainfall but declined during the post-monsoon season and maintained at a low level during winter. Abiotic factors like rainfall, soil temperature and soil moisture plays an important role in population dynamics of nematodes in the rhizosphere of banana. Population dynamics of *H. dihystera, M. incognita* and *Tyelnchorhynchus leviterminalis* showed a positive relationship with rainfall (Deori and Das, 2013). Neog and Borah (2015) reported that February-March and September-October were having the suitable climatic conditions for the fast multiplication of nematodes in the rhizosphere of banana. Lowest number of nematodes were recorded during December-January.

Cultural Control Method of Nematode Management

Biofumigation: Biofumigation is a practice by which nematicidal isothiocyanates (ITCs) are released in soil after incorporating glucosinolate-containing plant material. This practice is considered an ecological substitution of the soil fumigation with toxic fumigants such as methylbromide because these substances are fully biodegradable and less toxic (Kirkegaard *et al.*, 1993). Glucosinolates present in cruciferous plants get converted into various degradation products such as isothiocyanates, thiocyanates, and indoles after cutting or chewing of the plant parts. Through this process, they come in contact with the vacuolar enzyme myrosinase (Donkin *et al.*, 1995). Members of family Brassicaceae contain more than 350 genera which contains glucosinolates (Fahey *et al.*, 2001). Biofumigation with leaf materials of *Brassica juncea* @ 3.5 kg m^{-2} at 25°C resulted 66 per cent suppression of tomato root-knot disease at fruiting periods (Li Shi Dong *et al.*, 2007). Iapichino *et al.* (2008) reported that solarization followed by incorporation of *B. juncea* selection ISCI20 plants @ 20 t ha^{-1} decreased population of *Pyrenochaeta lycopersici* and *M. incognita* in tomato and increased the total yield. Glucosinolate degradation products activate the plant's resistance mechanism, produce toxins, and create defensive barriers around the roots of the host plant, thus preventing harmful pathogens like fungi to enter the host. The isothiocyanates (N=C=S) fate in soil is fundamental for the efficacy of bio fumigation. Residual glucosinolates are very weakly adsorbed, readily leached, and are microbially degraded and mineralized in soil. In contrast, isothiocyanates are strongly adsorbed by the organic matter in soil, react strongly with soil compounds bearing a nucleophilic group, and are prone to volatilization losses and microbial degradation and mineralization minimizing the risks of persistence in the environment or leaching (Mari *et al.*, 2008). Gomez *et al.* (2010) studied the effect of soil biofumigation with semi-rotted cattle manure @ 10 kgm^{-1} for the management of *Meloidogyne* sp.

on tomato and cucumber under sheltered conditions .The root knot index towards the end of each crop cycle was constantly below three along with a yield increase of 50 per cent over untreated. Biofumigation with mustard crop can effectively control *M. hapla* in gerbera under protected condition. Biofumigation with mustard followed by soil application of bioagents *viz., Pseudomonas fluorescence* resulted very good control of *Globodera pallida* encysted eggs (Anita *et al.,* 2011). Rodriguez *et al.* (2011) reported that biofumigation with fresh foliage mixture of *Cannavalia ensiformis* and *Azadirachta indica* with pig manure and organic materials such as rum and cured chicken manure decreased the root knot index and the number of *Meloidogyne* in grapevine. Biofumigation and organic materials improved the health conditions, physical and chemical characteristics of the soil along with increased yield. Incorporation of fresh crucifer residue (cabbage, cauliflower and radish) @ 1 kg 5 kg soil^{-1} to moist soil followed by covering with polyethylene sheets (50 micron thickness) was found to be effective in reducing the population of root knot nematode, *M. hapla* infecting celery and improved plant growth and yield (Anita, 2012).Volatile organic compounds (VOCs) from neem and mustard leaves were able to immobilize *M. incognita* J_2 when they were exposed to inoculated tomato seedlings. Irrigation performed directly after incorporation may trap the VOCs in soil water and thereafter retain nematode toxicity longer than incorporation that is performed late (Barros *et al.,* 2014). Lazzeri *et al.* (2014) tested 11 hydrolysis products of glucosinolates for their nematicidal properties. The glucosinolates *viz.,* 2-phenylethyl, benzyl, 4-methylthiobutyl, and prop-2-enyl isothiocyanate showed the stronger activity, with an LD_{50} at concentrations of 11, 15, 21, and 34 ìM, respectively. Based on these, new genotypes of Brassicaceae with high content of these glucosinolates which generates these most active isothiocyanates were selected. Seed meals got from *B. juncea, B. napus* and *Sinapis alba* were showed reduction in number of *P. penetrans* and *M. incognita* second-stage juveniles (Zasada *et al.,* 2014). *B. napus* and *B. juncea* as cover crops in a vineyard showed a consistent reduction of *Criconema xenoplax* and *M. incognita* in soil (Kruger, *et al.,* 2015). Ngala *et al.* (2015) reported that *B. juncea, Raphanus sativus* and *Eruca sativa* as soil amendments inhibited the viability of potato cyst nematode (PCN) (*Globodera pallida*). Concentration of glucosinolates correlated with PCN mortality. *B. juncea* and *R. sativus* can be used as green manures for the management of PCN.Curto (2016) reported that defatted seed of *B. carinata* can be applied as a biofumigant to manage *M. incognita* in tomato plants. Fourie *et al.* (2016) reported that members of family Brassicaceae having eminent potential to manage important plant parasitic nematodes *viz., Meloidogyne* sp., *Heterodera* sp., *Globodera* sp. and *Pratylenchus* sp.

Botanicals Method of Nematode Management

Soil application–Fresh and dry plant material: According to Kumar and Nair (1976) reported soil incorporation of leaves of *Calotropis* sp., *Eupatorium* sp., mango and cashew @ 5000 kg ha^{-1} at a depth of 25 cm three weeks before sowing seeds, reduced number of root galls incited by *M. incognita* and increased plant height and root weight in okra, cv. Pusa Sawani. Castillo (1985) reported reduction in *R. reniformis* population in pots where fresh leaves of *Asystacia gangetica* (L.)T. Anderson, *Polytrias amaura* (Buse) Kuntze, *Glyricidia sepium* and *Leucaena leucocephala* were added. Alam (1987) reported that chopped leaves of many weeds successfully suppressed the population of plant parasitic nematodes and improved plant growth. Mulching of green leaves of pongamia and neem in soil significantly reduced the incidence of root-knot nematodes and increased the plant growth as well as leaf yield in mulberry (Govindaiah *et al.*, 1989). Osman *et al.* (1989) reported that green and dry manuring of plant parts has been practiced as a method for the control of plant parasitic nematodes. Chopped leaves of *Glyricidia maculata* (H.B.K.) Steud. as green manure was found to reduce the population of *R. similis* and promote growth of black pepper under pot conditions (Jasy and Koshy, 1992). Root knot nematode can be controlled by application of green leaf manures to the infected soil (Wang and Chao, 1995). Ajith and Sheela (1996) reported addition of chopped green leaves of neem and eupatorium @ 15t ha^{-1} effectively reduced plant parasitic nematodes of okra and cowpea and subsequently increased crop yield during rainy and summer seasons. A study conducted by Khanna and Sharma (1998) revealed that application of leaves of *Azadiracta indica* and *T. patula* improved plant growth of tomato and reduced nematode count as well as gall index which were on par with that of nematicides. Ramakrishnan *et al.* (1999) reported that cassava leaf and tuber rind applied as soil amendments at 100 and 50 g $plot^{-1}$ significantly reduced *M. incognita* population and improved growth parameters of okra in pot experiments. *Lantana camara* soil-amendment caused significant suppression of *M. javanica* in mungbean (Syed and Imran, 2001). Nisha and Sheela (2002) reported that green leaf mulching with neem, chromolaena and glyricidia leaves @ 5 kg m^{-2} reduced nematode population and increased the yield of kacholam. Adediran *et al.* (2005) reported that either fallow dominated by *C. odorata* or the direct application of plant material as mulch reduced the population density of plant parasitic nematodes. Thoden *et al.* (2007) reported that pure 1, 2-Dehydropyrrolizidine alkaloids (PAs) extracted from roots of *C. odorata* have nematicidal effects on *M. incognita,* even at concentrations of 70-350 ppm.Application of green leaves of *C. odorata* and *A. indica* was found effective for managing nematodes associated with bhindi and cowpea (Sheela *et al.*, 2008). Wachira *et al.* (2009) reported that application of organic amendments (green leaf manure) to the soil acts as a stimulant of nematode destroying fungi which arrest the nematode population increase. Pakeerathan *et al.* (2009) reported that extent of galling (35.87), gall index (0.327), yield (17.87 Mt ha^{-1}), reproductive factor (0.411) and plant growth parameters *viz.*, height and dry matter (22.47 cm and 45.08 g) were significantly best in tomato plants treated with green leaf manures of *G. maculata* compared to *Thespesia populnea* (L.)Sol. ex Correa, *C. gigantea, A. indica, Glycosmis pentaphylla* (Retz.) DC. And control while *T. populnea* and *A. indica* ranked second and third, respectively in managing *M. incognita.* Wild sunflower leaves (*T. diversifolia*) @ 5kg $plant^{-1}$ in the rhizosphere of cardamon reduced the population of plant parasitic nematodes (Cyriac, 2013). Studies conducted by Odeyemi *et al.* (2013) revealed that treatment with *C. odorata* can significantly reduce the population densities of *Meloidogyne* sp., *Pratylenchus* sp., and *Helicotylenchus* sp. by 77.2, 75.3 and 81.3 per cent respectively. The population of free living nematodes (Rhabditids and *Dorylaimus* spp.) was also showed a considerable increase in the soil. The nematicidal phytochemicals discovered from the leaves and roots of *C. odorata* includes tannins (46.2±17.9 mg g^{-1}), saponins (81.5±76.8 mg g^{-1}), alkaloids (12.6±0.7 mg g^{-1}), flavonoids (5.3±2.6 mg g^{-1}), phenols (43.7±1.6 mg g^{-1}), cardenolides and anthraquinones. The phytochemical having highest concentrations were saponins followed by tannins (Agaba *et al.,* 2015). Alkaloids present in *C. odorata* are having inhibitory action on hatching of *M. incognita* eggs (Atungwu and Aruna, 2015).

Powder form: Patel *et al.* (1985) reported that the application of *Clerodendron inerme* (L.) Gaertn. in okra at 1.5 per cent ww^{-1} caused minimum galling and increase in growth of okra .Organic amendment with powdered leaves of the plants like curry leaf, (*Murray koenigii* (L.)Sprengel), Jasmine (*Jasminum sambac* (L.)Aiton), sour orange (*Citrus aurantifolia* (Christm.) Swingle), Patal garuda (*Rauwolfia serpentine* (L.) Benth. ex Kurz), Ber (*Zizyphus jujuba* Mill.), China rose (*Hibiscus rosa-sinensis* L.) and Justicia (*Justicia gendarussa* Burm.f.) were effective in reducing *M. incognita* population (Padhi and Behera, 2000). Siji *et al.* (2010) reported application of dried powder of *Cleome viscosa* L. @ 250g powder $plot^{-1}$ reduced gall formation and increased the fruit weight (61.76 per cent increase over untreated) of okra.

Plant extracts: Aqueous crude extracts of *C. odorata* showed nematicidal properties (Subramaniyan, 1985). Soil application of leaf extracts (5, 10 and 20 ml) of *Cymbopogon citratus* (DC.) Stapf, *E. crassipes* and *Ipomoea carnea* Jace. improved plant growth of chickpea (*Cicer arietinum* L.) var. P-256 seedlings (Siddiqui and Husain, 1990). Patel *et al.* (1993) reported that water hyacinch (*E. crassipes*) and congress grass (*Parthenium hysterophorus* L.) were moderately effective in reducing root-knot nematode numbers (25.1 and 28.9% respectively) in tomato. According to Mojumder and Raman (1996) seed treatment with neem products (nimbecidin, achook etc.) was effective as well as economical for nematode management in chickpea and other pulse crops.

Naik *et al.* (1998) reported that neem product extracts have no adverse effect on the growth of tomato plants, but significantly decreased the nematode development and reproduction. Maximum reduction in galls, egg masses and egg production was recorded in nimbecidine treated plants and found superior over seed kernel and cake extracts. Among neem based formulations (achook, neemark, nimbecidine), achook was found to be the most effective in reducing the penetration, number of galls and final soil population (Mojumder and Basu, 1999). The root leachate of *L. camara* was found to contain phenolic compounds, including *p*-hydroxybenzoic acid, vanillic acid, caffeic acid, ferulic acid and a quercetin glycoside, 7-glucoside (Shaukat *et al.*, 2003). Ahmad *et al.* (2010) reported that addition of freeze-dried aqueous extract of *L. camara* to sterile sandy substrate at three and five per cent concentration significantly decreased the root-knot infection (85 per cent reduction in root-knot count over untreated) to susceptible eggplants whereas second stage juveniles (J2) that penetrated roots of eggplant were able to complete development in sterile sandy substrate without treatment of freeze-dried aqueous extract. Botanicals such as *Azadirachta, Eucalyptus, Chromolaena, Sida acuta* Burm.f. and *Tagetes* have been found to be effective in the control of nematodes in cowpea, tomato and egg plant fields (Umar *et al.*, 2010).Organic extract of *C. viscosa* at 500 ppm showed moderate toxicity to *M. incognita* larvae (Williams *et al.*, 2003).

Physical Methods of Nematode Management

Hot water treatment: Integration of paring and hot water treatment of suckers along with neem cake and carbofuran application was found very effective in reducing the total population of *R. similis, H. multicinctus* and *M. incognita* infesting banana in both in soil (83.33 per cent) and roots (66.17 per cent) and in increasing the plant growth parameters and fruit yield (Subhadra *et al.*, 1998). Krishnappa *et al.* (2002) reported that paring of banana suckers and hot water treatment at 55°C for 20 minutes followed by application of neem seed cake at 1 kg plant $^{-1}$ reduced the soil and root population of *R. similis* in banana by 40 per cent. The same treatment was the most effective in increasing the yield by 101.94 per cent.

Organic soil amendments - Neem cake: According to Devakumar *et al.* (1985) reported that limonoids namely, azadirachtin, nimbin and salannin present in seed kernel oils of neem were the main nematicidal compounds present in neem. Azadirachtin is the major component of these (Mojumdar, 1995).Organic amendments can change the physical properties of soil which resulted inhibition of egg hatching, movement and survival of nematodes in soil. The soil pH, salinity, EC, carbon dioxide and oxygen concentrations, redox potential and soil structure were also altered by the application of organic amendments (Khanna *et al.*, 1997). Akhtar (1998) reported that the direct nematicidal activity of limonoids present in low concentrations in neem oil cakes has not been clear. So, other compounds (ammonia) which was formed during degradation of oil cake could be responsible for nematode mortality. Neem oilcake as soil-amendments could reduce the density of plant-parasitic nematodes *viz., H. indicus, Helicotylenchus indicus, R. reniformis* and *M. incognita* juveniles in chickpea. The populations of predatory and free-living nematodes were increased by the application of neemcake (Akthar, 2000).Neem cake, as fertilizer was lethal to parasitic nematodes. Treatment with 1 per cent neem cake resulted 67 – 90 per cent reduction in the number of *P. penetrans* and *M. hapla* nematodes in tomato roots. Number of free-living nematodes was either increased or not affected by the effect of neem cake (Abbasi *et al.*, 2005). Organic amendments enriched with microorganisms makes plants more tolerant to nematodes infestation. Development of specific microorganism inducers and exposure to natural compounds inducers are the two possible causes of plant tolerance or resistance provided by organic amendments (Bostock, 2005). Neem seed kernel extract containing 10 per cent azadirachtin successfully suppressed the population of *M. javanica* juveniles (Oka *et al.*, 2007)

Bioagents (Purpureocillium lilacinum): The action of fungal parasite *Purpureocillium lilacinum* (Thorn) Samson in reducing nematode population is a promising form of crop protection against *Meloidogyne* spp. The biocontrol potential of this parasitic fungus was reported against *Meloidogyne* spp. (Jatala *et al.*, 1980). Besides oviparasitism, the mortality of second stage juveniles of *M. incognita* by the action of culture filtrates of *P. lilacinum* was reported by Khan and Khan (1992). Khan *et al.* (1997) reported *P. lilacinum* as a potentially important fungal biocontrol agent capable of parasitizing nematode eggs, juveniles and females and reported to control a range of nematode species on a number of crops worldwide. Tropical conditions with high temperature and low pH values are favourable for the fast multiplication of the fungus (Laffranque *et al.*, 2003). Efficiency of *P. lilacinum* was more when applied before nematode inoculation or together with *M. incognita* but was not so effective to inhibit nematode reproduction when applied after nematode infestation (Pathan *et al.*, 2004). Kumar *et al.* (2008) reported that culture filtrates of *P. lilacinum* were found to be very effective in increasing the mortality and decreasing the hatching of root knot nematode, *M. incognita.*

Effect on nematodes infecting banana: Application of *P. lilacinum* @ 30g kg^{-1} soil at the time of planting reduced gall index, number of egg masses, percentage egg hatch and soil population of *M. incognita* in banana (Devrajan, and Rajendran, 2001). Vyas *et al.* (2001) reported that application *P. lilacinum* (25 kg ha^{-1}) in combination with carbofuran (1kg a.i ha^{-1}) just before planting of banana can significantly reduce root knot nematode population along with increased yield (42.02 t ha^{-1}). *P. lilacinum* acts as an egg parasite of several important endo parasitic nematodes such as *Meloidogyne* sp., *Globodera rostochiensis, R. similis, Pratylenchus* sp., *Heterodera* sp., *R. reniformis, Tylenchulus* *semipenetrans*. *P. lilacinum* strain 251 can be used in banana, tomato, tobacco, potato and other crops. Mendoza *et al*. (2007) evaluated the effect of *P. lilacinum* strain 251 (Bioact® WG) against *R. similis* in banana. Optimum dose found to be $6{\times}10^6$ cfu of *P. lilacinum* g dry soil^{-1} applied at three times; 6 days before planting, at-planting, and as a plantlet drench. Sundararaju and Kiruthika (2009) reported that treatments involving *P. lilacinum* alone and in combination with neem cake and botanicals significantly increased plant growth and reduced population of *R. similis* in banana. Thammaiah *et al*. (2012) reported that *P. lilacinum* at 10 g plant^{-1} + FYM at 500 g plant^{-1} and *P. lilacinum* + neem cake at 250 g plant^{-1}can suppress *R. similis* in banana along with a considerable increase in yield.

Effect on nematodes infecting other crops: According to Nisha and Sheela (2006) reported that integrated use of *P. lilacinum* with neem cake was found to be highly effective in reducing the multiplication of *M. incognita* in soil and increasing the plant growth characteristics of coleus. *P. lilacinum* significantly reduced the number of galls and increased plant growth characteristics of tomato plants inoculated with *M. incognita* (Kannan, and Veeravel, 2008). Soil application of *P. lilacinum* (50 g plant^{-1}) in combination with castor cake (1 kg plant^{-1}) recorded reduction in number of galls (37 galls 5 g root^{-1}) and nematode population (160 200cc^{-1}) also prevented the entry of wilt pathogen, *Ceratocystis fimbriata* in pomegranate (Somasekhara *et al*., 2012).Talc-based preparation of *P. lilacinum* when applied as seed treatment (10 g kg seed^{-1}) followed by soil application (10 kg ha^{-1}) with 1.5 t ha^{-1} FYM reduced the occurrence of *M. incognita* in okra with improved fruit yield (71 per cent) (Singh *et al*., 2014). Integrated use of soil fumigant dazomet and *P. lilacinum* (YES-2-14) reduced the population of root-knot nematodes and promoted the growth and yield of tomato (Nie Hai Zhen *et al*., 2016).Senapati *et al*. (2016) reported that combined application of *Pochonia chlamydosporia* and *P. lilacinum* (25 g each per m^2) significantly reduced the root knot count and nematode population in soil along with an increase in yield by 53.0 per cent in tomato.

CONCLUSION

Plant parasitic nematodes are one of the major treat for of banana cultivation throughout the world.The occurrence of three different trophic group of nematodes *viz*.phytoparasitic nematodes, predatory nematodes and large number of saprozoic nematodes were identified from the rhizosphere of banana. The major nematode pests of banana areroot knot nematode, *M.incognita*, reniform nematode, *R.reniformis*, spiral nematode, *H. dihystera*, cyst nematode, *H.oryzicola*, burrowing nematode, *R.similis*, lance nematode, *H.indicus*, lesion nematode, *Pratylenchus*sp., ring nematode, *Criconema*sp. and dagger nematode, *Xiphinema* sp.Besides direct damage, nematodes serve as predisposing agents in development of disease complexes with fungi, bacteria and viruses. During the past decade several agriculturally important nematicides have been deregistered or restricted in use because of concern about ground water contamination or adverse effect on human health alternative methods have to be developed for managing these notorious pest. Biofumigation is a practice by which nematicidalisothiocyanates (ITCs) are released in soil after incorporating glucosinolate-containing plant material.Glucosinolate degradation products activate the plant's resistance mechanism, produce toxins, and create defensive barriers around the roots of the host plant, thus preventing harmful pathogens to enter the host.Chopped leaves of many weeds like *Calotropis*sp., *Eupatorium* sp *Glyricidiasepium* and *Leucaenaleucocephala Azadiractaindica* and *Chromolaena. odorata* weres uccessfully suppressed the population of plant parasitic nematodes and improved plant growth. Integration of paring and hot water treatment of suckers along with neem cake application was found very effective in reducing the total population of *R. similis, H. multicinctus* and *M. incognita* infesting banana in both in soil and roots.Organic amendments enriched with microorganisms makes plants more tolerant to nematodes infestation. *Purpureocillium. lilacinum*as a potentially important fungal biocontrol agent capable of parasitizing nematode eggs, juveniles and females and reported to control a range of nematode species on a number of crops worldwide. Application of *P. lilacinum*at the time of planting reduced gall index, number of egg masses, percentage egg hatch and soil population of *M. incognita* in banana. Adopting these biorionale methods will not only suppress nematode population but also increase the plant growth parameters.

REFERENCES

Abawi, G.S. and Barker, K.R. (1984): Effects of Cultivar, Soil Temperature and Population Levels of *Meloidogyne Incognita* on Root Necrosis and *Fusarium* wilt of Tomatoes, *Phytopathol.*74(3): 433–438.

Abbasi, P.A., Riga, E., Conn, K.L., and Lazarovits, G. (2005): Effect of Neem Cake Soil Amendment on Reduction of Damping-off Severity and Population Densities of plant–Parasitic Nematodes and Soil Borne Plant Pathogens, *Can. J. Plant Pathol.* 27(2): 38–45.

Adediran, J.A., Adegbite, A.A., Akinlosotu, T., Agbaje, G.O., Taiwo, L,B., Owolade, O.F., and Oluwatosin, G.A. (2005): Evaluation of Fallow and Cover Crops for Nematode Suppression in three Agroecologies of South Western Nigeria, *Afr. J. Biotechnol.* 4: 1034-1039.

Agaba, T. A., Fawole, B., and Claudius-Cole, A. O. (2015): Screening of Siam Weed (*Chromolaena odorata*) and African Custard Apple (*Annona senegalensis*) for Nematicidal Activity, *J. Biol. Agric. Healthcare.* 5(14): 50-56.

Ahmad, F., Rather, M.A., and Siddiqui, M.A. (2010): Nematicidal Activity of Leaf Extracts from *Lantana Camara* L. against *Meloidogyne Incognita* (Kofoid and White) Chitwood and its use to Manage Roots Infection of *Solanum Melongena* L. *Brazilian, Arch. Biol. Technol.* 53(3): 543-548.

Ajith, K. and Sheela, M.S. (1996): Utilization of Green Leaves of Neem and Eupatorium for the Management of Soil Organisms in Bhindi and Cowpea, *Indian J. Nematol.* 26(2): 139-143.

Akhtar, M. (1998): Biological Control of Plant–parasitic Nematodes by Neem Products in Agricultural soil, *Appl. Soil Ecol.* 7: 219–223.

Akhtar, M. (2000): Nematicidal Potential of the Neem Tree *Azadirachta indica* (A. Juss), *Integrated Pest Manag. Rev.* 5: 57–66.

Akhtar, M. and Mahmood, I. (1993): Effect of *Mononchus Aquaticus* and Organic Amendments on *Meloidogyne Incognita* Development on Chilli, *Nematologia Mediterranea*. 21(2): 251-252.

Alam, M.M. (1987): Pollution free Control of Plant Parasitic Nematodes by Soil Amendment with Plant Waste, *Biol. Wastes*. 22: 75-79.

Ali, S. S., Pervez, R., Shaheen, A., and Ahmad, R. (2006): Community Analysis of Plant Parasitic Nematodes Associated with Pulse Crops in Hamirpur District (Uttar Pradesh), *Indian. J. Nematol* . 36(1): 99-102.

Anandi, Y., Mohilal, N., and Dhanachand, C. (2000): Community Analysis of Soil and Plant Nematodes Associated with Banana Plants in Manipur, *J. Agric. Sci. Soc.*, North-East India, 13 (2): 209-211.

Anita, B. (2012): Crucifer Vegetable Leaf Wastes as Biofumigants for the Management of Root knot Nematode (*Meloidogyne hapla* Chitwood) in Celery (*Apium graveolens* L.), *J. Biopesticides* 5: 111-114.

Anita, B., Selvaraj, N., and Vijayakumar, R. M. (2011): Associative Effect of Biofumigation and Biocontrol Agents in Management of Root knot Nematode *Meloidogyne hapla* in Gerbera, *J. Applied Hortic.*, 13(2): 154-156.

Atungwu, J. J. and Aruna, W. O. (2015): Phytochemical Analysis and Prospects of Some Indigenous Plants as Bionematicides: Implication for Organic Management of *Meloidogyne Incognita, International J. Nematol.*, 25(2): 200-207.

Bannon, J.H. (1977): Worldwide Dissemination of *Radopholus Similis* and its Importance in Crop Production, *J. Nematol.*, 9(1): 16–25.

Bapista, M.J., Souza, R.B. Pereira, W., Carrijo, O.A., Vidal, M.C. and Charchar, J.M. (2006): The Effect of Solarisation and Biofumigation on Tomatoes under Protected Cultivation, *Horticultura Brasileira*, 24(1): 47-52.

Barros, A. F., Campos, V. P., Silva, J. C. P. da, Pedroso, M. P., Medeiros, F. H. V., Pozza, E. A., and Reale, A. L. (2014): Nematicidal Activity of Volatile Organic Compounds Emitted by *Brassica juncea, Azadirachta indica, Canavalia Ensiformis, Mucuna pruriens* and *Cajanus Cajan* against *Meloidogyne Incognita, Applied Soil Ecol.*, 80: 34-43.

Bergh, I., Nguyen, T., Duong, T. M., Nguyet, H. H., and Nhi, W. D. (2005): Population Dynamics of *Pratylenchus coffeae* on Banana in North Vietnam, *J. Nematol.*, 7 (6): 891-900.

Bostock, R.M. (2005): Signal Crosstalk and Induced Resistance: Straddling the line between Cost and Benefit, *Annu. Rev. Phytopathol.*, 43(1): 545–580.

Cannayane, I., Jonathan, E. I., and Rajavel, D. S. (2007): Association of Plant Parasitic Nematodes and Antagonistic Microbes in Banana Rhizosphere, *Annals Plant Protection Sci.*, 15(2): 449-453.

Castillo, M.B. (1985): Some Studies on the Use of Organic Soil Amendments for Nematode Control, *Philipp. Agric.*, 68: 76-93.

Charles, J. S. and Venkitesan, T. S. (1984): New Hosts of *Heterodera oryzicola* Rao and Jayaprakash, 1978, in Kerala, India, *Indian J. Nematol.*, 14 (2): 181-182.

Charles, J. S. K., Rani, T. G., and Krishnan, S. (1996): Management of Banana Nematodes using Cultural and Chemical Strategies, *Pest Manag. Hortic. Ecosyst.*, 2(1): 19-22.

Chitamba, J., Manjeru, P., Chinheya, C. C., Mudada, N., and Handiseni, M. (2013): Plant-Parasitic Nematodes Associated with Banana (*Musa* spp.) in Rusitu Valley, Zimbabwe, *Nematropica*, 43 (1): 113-118.

Choudhury, B. N. and Phukan, P. N. (1990): Seasonal Fluctuations of Nematode Population in Banana, *Indian J. Nematol.*, 20(2):189-192.

Cobb, N.A. (1918): Estimating the Nematode Population of Soil, USDA Agriculture Technical Circle1.p.48.

Cochran, W. G. and Cox, G.M. (1965): Experimental Design (2nd Ed.), John Wiley and Sons Inc, New York, 182p.

Curto, G., Dallavalle, E., Matteo, R., and Lazzeri, L. (2016): Biofumigant Effect of New Defatted Seed Meals against the Southern Root-knot Nematode, *Meloidogyne incognita, Annals Applied Biol.*, 169 (1) :17-26.

Cyriac, A. (2013): Management of Nematodes Associated with Cardamom, M.Sc.(Ag) Thesis, Kerala Agricultural University, Thrissur, 80p.

Daykin, M. E. and Hussey, R.S. (1985): Staining and Histopathological Techniques in Namatology. In: Barker, K.R., Carter, C.C., and Sasser, J.N. (eds), An Advanced Treatise on *Meliodogyne*, North Carolina State University Press, Raleigh, North Carolina, pp.39-48.

De R.K., Ali, S.S., and Dwivedi, R.P. (2001): Effect of Interaction between *Fusarium Oxysporum* f.sp. *Lentis* and *Meloidogyne Javanica* on lentil, *Indian J. Pulses Res.*,14: 71–73.

De Vay, J.E., Gutierrez, A.P., Pullman, G.S., Wakeman, R.J., Garber, R.H., Jeffers, D.P., Smith, S.N., Goodell, P.B., and Roberts, P.A. (1997): Inoculum Densities of *Fusarium Oxysporum* f.sp. *Vasinfectum* and *Meloidogyne Incognita* in Relation to the Development of *Fusarium* wilt and the Phenology of Cotton Plants (*Gossypium hirsutum*), *Phytopathol.*, 87: 341–346.

Deori, A. and Das, D. (2013): Influence of Abiotic Factors on Nematode Population around Banana Rhizosphere, *Indian J. Nematol.*, 43 (2): 176-179.

Devakumar, C., Goswami, D.K., and Mukerjee, S.K. (1985): Nematicida Principles from Neem (*Azadirachta indica* A. Juss.). Part 1. Screening of Neem Kernel Fractions against *Meloidogyne incognita, Indian J. Nematol.*, 15: 121–124

Devi , G. (2007): Community Analysis of Plant Parasitic Nematodes in Pineapple Ecosystem in Meghalaya, *Indian J. Nematol.*, 37(1): 106-107.

Devrajan, K. and Rajendran, G. (2001): Effect of the Fungus *Paecilomyces lilacinus* (Thom.) Samson on the Burrowing Nematode *Radopholus similis* (Cobb) Thorne in Banana, *Pest Manag Hortic. Ecosyst.*, 7(2): 171-173.

Donkin, S. G., Etteman, M. A., and Williams, P. L. (1995): Toxicity of Glucosinolates and their Enzymatic Decomposition Products to *Caenorhabditis elegans*, *J. Nematol.*, 12(3): 112-114.

Eissa, M. F. M., Gindi, A. Y., Elgawad, M. M., Ismail, A. E., and Nagdi, W. A. (2003): Plant-Parasitic Nematodes Associated with Banana Crop in Egypt, *Bull. Natl Res. Cent.*, 28(5): 655-670.

Fahey, J.W., Zalcmann, A.T., and Talalay, P. (2001): The Chemical Diversity and Distribution of Glucosinolates and Isothiocyanates among Plants, *Phytochem.*, 56: 5-51.

FIB [Farm Information Bureau]. (2017): Farm Guide 2017 [on-line]. Available: http://fibkerala.gov.in/images/Farm_Guide/2016/farmguide16.pdf [14 June 2017].

Fourie, H., Ahuja, P., Lammers, J., and Daneel, M. (2016): Brassicacea-based Management Strategies as an Alternative to Combat Nematode Pests: a Synopsis, *J. Crop Prot.*, 80:21-41.

France, R.A. and Abawi, G.S. (1994): Interaction between *Meloidogyne Incognita* and *Fusarium Oxysporum* f.sp. *Phaseoli* on Selected Bean Genotypes, *J. Nematol.*, 26(4): 467–474.

Gantait, V. V., Bhattacharya, T., and Chatterjee, A. (2010a): Seasonal Fluctuation of Dorylaimid Population in Banana Plantation of West Bengal, India, *Indian J. Nematol.*, 40 (2):184-188.

Gantait, V. V., Bhattacharya, T., Chatterjee, A. (2011): Temporal Variation in Abundance of Nematodes in a Banana Plantation of West Bengal, India, *J. Nematologia Mediterranea*, 39(1): 9-15.

Gantait, V. V., Chatterjee, A., and Bhattacharya, T. (2010b): Trophic Groups of Nematodes Associated with Banana Plantation in Paschim Medinipur district of West Bengal, India, *Tropical Ecol.*, 52(3): 331-335.

Gantait, V. V., Tanmay, B., and Amalendu, C. (2010c): Community Analysis of Soil and Plant Parasitic Nematodes in a Banana Plantation of West Bengal in India, *International J. Nematol.*, 20(1): 119-124.

Ghosh, S. and Khan, M. R. (2010): Integrated Approach for Management of Major Insect Pests and Nematode Problems of Okra, *Abelmoschus esculentus* (L.), *Annals Plant Prot. Sci.* 18 (2): 388-393.

Gomez, L., Gonzalez, E., Enrique, R., Hernandez, M. A., and Rodriguez, M. G. (2010): Use of Biofumigation for the Management of *Meloidogyne* spp. in Vegetable Sheltered Production, *J. Revista de Protección Vegetal.*, 25 (2): 119-123.

Goswami, B.K., Rao, U., and Singh, S. (1998): Potential of Some Fungal Bioagents against Root-knot Nematode, *Meloidogyne incognita* Infecting Tomato. In: Reddy, P.P., Kumar, N.K.K. and Verghese, A. (eds.), Proceedings of First National Symposium on Pest Management in Horticultural Crops, 15-17 October 1998, Bangalore. Association for Advancement of Pest Management in Horticultural Ecosystems, Indian Institute of Horticultural Research, Bangalore, pp. 304-307.

Govindaiah, S., Sharma, N., and Gargi, D.D. (1989): Effect of mulching of Green Leaves for the Control of Root-knot Nematode in Mulberry, *Indian J. Nematol.*, 19(1): 25-28.

Gowda. M, Gajbhiye, V. T., and Gautam, C. (2014): Carbosulfan Absorption by *Polianthes tuberosa* L. Bulbs and its Effect on Root-knot Nematode, *Meloidogyne Incognita, Indian J. Nematol.*, 44 (2): 164-171

Gowen, S.R. and Queneherve, P. (1990): Nematode Parasites of Bananas, Plantains and Abaca. In. Plant Parasitic Nematodes in Tropical and Subtropical Agriculture (Eds. Luc, M., Sikora, R.A. and Bridge, J.). CAB International, Wallingford, UK. pp.431-60.

Huang,J.S. (1985): Mechanism of Resistance to Root-knot Nematodes. In: An Advance Treatise on Meloidogyne Vol.I. Biological Control (Eds.Sasser, J.N and carter, C.C.) North Carolina State University, Graphics, pp.165-74.

Hugon, R., Ganry, J., and Berthe, G. (1984): Population Dynamics of the Nematode *Radopholus similis* in Relation to the Development of the Banana and to the Climate, *Fruits*, 39 (4): 251-253.

Iapichino, G., Puleo, L., Vetrano, F., and Sciortino, A. (2008): Effects of Solarization and Biofumigation on Tomato Greenhouse Production in the Southern Coast of Sicily, *Acta Hortic.*, 801(2) : 1557-1562.

Jasy, T. and Koshy, P.K. (1992): Effect of Certain Leaf Extracts and Leaves of *Glyricidia maculata* (H.B & K) Steud. as Green Manure on *Radopholus similis*, *Indian J. Nematol.*, 22(2): 117-121.

Jatala, P., Kaltenbach, R., and Bocangel, M. (1980): Biological Control of *Meloidogyne Incognita* and *Globodera pallida* on potatoes, *J. Nematol.*, 11: 303.

Jonathan, E. I.and Rajendran, G. (2000): Assessment of Avoidable Yield loss in Banana due to root-knot Nematode *Meloidogyne incognita, Indian J. Nematol.*, 30(2): 162-164.

Jonathan, E.I. and Rajendran, G. (1998): Interaction of *Meloidogyne Incognita* and *Fusarium Oxysporum* f.sp. *Cubense* on Banana, *Nematologia Mediterranea*, 26: 9–12.

Kadela, P. (2008): Community Analysis of Nematodes in Village Kawas, Barmer, Rajasthan, *Indian J. Nematol.*, 38(1): 117-118.

Kalaiarasan, P., Sudheer, M. J., and Senthamarai, M. (2010): Community Analysis of Nematodes Associated with Banana in different districts of Andhra Pradesh, *Indian J. Nematol.*, 40 (1): 35-37.

Kamira, M., Hauser, S., Asten, P., Coyne, D., and Talwana, H. L. (2003): Plant Parasitic Nematodes Associated with Banana and Plantain in Eastern Angand Western Democratic Republic of Congo, *Nematropica,* 43(2): 216-225.

Kannan, R. and Veeravel, R. (2008): Dose Optimization of *Paecilomyces Lilacinus* Bainer for the Management *of Meloidogyne incognita* Chitwood in Tomato, *Plant Archives, 8(2): 841-844.*

Kasapoglu, E. B., Yoraz, G., and Elekcioglu, I. H. (2015): Investigation on Population Dynamics of Important Plant Parasitic Nematodes (*Helicotylenchus Multicinctus, H. Dihystera* and *Meloidogyne* spp.) (Nemata) in Banana Greenhouses Grown in Bozyazý (Mersin), *Turkiye Entomoloji Dergisi* 39(2): 199-207.

KAU-Kerala Agricultural University. (2011): Package of Practices Recommendations: Crops. (14th Ed.), Kerala Agricultural University, Thrissur, 360p.

Kaur, H., Kaur, H., and Kumari, N. (2010): Plant Parasitic Nematodes Associated with Banana Crops (*Musa* AAA) in district Patiala, Punjab in India, *Trends Biosci.*, 3(2): 147-148.

Khan, M. R. and Hasan, M. A. (2011): Nematode Diversity in Banana Rhizosphere from West Bengal in India, *J. Plant Protection Res.*, 50(3): 263-268.

Khan, M.M.A., Holland, R.J. and Williams, K.L. (1997): Recent Studies on *Paecilomyces lilacinus* as a Bionematicide. Suppression of *Heterodera avenae* Populations, Infection of *Meloidogyne javanica* eggs, Females and Juveniles in a Pot Trial and *Radopholus Similis* eggs in Laboratory Studies, *Austalasian Nematol., Newsl.* 8: 11-12.

Khan, M.R. (1999): Distribution of Radopholus Similis in India, its Spread in New Regions and an Analysis of the Nematofauna of Banana Crop Pathosystem, *J. Nematologia Mediterranea,* 27(2): 239-245.

Khan, M.R. and Goswami, B.K. (1999): Nematicidal Effect of Culture Filtrates of *Paecilomyces Lilacinus* Isolates on *Meloidogyne Incognita, Indian J. Nematol.*, 39(2): 201-206.

Khan, S.T. and Khan, T.A. (1992): Effect of Culture Filtrates of Soil Fungi on the Hatching Mortality of Root Knot Nematode (*Meloidogyne incognita*), *Curr. Nematol.*, 3(1):53-60.

Khanna, N., Cressman III, C.P., Tatara, C.P., and Williams, P.L. (1997): Tolerance of the Nematode *Caenorhabditis elegans* to pH, Salinity, and Hardness in Aquatic Media, Arch. *Environ. Contam. Toxicol.*, 32: 110–114.

Khanna, S.A. and Sharma, K.N. (1998): Phytotherapeutic Effect of Some Indigenous Plants/ Nemat Icides on *Meloidogyne Incognita* Infesting Tomato. In: Proceedings of National Symposium on Rational Approaches in Nematode Management for Sustainable Agriculture, 23-25 November 1998, Indian Agricultural Research Inst Institute, New Delhi, Nematological Society of India, Indian Agricultural Research Institute, New Delhi , pp.4-6.

Kirkegaard, J.A., Gardner, P.A., Desmarchelier, J.M. and Angus, J. F. (1993): Biofumigation using *Brassica* species to Control Pests and Diseases in Horticulture and Agriculture, In: Wratten, N. and Mailer, R.J. (eds). Proc. 9th Australian Research Assembly on Brassicas, Agricultural Research Institute, Wagga Wagga. pp. 77–82.

Kloepper, J.W., Rodriguez -Kabana, R., McInroy, J.A. , and Col l ins , D.J. (1991): Analysis of Populat ions and Physiological Characterization of Microorganisms in Rhizosphere of plants wi th Antagonistic Properties to Phytopathogenic Nematodes, *Plant Soil.*, 136(1): 95-102.

Krishnappa, K., Reddy, B. M. R., Ravichandra, N. G., and Karuna, K. (2002): Integrated Management of Nematode Complex in Banana, Proceedings of National Symposium on Biodiversity and Management of Nematodes in Cropping Systems for Sustainable Agriculture, Jaipur, India, 11-13 November, 2002. pp. 223-227.

Kruger, D. H. M., Fourie, J. C., and Malan, A. P. (2015): The Effect of Cover Crops and their Management on Plant-parasitic Nematodes in Vineyards, *South African J. Enol. Vitic.*, 36 (2) :195-209.

Kumar, M.R., Rani ,J.S., and Sudheer, J.M. (2008): Effect of Culture Filtrates of *Paecilomyces lilacinus* on the Mortality and Hatching of Root-knot Nematode, *Indian J. Nematol.*, 38 (1): 90-93.

Kumar, R., Ahmad, S., and Saxena, S.K. (1988): Disease Complex in Chickpea involving *Meloidogyne Incognita* and *Fusarium Oxysporum*, *Int. Nematol. Network Newsl.*,5: 12–4.

Kumar, S. (2002): Population Dynamics and Seasonal Incidence of Nematodes in Banana, *Indian J. Nematol.*, 32 (1): 93.

Kumar, T.P. and Nair, M.R.G.K. (1976): Effect of Some Green Leaves and Organic Wastes on Root-knot Nematode Infestation on Bhindi, *Agric. Res. J. Kerala*, 14(1): 64-67.

Laffranque, J. P., Pi, M. O., Decroos, Y., and Aertens, F. (2003): Biological Control of Nematodes with the Soil Borne Fungus *Paecilomyces lilacinus* Strain 251. Colloque International Tomate Sous Abri, Protection Integree- Agriculture Biologique, Avignon, France, 17-18 et 19 Septembre 2003 pp.126.

Lazzeri, L., Curto, G., Leoni, O., and Dallavalle, E. (2014): Effects of Glucosinolates and their Enzymatic Hydrolysis Products via Myrosinase on the root-knot nematode *Meloidogyne incognita* (Kofoid and White) Chitwood, *J. Agric. Food. Chem.*, 52: 6703 6707.

Li ShiDong, Li MingShe, Miao ZuoQing, Guo RongJun. (2007): Soil Biofumigation for Management of Vegetable root-knot Nematode Disease, *Plant Prot.*, 33 (4): 68-71.

Li ShuQing., Liu ZhiMing., and Wei Gang. (2003): A Study on the Biological Characters of Banana root-knot Nematode, *Meloidogyne incognita* Chitwood, *Southwest China J. Agric. Sci.*, 16(2): 66-69.

LiXunDong, Y., LiuXiang. Z., and Qin, L.(1998): Study on the Populations of Rhizosphere Nematodes of Banana, *J. South China Agric. University*, 19(4): 32-35.

Maheswari, U.T., Sharma, S.B., Reddy, D.D.R., and Haware, M.P. (1997): Interaction of *Fusarium oxysporum* f.sp. *ciceri* and *Meloidogyne javanica* on *Cicer arietinum*, *J. Nematol.*, 29: 117–26.

Maina, M.J. (2011): Plant Parasitic Nematodes Associated with Cabbage in different Agroecological Zones in Nyandarua and Embu Counties, Kenya, M.Sc.(Plant Pathology) thesis, Kenyatta University, Kahawa, 35p.

Mari, M., Leoni, O., Bernardi, R., Neri, F., and Palmieri, S. (2008): Control of Brown rot on Stone fruit by Synthetic and Glucosinolate-derived Isothiocyanates, *Postharvest Biol. Technol.*, 47: 61 67.

Meher, H. C., Gajbhiye, V. T., Singh, G., and Sharma, H. K. (2008): Nematicidal Efficacy and Persistence of Carbosulfan, Fenamiphos and Triazophos in Chickpea Following Seed Treatment, *Nematologia Mediterranea*, 36 (2):203-210

Mendoza, A. R., Sikora, R. A., and Kiewnick, S. (2007): Influence of *Paecilomyces Lilacinus* Strain 251 on the Biological Control of the Burrowing Nematode *Radopholus Similis* in banana, *Nematropica*, 37 (2): 203-213

Mojumdar, V. (1995): Effects on Nematodes. In: Schmutterer, H. (Ed.), The Neem Tree, *Azadirachta indica* A. Juss. and Other Meliaceous Plants: Source of Unique Natural Products for Integrated Pest Management, Industry, and other Purposes, VCH, Weinheim, pp. 129–150.

Mojumder, V and Basu, R. (1999): Seed Coating of Chickpea with Neem based Pesticidal Formulations for the Management of *Meloidogyne incognita, Indian J. Nematol.*,29 (1): 28-32.

Mojumder, V and Raman, R. (1996): Comparative Efficacy of Neem based Nematicidal Products for the Management of Nematode Pests of Pulse Crops, in: Proceedings of International Neem Conference, 4-9 February, 1996, Queensland, Gatton College, Australia, pp.46.

Musabyiman. Y., Saxena.R.C., Kairu. E.W, Ogol.C.K., and Khan. Z.R. (2000): Powdered Neem Seed and Cake for Management of the Banana Weevil, *Cosmopolites Sordidus*, and Parasitic Nematodes, *Phytoparasitica*, 28(4):321-333.

Naidu, P. H., Haritha, V., and Sudheer, M. J. (2007): Community Analysis of Plant Parasitic Nematodes in Chittoor district of Andhra Pradesh, *Indian J. Nematol.*, 37(2) : 207-211.

Naik, B.G., Nanjegowda, D., Ravi, K., Reddy, P.P., Kumar, N.K.K., and Varghese, A. (1998): Effect of Neem Products and a Nematicide for Management of Root-knot Nematode *Meloidogyne Incognita*, in Tomato, In: Proceedings of First National Symposium on Pest Management in Horticultural Crops: Environmental Implications and Thrusts, Bangalore, 15-17 October 1997, Bangalore, Indian Institute of Horticultural Research, Bangalore, pp.321-322.

Nair, M.R.G.K., Das, N. M. and Menon, M. R. (1966): On the Occurrence of Burrowing Nematode, *Radopholus Simils* (Cobb, 1893) Thorne 1949 on Banana Kerala, *Indian J. Entomol.*, 28: 553-554.

Nandwana, R.P., Varma, M.K., and Lal, A. (2005): Community Analysis of Phytonematodes in the Sugarcane Ecosystem in Bundi District of Rajasthan, .*Indian J. Nematol.*, 35(2): 221.

Narayana, R. (2012): Biodiversity of Nematodes Associated with Cardamom in Cardamom Reserve Hills of Idukki district, In: Proceedings of Nat ional Seminar on Watershed Planning for Natural Resource Management, 15-16 February 2012, Thiruvanathapuram. Kerala State Land Use Board, Government of Kerala, pp.208-209.

Nath, R. C., Brindaban, M.,and Dasgupta, M. K. (1998): Population Behaviour of *Helicotylenchus multicinctus* in Soil and Roots of Banana in Tripura, *J. Fundamental Applied Nematol.*, 21(4): 353-358.

Neog, P. P. and , Borah,D. (2015): Seasonal Population Fluctuation of Important Plant Parasitic Nematodes in the Rhizosphere of Banana, *J. Crop Res.*, 49(3): 45-47.

Ngala, B. M., Haydock, P. P. J., Woods, S., and Back, M. A. (2015): Biofumigation with *Brassica Juncea, Raphanus Sativus* and *Eruca Sativa* for the Management of Field Populations of the Potato Cyst Nematode *Globodera pallid, Pest Manag. Sci.*, 71 (5): 759-769.

NHB [National Horticulture Board]. (2017): Horticultural Statistics at a Glance 2015 [on-line]. Available: http://nhb.gov.in/area-pro/horst_galance_2016.pdf [14 June 2017].

Nie HaiZhen, Sun ManHong, Li ShiDong, Zhong ZengMing. (2016): Integrated Control of Root-knot Nematode Disease of Tomato by Dazomet and *Paecilomyces lilacinus, Acta Phytophylacica Sinica*, 43(4): 689-696.

Nisha M.S., Narayana, R and Nimisha, A.M. (2017): Biofumigation using crop residues of cruciferous vegetable wastes for the management of nematodes in okra, In: Proceedings of National Seminar on Biodiversity Conservation and farming systems for Wetland Ecology,22-23February,2017, Kumarakom, Kerala, pp.121-122.

Nisha, M. S. and Sheela, M. S. (2002): Effect of green leaf mulching for the management of root-knot nematode in kacholam, *Indian J. Nematol.*, 32 (2): 211-212.

Nisha, M. S. and Sheela, M. S. (2006): Bio-management of Meloidogyne incognita *on Coleus,* Solenostemon rotundifolius *by integrating solarization,* Paecilomyces lilacinus, Bacillus macerans *and neemcake, Indian J. Nematol.*, 36 (1): 136-138.

Nisha, M.S. (2005): Integrated management of root knot nematode *Meloidogyne incognita* in coleus, *Solenostemon rotundifolius* (Poir) Morton, Ph.D. (Ag) thesis, Kerala Agricultural University, Thrissur,181p.

Nisha, M.S. and Sheela, M.S. (2002): Effect of green leaf mulching for the management of root-knot nematode in kacholam, *Indian J. Nematol.*, 32(2): 183-233.

Nisha, M.S., Sheela M.S., and Narayana, R. (2015): Biomanagement of root knot nematode *Meloidogyne incognita* on brinjal by *Paecilomyces lilacinus* [abstract] In:*Abstracts Twentys eventh Kerala Science Congress;* 27-29 January 2015, Alappuzha, Kerala State Committee on Science, Technology and Environment, Government of Kerala.pp.12.Abstract No.1.18.

Norton, D.C. (1978): Ecology of plant parasitic nematodes, John -Wiley and Sons, New York, 268p.

Odeyemi, I. S., Afolami, S. O., Adigun, J. A. (2013): Plant parasitic nematode relative abundance and population suppression under *Chromolaena odorata* (Asteraceae) fallow, *International J. Pest Management* 59(1): 79-88.

Oka, Y., Tkachi, N., Shuker, S., and Yerumiyahu, U. (2007): Enhanced nematicidal activity of organic and inorganic ammonia-releasing amendments using neem extracts, *J. Nematol.*, 39: 9–16.

Oliveira, U. L. C., Silveira, A. J., Soares, P. L. M., and Bittencourt, M. A. L. (2015): Plant parasitic nematodes associated with bananas plantings in the south region of Bahia, *Agrotropica,* 27 (1): 5-14.

Osman, A.A., Farhat, A.A., and Wafdi, A.W. (1989): Organic amendments as co-agent with systemic nematicides to control nematodes infecting cowpea, *Bull. Zool. Soc.Egypt.*, 38: 49-63.

Ozarslandan, A. and Dincer, D. (2015): Plant parasitic nematodes in banana fields in Turkiye, *Bitki Koruma Bülteni,* 55(4): 361-372

Padhi, N.N. and Behera, G. (2000): Evaluation of nematicidal potential in ten indigenous plant species against *Meloidogyne incognita, Indian Phytopathol.*, 53: 28-31.

Pakeerathan, K., Mikunthan, G., and Tharshani, N. (2009): Eco-friendly management of root-knot nematode *Meloidogyne incognita* (Kofid and White) Chitwood using different green leaf manures on tomato under field conditions, *Am.-Eurasian J. Agric. and Environ. Sci.*, 6(5): 494-497.

Patel, A. D., Bindu, K. P., Patel , B.A., and Patel, D. J. (2008): Community analysis of plant parasitic nematodes associated with agricultural crops in Junagadh district of Gujarat and Diu -Union territory, *Indian J. Nematol.*, 38(1): 53-56.

Patel, D.J., Patel, H.V., Patel, S.K., and Patel, B.A. (1993): Nematicidal properties of some plant materials for the management of root knot nematodes in tomato nursery. *Indian J. Plant Prot.*, 21(2): 242-244.

Patel, H.R., Thakar, N.A., and Patel, C.C. (1985): Inhibitory effect of *Clerodendron inermi* on root-knot of okra, *Madras Agric. J.*, 72: 470-472.

Pathak, K.N. and Keshari, N. (2004): Interaction of *Meloidogyne incognita* with *Fusarium oxysporum* f.sp. *conglutinans* on cauliflower, *Indian J. Nematol.*, 34(1): 85-87.

Pathan, M. A., Soomro, S. H., Jiskani, M. M., Wagan, K. H., and Memon, J. A. (2004): Evaluation of Paecilomyces lilacinus *for the management of* Meloidogyne incognita, *Pakistan J. Nematol.*, 23 (1): 61-65.

Posadas, L.A. V., Nunez, S. A., Lopez L.D., and Carrion, G. (2016): Plant parasitic nematodes associated to banana roots (Musa acuminata AA) in central Veracruz, Mexico, *Revista Mexicana de Fitopatologia*, 34 (1): 116-130.

Rajendran, G., Cannayane, I.,and Shobana, N. J. (2002): Survey on plant parasitic nematodes associated with banana in Coimbatore, Tamil Nadu, India, *Current Nematol.*, 13(1): 73-76.

Rajinikanth, R. (2011): Production of nematode free bioagent colonised seedlings of cabbage, In: *Abstracts, National Symposium, Nematodes: A challenge under changing climate and agricultural practices;* 16-18, November, 2011, Kovalam, Nematological Society of India, New Delhi. pp.137-138.

Ramakrishnan, S., Sreeja, P., and Mohandas, C. (1999): Cassava wastes for management of root-knot nematode, In: Dhawan, S.C., Kaushal, KK., and Ganguly, S. (eds), Proceedings of National Symposium on Rational Approaches in Nematode Management for Sustainable Agriculture, 23-25 November 1998, Anand, Gujarat Agriculture University, Anand, pp.23-25.

Ramana, K. and Dasgupta, M. K. (1998): Population ecology and community structure of plant parasitic nematodes associated with ginger in West Bengal, *Indian J. Nematol.*, 28 (1): 10-14.

Ramclam, W. and Araya, M. (2006): Frequency of occurrence and abundance of root nematodes on banana (*Musa* AAA) in Belize, *International J. Pest Management*, 52 (1):71-77.

Ravishankar, M., and Singh, R. V. (2005): Effect of carbosulfan (25 STD) and neem seed kernel powder as corm dressing for the management of root-knot nematode (*Meloidogyne incognita*) infecting gladiolus, *Indian J. Nematol.*, 35 (1): 53-55.

Ray, S. and Parija, A. K. (1987): Community analysis of nematodes in the rhizosphere of banana in Puri district, Orissa, *Indian J. Nematol., 17(2): 159-161.*

Reddy, P. P., Khan, R. M., and Rao, M. S. (1991): Evaluation of chemicals for the management of the burrowing nematode, *Radopholus similis* infecting banana, *Current Nematol.*, 2 (1): 1-2

Rodriguez, A., Munoz, Y., and Pocasangre, L. E. (2012): Evaluation of free-living nematodes as indicators of soil quality in three banana production systems, Tierra Trop: Sostenibilidad, Ambientey Sociedad, 8(1): 115-125.

Rodriguez, H.M.G., Viruliche, L. P., Hernandez, O., Hernandez, J., Enrique, R., Gomez, G., Miranda C.I., Rosales, C., and Suarez, H.Z. (2011): Impact of biofumigation and organic materials on recovery of one vineyard infested with root knot nematodes, *Agronomia Trop.*, 61 (2): 113-124.

Roy, K., Roy, S., Sarkar, S., Rathod, A., and Pramanik, A. (2014): Diversity of migratory nematode endoparasites of banana, *J. Crop Weed*,10 (2): 375-391.

Saeed, M. and Ashrafi, S. H. (1971): The influence of rainfall on the population of nematodes in banana field, *Pakistan J. Scientific Indus. Res.*, 14 (5): 403-404.

Schindler, A.F. (1961): A Simple Substitute for a Baermann Funnel, *Plant dis. Reporter*, 45: 747-748.

Seinhorst, J.W. (1965): The Relation between Nematode Density and Damage to Plants, *Nematologica*, 11: 137-154.

Senapati, S., Sahoo, S., and Mahalik, J. K. (2016): Field Efficacy of Bioagents for Management of Root Knot Nematode (Meloidogyne Incognita) in Tomato, *Annals Plant Prot. Sci.*, 24 (1):152-156.

Senthamizh, K. , Sivakumar, M. , and Sivakumar , C.V. (2005): Community Analysis of Plant Parasitic Nematodes Associated with Groundnut in Erode district of Tamil Nadu, *Indian J. Nematol.*, 35(2): 209-210.

Shaukat, S.S., Siddiqui, I.A., Ali, N. I., Ali, S.A., and Khan, G.H. (2003): Nematicidal and Allelopathic Responses of *Lantana camara* root extract, *Phytopathologia Mediterranea*, 42(1): 71-78.

Sheela, M.S., Ajith, K., and Nisha, M.S. (2008): Impact of Green Leaf Application on the Management of Plant Parasitic Nematodes and its Effect on the Population of Predatory and Saprophytic Nematodes and Micro Flora in Soil, In: Proceedings of Fifth International Congress on Nematology, 13-18 July 2008, Brisbane. Australasian Association of Nematologists, Ausrtral ia, pp.37-38.

Shendge, A. G., Mhase, N. L., Landge, S. A., and Kadu, R. V. (2010): Integrated Management of root-knot Nematode, *Meloidogyne Incognita* Infesting Okra [*Abelmoschus esculentus* (L.) Moench], *Int. J. Plant Prot.*, 3(2): 369-371.

Shreenivasa, K. R., Krishnappa, K., Reddy, B. M. R., and Ravichandra, N. G. (2002): Influence of some Ecological Factors on Biodiversity of Nematode Complex on Banana, In: Proceedings of National Symposium on Biodiversity and Management of Nematodes in Cropping Systems for Sustainable Agriculture, Jaipur in India, 11-13 November, 2002, pp.104-107.

Siddiqui, Z.A. and Husain, S.I. (1990): Herbal Control of Root-knot and Root-rot Diseases of Chickpea, I. Effect of Plant Extracts, *New Agric.*, 1(1): 1-6.

Siddiqui, Z.A. and Mahmood, I. (1999): Effects of *Meloidogyne incognita, Fusarium Oxysporum* f.sp. *pisi, Rhizobium* sp. and different Soil Types on Growth, Chlorophyll, and Carotenoid Pigments of Pea, *Israel J. Plant Sciences*, 47: 251–256.

Siji, J.V., Jayaprakash, C.A., Sheela, M.S., and Mohandas. C. (2010): Efficacy of *Cleome Viscosa* L. against *Meloidogyne Incognita* Infestation in Okra (*Abelmoschus esculentus* L.), *Thai J. Agric. Sci.*, 43 (3): 151-156.

Singh, S., Singh, B., and Singh, A. P. (2014): Integrated Management of Root-knot Disease of Okra caused by Root-knot Nematode, Meloidogyne incognita, *Indian J. Nematol.*, 44(2): 172-178.

Somasekhara, Y. M., Ravichandra, N. G., and Jain, R. K. (2012): Bio-management of Root Knot (*Meloidogyne incognita*) Infecting Pomegranate (*Punica granatum* L.) with Combination of Organic Amendments, *Res. Crops*, 13(2): 647-651.

Southey, J. F. 1(986): Extract of *Meloidogyne* egg Masses, In: Southey, J.F. (ed.), Laboratory Methods for Work with Plants and Soil Nematodes, HMSO, London, pp.42-44.

Sreeja, C.A. (2011): Effect of Biodynamic Preparations on Growth of Cardamom and Improvement of Soil Microbial and Nematode Dynamics, M.Sc. Thesis, Sree Narayana Arts and Science College, Kumarakom, Mahatma Gandhi University, Kottayam, 39p.

Stirling,G.R. (1991): Biological Control of Plant Parasitic Nematodes, Chichester, England, p.282.

Subhadra, B., Krishnappa, K., and Reddy, B. M. R. (1998): Integrated Management of Nematode Complex on Banana using Physical, Cultural and Chemical Methods, *Mysore J. of Agric Sci.*, 32(2): 48-153.

Subramaniyan, S. (1985): Effect of *Eupatorium Odoratum* Extracts on *Meloidogyne Incognita, Indian J. Nematol.*, 15(2): 247.

Sudheer, M. J., Kalaiarasan, P., Senthamarai, M., Prabhu, S., Rao, G. M. V. P., Priya, P., Naidu, P. H., Haritha, V., Kumar, M. R., and Sailaja, R. (2008): Diversity and Community Structure of Major Plant Parasitic Nematodes in Selected Districts of Andhra Pradesh in India, *Indian J. Nematol.*, 38(1): 68-74.

Sundararaju, P. (2002): Seasonal Fluctuations of *Radopholus Similis* and *Pratylenchus Coffeae* in Certain Cultivars of Banana, *Infomusa,* 11 (1): 16-18.

Sundararaju, P. (2006): Community Structure of Plant Parasitic Nematodes in Banana Plantations of Andhra Pradesh in India, *Indian J. Nematol.*, 36(2): 226-229.

Sundararaju, P. (2009): Vertical and Horizontal Distribution of Plant Parasitic Nematodes Associated with Banana, *Indian J. Nematolo.*, 39(1): 80-84.

Sundararaju, P., Banu, G., and Ratnakaran, K. (1999): Effect of Various Plant Extracts on Mortality of *Radopholus similis, Indian J. Nematol.*, 29 (1): 78-111.

Sundraraju, P. and Kiruthika, P. (2009): Effect of Bio-control Agent, *Paecilomyces Lilacinus* along with Neemcake and Botanicals for the Management of *Meloidogyne Incognita* on Banana, *Indian J. Nematol.*,39 (2): 201-206.

Syed, S. and S. Imran. (2001): *Lantana Camara* in the Soil Changes the Fungal Community Structures and Reduces Impact of *Meloidoyne javanica* on Mung bean, *Phytopathol. Mediterr.* 40: 245-252..

Thammaiah, N., Kanamadi, V. C., Shirol, A. M., Devappa, V., Swamy, G. S. K., and Basavarajappa, H. R. (2012): Biological Control of Burrowing Nematode (*Radopholus similis*) in banana, *J. Mycol. Plant Pathol.*, 42(4): 509-512.

Thoden, T. C., Boppré, M., Hallmann, J. (2007): Pyrrolizidine Alkaloids of *Chromolaena odorata* act as Nematicidal Agents and Reduce Infection of Lettuce Roots by *Meloidogyne Incognita, Nematol.*, 9(3): 343-349.

Tiwari, S. P., Vadhera, I., and Deve, G. S. (2000): Burrowing Nematode *Radopholus Similis* Associated with Banana Crop in Madhya Pradesh, *Indian. J. Nematol.*, 30 (1):38-41.

Tzortzakakis, E. A. (2008): Plant Parasitic Nematodes Associated with Banana Crop in Crete, Greece, *Acta Agriculturae Slovenica* .91(1): 97-101.

Umar, I., Muhammad, Z., and Okusanya, B.A.O. (2010): Effect of Organic Amendments on the Control of *Meloidogyne Javanica* (Kofoid and White, 1919) Chitwood, 1949 on Tomato (*Lycopersicon Lycopersicum,* Mill), *Agric. Business and Technol. J.*8: 63-77.

Varghese, A.P. (2015): Nematode Association in Cabbage, *Brassica oleracea* L. var. *Capitata* and its Management using Botanicals, M.Sc.(Ag) thesis, Kerala Agricultural University, Thrissur,144p.

Varghese, K. C. and Nair, M. R. G. K. (1968): Studies on the Population Fluctuations of Soil Nematodes Associated with Banana in Kerala State, *Agric. Res. J. Kerala,* 6:108-112

Vyas, R. V., Patel, N. B., and Patel, D. J. (2001): Management of Root-knot Nematodes in Banana, *Indian J. Nematol.*, 31(1): 86-87.

Wachira, P.M., Okoth, S., Kimenju, J., and Mibey, R.K. (2009): Influence of Land use and Soil Management Practices on the Occurrence of Nematode Destroying Fungi in Taita Taveta, Kenya, *Trop. Subtropical Agro. Ecosyst.*, 10: 213-223.

Walksman, S. A. (1922): A Method for Counting the Number of Fungi in Soil, *J. Bacteriol.*,1: 339-341.

Wang, Y. and Chao, C.C. (1995): The Effect of Organic of Six Tomato Cultivars to the Root knot Nematode, Farming Practices on the Chemical, Physical and Biological Properties ofSoil in Taiwan, Vol. 6. FFTC Book Series, 33-39p.

Widmer, T.L. and Abawi, G.S. (2000): Mechanism of Suppression of *Meloidogyne hapla* and its damage by a Green Manure of Sudan Grass, *Plant Dis.*, 84: 562-568.

Williams, L.A.D., Vaques, E., Reid, W., Porter, R.., and Kraus, W. (2003): Biological Activities of an extract from *Cleome viscoza* L. (Capparaceae), *Sci. Nat.*, 90: 468-472.

Zasada, I. A., Meyer, S. L. F., and Morra, M. J. (2014): Brassicaceous Seed Meals as Soil Amendments to Suppress the Plant-parasitic Nematodes *Pratylenchus Penetrans* and *Meloidogyne Incognita*, *J. Nematol.*, 41: 221 227.

Zhao, Y., Zhang X. B., Ruan, Y. Z., and Wang, Y. N. (2013): Types and Occurrence of Banana *Meloidogyne* spp. in Hainan, *Jiangsu Agric. Sci.*, 43(2): 128-130.

Pest and Parasites : *Control & Elimination Strategies* **Pages 48–53**
Edited by: Dr. Pawan Kr. 'Bharti'
ISBN: 978-93-86841-99-5
Edition: 2019
Published by: Discovery Publishing House Pvt. Ltd., New Delhi (India)

3

Integrated Pest Management for Rodent in Buildings

[1]Abd El-Aleem Saad Soliman Desoky

ABSTRACT

The objectives of the study is to provide an integrated control program for rodents in buildings and to clarify the most important preventive methods that can be used in the control process and to make some important observations when the application of control methods such as mechanical control, biological and chemical to get the best anti-rodent program inside buildings.

Keywords: integrated control program, preventive methods, control process, anti-rodent

INTRODUCTION

Rats and mice can be a major pest problem in buildings. They damage food, books, documents, and clothing. Damage to a structure occurs when rats and mice gnaw on structural components, including wiring, wood, and plastics. The gnawing on wire insulation can result in electrical shorts and fires. Rodents have also been implicated in the spread of dangerous human diseases. In short, structural risks, health risks, and a general lowering of environmental quality accompany any rodent infestation.

All rodents require food, shelter, and water. The shelter provides protection from predators, inclement weather, and a favorable place to bear and rear their young. Although rodents require water, those water requirements vary greatly by species. Because rodent food and cover (i.e., vegetation) can be influenced by human activities, there has been considerable development of strategies to reduce populations and damage by manipulating vegetation (e.g., Barras and Seamans 2002 & Desoky 2007).

Follow the tips in the sections below and you will be one step closer to keeping your home permanently free of rats and mice(SRC).

[1] Plant protection Department (Agriculture Zoology), Faculty of Agriculture, Sohag University, Egypt.

1. Preventive methods

The most important steps in controlling rodents are preventive methods because prevention is better than control

The following means:

- Healthy buildings should be constructed to prevent the entry of mice and rats.
- In occupied buildings, all possible access areas should be identified by rodents.
- Repair / seal any cracks or holes small diameter or inch or larger in the foundation, walls.
- Repair broken windows and doors - Make sure that the door seals are tight for any inhabited buildings.
- Place the wire on all building windows.
- All edible foods (lunch and snacks) will be stored in rodent-resistant containers and not in office drawers.
- Cracked or unusual food will be cleaned and removed from the intake area at the end of each day.
- Garbage containers are emptied in the dining areas daily or have narrow blankets.
- There will be no garbage dumps in the uninhabited buildings.
- The external garbage areas will remain clean and devoid of organic debris on the ground.
- Remove rodent attractions such as food or shelter by ensuring that the food is stored safely and that the surrounding environment is clean.
- Rinse food and beverage containers before disposing or recycling.
- Keep at least two feet between bushes, shrubs, fences and buildings. Also, remove the limb within 3 feet of the structure or ceiling.
- Keep firewood away from the ground and away from structures as much as possible to mitigate shelter opportunities.
- Fruit trees will be free of fruit that has fallen to the ground during summer and fall.
- Birds, squirrels and other wildlife will not be fed within 200 feet of any building in the province.
- Prevent the entry of animals into warehouses and houses.
- Keep stove tops clean and free of food scraps.
- Separate your home from paper, fabric, and any similar materials that attract rodents to nest.

METHODS OF TREATMENT

Mechanical Control

Using Traps

Using traps instead of rodent poisons gives you clear confirmation of a captured rodent and allows you to better gauge the effectiveness of treatment. You are also able to dispose of rodents immediately rather than dealing with the foul odor of rotting carcasses from poisoned rodents inside your walls or otherwise out of reach. Most important, using traps allows you to avoid rodenticides, which pose a greater threat of exposure to children, pets, and non-target wildlife, including natural predators. (SRC)

- Traps Description

Live-Animal Trap

This is a catch and release system that avoids killing a rat or mouse. Some states prohibit releasing rodents into the wild. The Center for Disease Control (CDC) warns that captured rats or mice might urinate and increase risk of spreading disease.Muhammad Sarwar (2015)

Snap Trap

This is the oldest type of trap and uses a spring-loaded bar to kill a rodent on contact. Some modern snap traps prevent risk to children and pets by enclosing the device in a plastic box.

Multiple-Catch Live Mouse Trap

This is a catch and release system that allows for capture of multiple mice.

Glue Trap

Glue traps are not recommended because the adhesive plate that is used to capture rodents can also trap birds, baby animals, lizards, and even pets. These traps also cause undue suffering to rodents. The CDC warns that captured rats or mice might urinate and increase the risk of spreading disease.

Enclosure boxes are plastic boxes that can fit a single snap trap, sometimes more, in order to provide an additional layer of protection for kids and pets. These boxes also hide the dead rodent, making for easier disposal of rodent, and can be re-used (SRC)

Electronic Trap

This battery-powered trap delivers an electric shock that kills rodents quickly. This is a newer type of trap, and models are available for both rats and mice.

Important Notes

- Be sure to place traps in locations where children and pets cannot access them or place traps in safety enclosure boxes.

- Place the trap sideways next to the walls.
- Do not place the trap continuously.
- Wash the trap after the fishing process.
- Remove rodents by using traps be cautious with live traps as rodents might urinate which increases the risk of spreading disease.
- Use gloves when disposing of dead rodents, nests, or any nesting material.
- Spray the dead rodent or nesting material with a disinfectant solution and allow them to soak for 5 minutes before disposing rodent or materials in a secure plastic bag.
- Spray and wipe up the area surrounding dead rodent or nesting material with a disinfectant.
- Place the plastic bag with rodent or nesting material into another plastic bag along with any wipes or rags that were used to sanitize the surrounding area.
- Be sure to wash your hands thoroughly with soap and water. (SRC)

Destruction of Burrows

Pruning both for adult trees or foliage with disposal of pruning products so as not to be a cache of mice to form a nest on these wastes.

Biological Control

Using Natural predators such as cats can help to control rodent populations by feeding on rats and mice. (SRC)

Chemical Control

Conditions to be Available before Rodent Control

- The control process should be carried out in case of the presence of mice or their effects.
- You must know the type of rodent present because each type has a control method. Witmer*et al.*(1995)
- You should use bre-baiting so that avoidance of poison bait does not occur.
- The control should be performed when the population density is as low as possible.Buckle and Smith (1994)
- The food available should be as low as possible.
- The control method varies depending on the location and food available.
- You must use a bait different from the food available in the place.
- Use attractants if necessary.

Using Rodenticides

Rodenticides consist of different types of poisons used to kill rodents. Rodenticide baits can be lethal for any mammal or bird that ingests them and are not only poisonous for rodents. As a result, all baits pose a high risk of poisoning for non-target animals that might eat the bait or consume a poisoned rat or mouse. Buckle (1999)

- The use of rodenticides has to be used with preventive measures such as gloves.
- If you choose to use rodenticides, you should be ready to deal with these potential consequences:
- Rodents are likely to die in locations where they cannot be retrieved
- The smell of a dead animal will persist for several weeks to several months.
- Always read and follow the label instructions on the pesticide product. The label is the law and you could be liable for any damage resulting from not following the label instructions.
- Indoors, only place rodenticide bait stations in locations that are completely inaccessible to children and pets—inside walls, under heavy appliances, or in enclosed crawlspaces. (Desoky, 2014)
- It is best to use anticoagulants because they are environmentally safe. (Desoky, 2016)
- Passage on the baits stations in the early morning or before sunset.
- The lids of all bait stations must be securely.
- All bait stations should be numbered and their location marked on a simple floor plan map.
- Bait stations should be inspected during every service visit for monitoring purposes and to ensure stations are not providing harborage to non-target pests.
- When dead mice have to be disposed of quickly because they have dangerous external parasites.
- Once all signs of rodents are gone, remove bait stations promptly by placing in a secure plastic bag. (UCDIO)

REFERENCES

Barras, S.C. and T.W.Seamans (2002). Habitat Management Approaches for Reducing Wildlife use of Airfields. Proceedings of the Vertebrate Pest Conference 20:309-315.

Buckle, A.P. (1999). Rodenticides their Role in Rodent Pest Management in Tropical Agriculture. In: Singleton, G.R., Hinds, L.A., Leirs, H., Zhang, Z.(Eds.), Ecologically based Management of Rodent Pests. ACIAR, Canberra, pp. 163–177.

Buckle, A.P. and R.H. Smith (1994). Rodent Pests and their Control. CAB International, Wallingford, U.K.

CDC, Center for Disease Control

Desoky, A.S.S.(2007). Management Strategies for Rodents within different Ecosystems. M. Sc. Thesis, Fac. Agric. Assiut Univ. 124.

Desoky, A.S.S (2014) Strategies of Rodent Control Methods at Airports, Global Journal of Science Frontier Research.

Desoky, A.S. S. (2016) Rodenticides (Anticoagulant), International Journal of Research Studies in Zoology, Volume 2, Issue 3, PP1-6

EPA, Environmental Protection Agency

Muhammad Sarwar(2015). The Rodents (Mammalia: Rodentia) – Gnawing Away on Crops and Options for the Integrated Pest Management at Field, American Journal of Marketing Research Vol. 1, No. 3, 2015, pp. 136-141.

SRC, Safe Rodent Control https://t.co/6SOqjYp2M7

UCDIO,University of California, Davis IPM Online.

Witmer, G. W.; M. W. Fall and L. A. Fiedler (1995). Rodent Control, Research Needs, and Technology Transfer. International Wildlife Management Congress, 16-26.

Pest and Parasites : *Control & Elimination Strategies* **Pages 54–60**
Edited by: **Dr. Pawan Kr. 'Bharti'**
ISBN: 978-93-86841-99-5
Edition: **2019**
Published by: **Discovery Publishing House Pvt. Ltd., New Delhi (India)**

4

Global Scenario of Tomato Pin Worm, Tuta Absoluta (Meyrick) and their Management

[1]V.K. Mishra, N.N. Singh and [2]Varucha Misra

INTRODUCTION

Alien species are species of plants, insect pests that inter a country or region accidentally outside their natural habitat. Invasive alien species is an alien species which becomes established in natural or semi-natural ecosystems an agent of change and threats native biological diversity. This pest does not belong to that area where the occurrence of damage has been reported and so these are considered to be the invasive ones. *Tuta absoluta* is a neotropical, oligophagous pest which infests more several solanecous crops and others too. Since 1960s, this moth has attained the position amongst the key pests of tomato in South America. An invasive species can be any kind of living organism that is not native to an ecosystem which causes harm. They can harm the economy, environment, human health. South American tomato pin worm, *Tuta absoluta* (Meyrick, 1917) (Lepidoptera: Gelechiidae) commonly called as tomato leaf miner is amongst one of the critical invasive pest seen for the first time infesting tomato crop in Maharashtra, India. On basis of classification it is the most severe danger for tomato all through world. This pest has covered South America to many parts of Europe, entire Africa and is now being spreading at a rapid pace in India. The infestation of this pest on plants is either direct or through sites of infection of other pest. Reports have shown that 90 per cent of yield losses and poor quality of fruit due to this pest attack on tomato. Its occurrence in India was reported for the first time by different workers in different parts of India. Its occurrence in and around Bangalore was reported by Sridhar *et al.* (2014); around Pune by Shashank *et al.* (2015); in Malnad and Hyderabad-Karnataka region by Kalleshwaraswamy *et al.* (2015) and in Telangana by Kumari *et al.* (2015). EPPO (2010) had showed that propagation of *T. absoulta* could be due to transportation of packaging materials from country to country. Occurrence of this pest in any country had been reported to be the most damaging pest in respect to tomato plant

[1] Department of Entomology and Agricultural Zoology, Institute of Agricultural Sciences, Banaras Hindu University, Varanasi, 221005 (Uttar Pradesh) – India

[2] ICAR-Indian Institute of Sugarcane Research, Lucknow- 226 002 (U.P.), India.

(Germain *et al.*, 2009). In India, recent reports stated the attack of this pest in tomato but due to Oligo- phagous nature of this pest, it can cause damage to other solanaceous plants which makes this pest of utmost importance. In this chapter, focuses have been made on its life cycle, symptoms, damage per cent and management strategies which will be helpful for awaring the farmers from this problem.

Global Spread

Tuta absoluta was only present in South America at the end of 2006. It was first detected in the province of Castello (Spain) where significant damage is reported (Urbaneja *et al.*, 2007). The incidence of *T. absoluta,* a new pest in Integrated pest management tomato fields in the northeast of Spain and also its natural enemies were observed (Arno *et al.*, 2009). The occurrence of *T. absoluta* in Bulgaria, for the first time was noticed in a glasshouse with tomato plants and severe infestation by the pest was observed which had rapidly spread after the last treatment with pesticides. The leaves were the most heavily damaged plant parts with an average of 9.42 and 8.75 mines per leaflet on the middle and upper layer of the canopy, respectively (Harizanova *et al.*, 2009). The occurrence of *T. absoluta* (Meyrick) (Lepidoptera: Gelechiidae)

The pest that's infesting tomato crops

Since 2008, tuta absoluta has spread to 15 african countries and driven up costs for both formers and consumers

Sources: European and Mediterranean Plant Protection Organization (2005), Office of international research, Education, and Development, Virginia Tech

Fig. 4.1: Incidence of *T. absoulta* in Tomato plant in the world (Source: EPPO and Office of international research, education and development, Virginia Tech)

in the Bosnia and Herzegovina was noticed based on the moths trapped from pheromones placed in the greenhouses and open field. From Spain it had spread to European and Mediterranian countries (Urbaneja *et al.*, 2009), later it was noticed in Turkey and then in Iraq later it was reported in east of Iran (Desneux *et al.*, 2010). Due to its exceptional speed of spread, Desneux *et al.* (2011) predicted it might reach India. Following its introduction to Afro-Eurasia in 2010 it was in the quarantine watch-list of India. In 2014, *T. absoluta* was first time noticed in Pune, India (Shashank *et al.*, 2015).

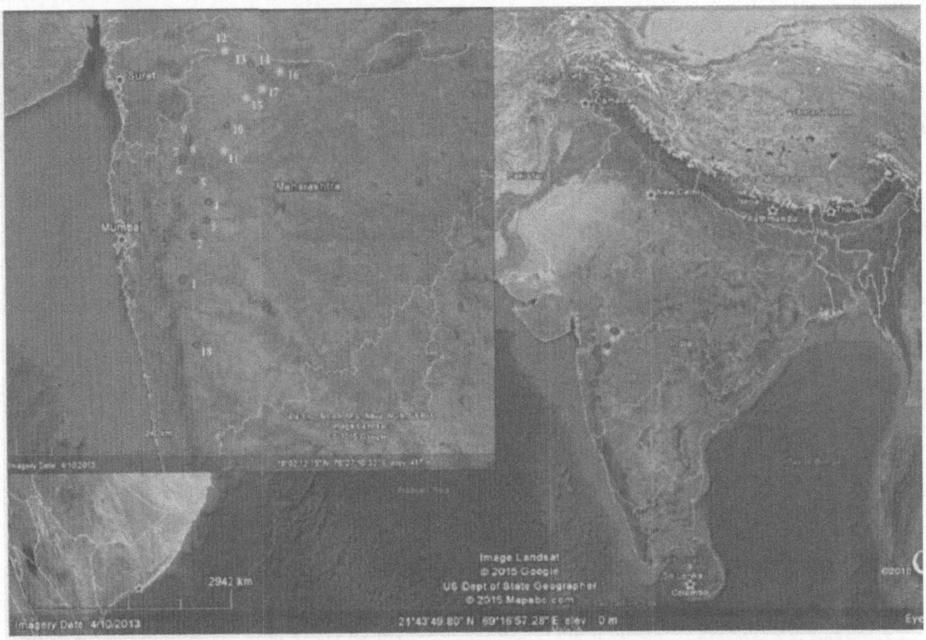

1. Map depicting surveyed localities in Maharashtra (light blue dots indicate absence) (1-Pune, 2-Nerayamgaon, 3-Ghargaon, 4-Sangamner, 5-Sinnar, 6-Dakambae, 7-Talegaon, 8-Vani, 9-Saptashrungi, 10-Malegaon, 11-Manmad, 12-Shahada, 13-Shirpur, 14-Saver, 16-Dhule, 16-Chopda, 17-Amalner, 18-Satara).

Fig. 4.2: Incidence of *T. absoluta* in Tomato plant in India (Source- Shashank *et al.* 2015)

In India, this pest was first recorded from states like Karnataka and Maharastra in October 2014. Later, it spread to neighbouring states like Andhra Pradesh, Telangana and Tamil Nadu. Recently its incidence is also reported from Delhi and mid-hills of Himachal Pradesh. Now this new invasive pest has crossed all the borders and spread to Varanasi and Mirzapur areas of Uttar Pradesh. So, it is important to keep a vigil on incidence, extent of damage by this new pest in tomato and its spread to other vegetable crops in the regions.

Reason for Spread and Distribution

Fruit import & commercialization of the crop. Long distance dissemination – packaging boxes through infested countries Wind currents seem to be especially favourable for its dispersal in Spain, International trade & movement of materials –Increased risk of alien species invasion. Import of Tomato to fulfill domestic needs of Kathmandu valley has led to introduction of *T. absoluta* to Nepal from India during 2014.

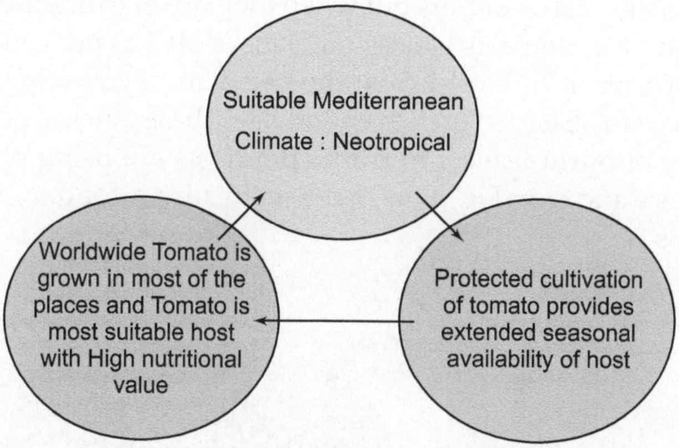

Fig. 4.3: Favorable conditions in invading places

Host Range

Tomato (*Solanum lycopersicon*) Potato (*Solanum tuberosum*), Eggplant, Tobacco, Poplar, Sweet cucumber, Beans etc., Other alternate hosts : *Solanum nigrum, S. eleagnifolium, S. bonariense, S. sisymbriifolium, S. saponaceum, S. lyratum, Lycopersicum puberulum, Datura stromanium, D. ferox, Nicotiana glauca.* The larvae of *T. absoluta* preferred tomato leaves at the most followed by brinjal leaf and tomato fruit and Chilli was least preferred.

Identification

The moth has a grey-brown colour, is approximately 6 mm in size and has a wingspan of about 10 mm Newly-hatched caterpillars are approximately 0.5 mm in size and have a yellowish colour. When maturing, caterpillars turn yellow-green and a black band develops behind the head. Fully grown caterpillars are approximately 9mm in size with a pinkish colour on the back. The pupa is light brown and approximately 6mm in size.

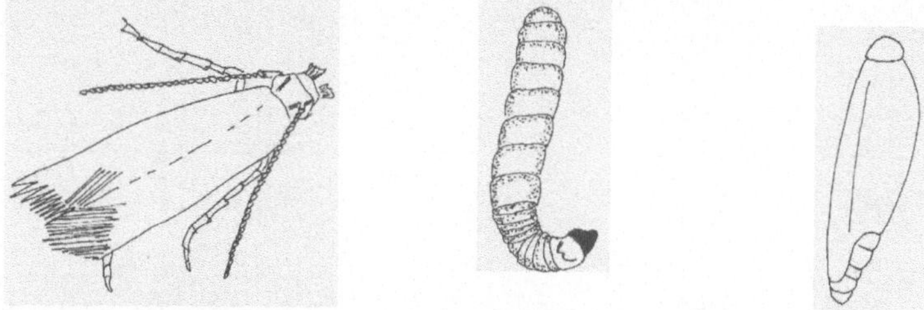

(A) (B) (C)

Fig. 4.4: Different stages of *Tuta absoluta* a. Adult b. Larva c. Pupa

Nature of Damage and Symptoms

This pest loves to feed on Solanaceous vegetables but it feeds on other vegetables too. The young stage of this pest nourishes on stems, leaves, buds, calyces and even on fruits (young ones/ripened ones). When larva feeds on stems of plants they act as miners but when they do on fruits, they act as borer. The infestation of these pests causes damage of 50-100 per cent loss in yield and quality of fruit. ETL level 2-5 larvae per plant. Symptoms revealed that white patches were observed on leaves and later these patches get dried giving an appearance of burnt leaves. In fruits, pin holes are being observed at the point of entrance and exit (Fig. 4.5). These sites cause secondary infections and rotting in fruits.

(A) (B) (C)

Fig. 4.5: Symptoms of *Tuta absoluta* on tomato plant
(a) Infected leaves (b) Infected fruits (c) Larva infesting on tomato

Life Cycle of *Tuta Absoluta*

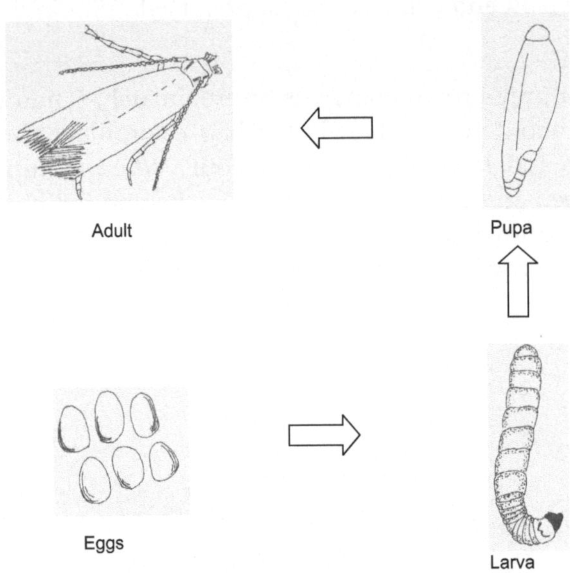

Fig. 4.6: Life Cycle of IUTA Absoluta

Management Strategies

Integrated pest management (IPM) strategies are the effective ones for controlling of *Tuta absoluta* insect. The integrated control method recommended employs the following (1) Use light traps and pheromone traps for monitoring (2) Deep summer plough in to expose the resting stage of pests (3) Removing of crop residues and alternate hosts (4) Crop rotation with non- solanaceous crops (5) Destroy the affected plants and damaged fruits (6) Selection of pest (whitefly/spider) resistant wild tomato varieties for resistance of this pest (7) Biological control agent such as *Egg parasitoid Trichogramma pretiosum has been widely used to control Tuta absoluta* (8) The usage of chemicals for controlling this pest such as imidacloropid in the irrigation water after 8-10 days of planting, chlorantranilprole 20SC (Rynaxpyr) @ 0.35 ml/l or cyantraniliprole 10 OD (Cyzapyr) @ 1.8 ml/l or indoxacarb 14 SC @ 75 (g a.i,/ha) or dimethoate 30 EC @ 275 (g a.i./ha) sprayed at 10 days interval for control of this pest.

CONCLUSION

Tuta absoluta is a damaging pest for tomato plant. Attack of this pest causes heavy losses in crop yield. It feeds on every part of the plant either stem or calyces or fruits. Controlling this pest is important. Application of integrated control method is an effective method against *Tuta absoluta* of tomato. There is a need for using such combination products as a pest management strategy for achieving expected results. New insect management strategies should be based on treatments that have been already established not on occurrence (presence/absence) of pest. This will help in reducing the costs. Effective use of these management strategies in combination with intensive exploration of population quantity of pests will enhance sustainability of the tomato.

REFERENCES

Arno J, sorribas R, Prat M., Matas M, Pozo C and Gomez A . *Tuta Absoluta*, a New Pest in IPM Tomatoes in the North-east of Spain. *IOBC/WPRS Bulletin*, 2009; 49: 203-208.

Desneux N, Wajnberg E, Kris A G, Wyckhuys Burgio G, and Arpaia S. Biological Invasion of European Tomato Crops by *Tuta absoluta*: Ecology, Geographic Expansion and Prospects for Biological Control. *J Pest Sci.*, 2010; 83: 197–215.

EPPO. First Report of *Tuta Absoluta* in Hungary. *EPPO Reporting Service*, 2010, 3(52): 2.

Germain J F, Lacordaire A I, Cocquempot C, Ramel JM and Oudard E. Un Nouveau Ravageur de la Tomateen France: *Tuta absoluta. PHM-Revue Horticole*, 2009; 512: 37-41.

Harizanova V, Stoeva, A and Mohamedova M. Tomato leaf miner, *Tuta absoluta* (Povolny) (Lepidoptera: gelechiidae) – First Record in Bulgaria. Agril. Sci. And Tech. 2009; 1, (3), 95–98.

Kalleshwaraswamy CM, Murthy M S, Viraktamath CA and Kumar N K K. Occurrence of *Tuta Absoluta* (Lepidoptera: Gelechiidae) in the Malnad and Hyderabad-Karnataka Regions of Karnataka, India. *Florida Entomologist*, 2015; 98(3): 970-971.

Kumari D A, Anitha G, Anitha V, Lakshmi B K M, Vennila S and Rao N H P . New Record of Leafminer, *Tuta Absoluta* (Meyrick) in Tomato. *Insect Environment*, 2015, 20(4): 136-138.

Molla, O., Monton, H., Vanaclocha, P., Beitia, F. and urbaneja, F. Predation by the Mirids, *Nesidiocoris Tenuis* and *Macrolophus Pygmaeus* on the Tomato Borer, *Tuta Absoluta. IOBC/ WPRS Bulletin*, 2009, 49: 209-214.

Shashank, P. R., Chandrashekar, K., Naresh, M. and Sreedevi, K. Occurrence of *Tuta Absoluta* (Lepidoptera: Gelechiidae): An Invasive Pest from India. *Indian Journal of Entomology*, 2015, *S*77(4): 323-329.

Sridhar, V., Chakravarthy, A. K., Asokan, R., Vinesh, L. S., Rebijith, K. B. and Vennila, S. 2014. New Record of the Invasive South American Tomato Leaf Miner, *Tuta absoluta* (Meyrick) (Lepidoptera: Gelechiidae) in India. *Pest Management in Horticultural Ecosystems*, 20(2): 148-154.

Sridhar, V., Onkaranaik, S. and Nitin, K. S. 2016. Efficacy of New Molecules of Insecticides against South American Tomato Moth, *Tuta Absoluta* (Meyrick) (Lepidoptera: Gelechiidae). *Pest Mngt. Hortic. Eco.*, 22(2): 137-145.

Pest and Parasites : *Control & Elimination Strategies* **Pages 61–135**
***Edited by:* Dr. Pawan Kr. 'Bharti'**
ISBN: 978-93-86841-99-5
***Edition:* 2019**
***Published by:* Discovery Publishing House Pvt. Ltd., New Delhi (India)**

5

Ecto-Parasites of Farm Animals
Alleviation and Control Measures

[1]Dr. Abd El-Aleem Saad Soliman Desoky

INTRODUCTION

Ruminants such as cattle, sheep and goats are worldwide important sources of human food and different economically important goods such as leather and/or wool, etc. Therefore, they are reared often in masses and in monocultures, which are highly attractive for many ectoparasites (Eckert *et al.,* 2009 and Schnieder, 2008). Many of these ectoparasite species have their breeding sites very close to their hosts, so that they are practically always present. Of course, the speed of the development of ectoparasites is temperature dependent. This implicates that their presence and numbers vary according to the different seasons during the year (especially in milder and temperate climates).

Many ectoparasites harm the health of their hosts by blood sucking (e.g., ticks, mite, simuliids, midges, biting flies, fleas, lice and bugs). This leads primarily to often enormous losses of blood. Furthermore, the biting sites become super infected with bacteria, and these wounds attract licking flies. In addition, some of the blood-sucking ectoparasites may act as vector of some diseases, such as ticks may transmit stages of Babesia, Theileria, Rickettsiales, Anaplasma, several bacteria, and viruses, which causes several diseases or even death to the hosts (Raether and Harder, 2008; Mehlhorn *et al.,* 2008; Eckert *et al.,* 2009). Blood-sucking insects such as biting flies, simuliids, or midges are known vectors of similar agents of disease, as midges turned out as vectors of the Bluetongue virus serotype 8, which overwhelmed cattle and sheep in Europe during the outbreak of 2006-2009 (Mehlhorn *et al.,* 2009; Conraths *et al.,* 2007; Hoffmann *et al.,* 2009). Simuliids are known to transmit filarial worms as well as causes painful bites to cattle (Dettner and Peters, 2010). Non-blood sucking insects may introduce several diseases to the animal. Licking flies may transport a great variety of causes of diseases on their labellae (=the terminal saliva-containing parts of their mouthparts) onto wounds or lips and nose and thus they may initiate several diseases (bacteriosis, virusis, or even parasitosis) (Förster *et al.,* 2009).

[1] Department of Plant Protection, Faculty of Agriculture, Assiut University, Egypt.

Some other ectoparasites just found in the skin of ruminants, such as the mallophaga feed on skin and at the basis of hair and induce harmful effect in its structure which lead to lowering its quality as a leather when used . Many mite species (Sarcoptes, Psoroptes, Chorioptes) enter the skin either totally or at least in parts, thus causing wounds and hindering the further use of the skin as leather of high quality. The same is true for the members of the scaled bot flies (Hypoderma, Oestrus), which leave large hollows in the skin along the back of the animal, where the Hypoderma larvae have their final breeding sites just before falling down to earth in order to pupate there.

All these different attacks of ectoparasitic and/or part time endoparasitic ticks, mites, or insects made it necessary to block their aggressive attacks by repellents to be placed onto the animals and to decrease the number of aggressors in the surroundings of herds by application of insecticides and acaricides on the skin of farm animals and/or on the breeding sites of the ectoparasites. Such activities of prophylaxis or control need knowledge of the developmental of life cycle and on the periods of occurrence of the ectoparasites as well as on their breeding sites.

Unfortunately, research on entomological topics has been decreased during the last 30–40 years so that basic data of many important ectoparasites are rather old or even lacking. Thus, there is an extreme need to update such data in order to get the most efficient control and to avoid development or increase of potential resistances. (Eckert *et al.*, 2009; Dettner and Peters, 2010)

The economic impact from changes in animal husbandry and the need for increased parasite surveillance and control have increased the need for a better understanding of the current distribution and prevalence of livestock and domesticated animal ectoparasites, the success in using the effective pesticides and some recent trends for controlling as main step in ectoparasites eradication. Ectoparasites controlling program depends on identifying the species of the parasites under local environmental conditions.

Objectives

The parasitic arthropods infesting farm animals have not gained much attention in upper Egypt. So, the present work of investigations aims to study the following topics:

1. Survey of animal farm pests in the studied area, in addition to animal farm ectoparasites.
2. Survey of rodents and their ectoparasite as carriers.
3. Determination of population density of ectoparasites.
4. Control of ectoparasites on buffaloes, cattle and sheep.
5. Studies the effect of attractant and repellent baits on rodent.
6. Evaluation of some rodenticides used in a large scale.

RESEARCH ON ECTO-PARASITES AND FARM ANIMALS

Ecological Studies

General Survey of Pests Inhabiting Farm Animals in the Area of Study

Byford *et al.* (1992) found that the horn fly, *Huernatobia irritans* (L.), is the most important pest of cattle throughout the United States and discussed its greatest economic importance to pastured cattle.

Abo Elmaged (1998) recorded five species of rodents, twenty six species of mites (Astigmata and Mesostigmata), three species of ticks, thirteen species of flies, three species of mosqutoes, three species of fleas, two species of lice, two species of ants, two species of cockroaches, one species of scorpion and one species of spiders in animal farm of the Faculty of Agriculture in Assiut University throughout three years.

Grabovac and Petriæ (2003) identified Flies of five families and nine genera on stock farms during their study. The families were represented: Muscidae, Calliphoridae, Tachinidae, Sarcophagidae and Drosophilidae. They found the larvae of most species during the study are coprophagous, detritophagous or necrophagous while adults are hematophagous (*Stomoxys calacitrans* L.), molestants, and have a vector role.

Peter *et al.* (2006) in South Africa, found that many blood feeding flies and mosquitoes parasitise humans and/or pastured livestock, such as horn flies (*Haematobia irritans*) and the buffalo fly (*Haematobosca stimulans*), are major pests, and stable flies (*Stomoxys calcitrans*).

Meerburg *et al.* (2007) found that flies can be considered as a serious pest in animal production, for example, stable flies (*Stomoxis calcitrans*), the common housefly (*Musca domestica*) and the lesser housefly (*Fannia canicularis*). Also they found, the housefly is the most frequently encountered around pig houses.

Survey and Population of Ectoparasites

Animal Ectoparasites

Harris *et al.* (1982) studied insect fauna which were collected from cattle droppings at 2 locations in Oahu, Hawaii, one in the wet east side (Kualoa) and another in the dry northwest side (Poamoho). From these areas, 7 species of Scarabaeidae were collected. The most numerous species were *Onthophagus gazalla* F., *Onthophagus Sagittarius* (L.), and *Aphodius lividus* (Oliver). Four species of Hydrophilidae were collected of which *Cercyon quisquilius* (L.) was the most numerous of the predator beetles, 9 species of Staphylinidae [*Oxytelus* sp., *Philonthus* (probably *longicornis* Steph.), *Philonthus rectangulus* Shp., *Philonthus discoideus* Grav., *Philonthus* sp., *Platystethus* sp., *Lithocharis* sp., *Eulissus* sp., and *Xantholininae* sp.] and 2 Histeridae [*Pachylister caffer* (Erich.) and *Hister nomus* Erich.]; all in low numbers except the *Oxytelus* species. Dipterous larvae, in

6 families and other unidentified families, were collected. In general, beetles were more abundant at Poamoho than at Kualoa and dipterous larvae were more abundant at Kualoa.

Milnes *et al.* (2003) followed over two winter periods a group of 61 cattle which were naturally infested with lice. Data were collected on the number of lice found at various body sites over this period. Summary statistics were produced and due to the repeated measured and hierarchical structure of the data, multi-level analysis was used to model the population dynamics of *Bovicola bovis* and assess the influence of the various hierarchical levels. A four level Poisson model was produced-level one, the individual number of lice at each parting; level two, the body site examined (shoulder, midline or rump); level three, the time of the inspection and level four, the animal. Seasonal fluctuation in lice numbers was modelled using a cosine function transformation of time. A seasonal pattern was seen in both year's with lice counts higher in the first than the second year. The midline area was the most sensitive to detection of *B. bovis*. Variance contributed by the individual animal was less than that contributed by the body site examined and the time of the inspection. The model suggested that lice numbers within the shoulder and rump sites were near random following a Poisson distribution, but aggregation of lice occurred at the midline site with the distribution between animals following a Negative Binomial Pattern. The midline site was the most sensitive site for detecting *B. bovis*. Infestation numbers were higher in the first winter when cattle were younger. In the second winter, there was no difference in lice numbers between cattle exposed to infection for the first or second time.

Deem *et al.* (2005) collected *Amblyomma* sp. (larvae) and *Rhipicephalus ziemanni* Neumann from dead forest buffalos in Congo.

Hussain *et al.* (2005) found during their study for chemotherapeutic control of lice infestation in cattle and buffaloes that sucking lice were the most common ectoparasites of cattle and buffaloes.

Sargison (2005) found that sheep scab is a highly contagious and rapidly progressive disease of sheep of all ages, caused by infestation with the non-burrowing mite *Psoroptes ovis*. The disease occur in most sheep-producing countries, with the notable exceptions of Australia and New Zealand.

Kaal *et al.* (2006) conducted epidemiological and clinical study of flea infestations in farm animals in northern Libya. They found that 150 sheep out of 12, 130 sheep, 23 goats from 2981 examined and 11 calves out of 1124 cattle were infested with fleas.

Reeves *et al.* (2006) collected 6 species of lice, *Anaplasma marginale, Bartonella* spp., *Brucella* spp., *Borrelia recurrentis, Coxiella burntii, Francisella tularensis*, from rats and domestic cattle throughout 13 governorates in Egypt in there study for testing these species for as pathogens.

Yakhchali and Hosseine (2006) studied the ectoparasites of sheep and goats in the northwest region of Iran. They found that ectoparasites (ticks, mites, lice, and fleas) were collected from 77 sheep (6.4%) and 119 goats (9.9%), with an overall prevalence of 8.2%. Ticks were the most frequent ectoparasites. Adult ticks (849) were collected and identified: the highest number belonged to the *Rhipicephalus bursa* (90.7% of sheep and 88.8% of goats), followed by *R. sanguineus* (6.9%), *Boophilus annulatus* (2.4%), plus *Ornithodoros lahorensis* (2.6%). Fifty-two sheep (67.5%) and 85 goats (71.4%) were infested with three species of lice. These were *Damalina ovis* (58.8%) and *D. caprae* (71.4%), *Haematopinus species* (on sheep 76.6% and on goats 62.2%), *Linognathus stenopsis* (36.1%), *L. ovillus* (29.4%). The seasons of highest infestation were fall and winter (50%), the least being spring and summer. Of these, two sheep (2.6%) were infested by *Sarcoptes scabiei*, maximum infestation occurring in winter. *Ctenocephalides felis felis* comprised of all the fleas collected (16.8% of goats, and 13% of sheep). Flea infestation was more widespread in fall and winter (10.2%) than in spring and summer (6.1%).

Tefera and Abebe (2007) studied the ectoparasites of small ruminants in three districts (woredas) of the eastern part of Amhara Regional State, Ethiopia, from November 2003 to March 2004, with the objectives of determining the prevalence of ectoparasites and identifying the potential risk factors associated with the problem. Out of 752 sheep and 752 goats examined, 50.5% of sheep and 56.4% of goats were infested with one or more ectoparasites. The ectoparasites identified in sheep were *Damalina ovis* (38.5%), *Melophagus ovinus* (12.5%), tick infestations (3.4%) and *Linognathus* spp. (2.4%). In goats, parasites such as *Linognathus* spp. (28.3%), ticks (22.2%), sarcoptic mites (6.1%) and *Ctenocephalides* spp. (8.1%) were identified.

Veneziano *et al.* (2007) examined 762 water buffaloes in Italy, in order to detect the presence of lice, they found *Haematopinus tuberculatus* in 11.0% (14/127) of the farms and 4.5% (34/762) of the animal.

Kakar and Kakarsulemankhel (2008) examined 404 cows and 386 buffaloes in Pakistan. They found that 28.96 and 25.64% respectively, gave positive results for ectoparasites. The prevalence of ticks, lice, mites and mixed infection was found to be 10.14, 7.17, 5.19 and 6.43%, respectively in cows and 6.99, 9.84, 4.92 and 3.88% respectively in buffaloes. It was concluded that the prevalence of ectoparasites in cows was higher than in buffaloes due to differences in feeding habits and hygienic habitats of the two species

Muhammad *et al.* (2008) found that the infestation rates of important genera of ticks infesting cattle in Frontier Region, Peshawar, Pakistan were as follows: *Boophilus* (43.40%), *Hyalomma* (36.65%), *Rhipicephalus* (16.88%) and *Amblyomma* (3.05%), while infestation rates by ticks of these genera in buffaloes were 53.12, 31.25, 15.62 and 3.05%, respectively on different livestock species in Faisalabad (Pakistan).Generally, Infestation rates were 28.2 and 14.7% in cattle and buffaloes, respectively. Most livestock species carried more than one genera of ticks. Ticks of the genus *Hyalomma* were the most prevalent in cattle and buffalo, followed by those belonging to *Boophilus*.

Rahbari *et al.* (2008) found that one hundred fifty six species of *Pulex irritans* were collected from sheep, goats, cattle, chicken and human, which consisted of 92.8% of all recovered fleas. Chickens infested by three species of fleas including *Pulex irritans* (84.6%), *Ctenocephalides canis* (12.9%) and *Ceratophilus gallinae* (2.5%).Two hundred and eighty nine cases of animal and 244 cases of human infestation were recorded among the suspicious populations, the most prevalence of infestation was found in sheep and goat herds whilst chicken flocks infested with the lowest rate and cattle were infested moderately.

Ramzan *et al.* (2008) found that the main species of ecto-parasites observed on cattle in Dera Ghazi Khan (Pakistan), were *Boophilus microplus, Boophilus annulatus, Hyalomma aegyptium, Psorcoptes bovis, Sarcoptes Scabies var bovis, Haematopinus tuberculates* and *Linognathus vituli.*

Tasawar *et al.* (2008) studied the lice infestation at a private cattle farm, situated in Multan, Pakistan,and found that ninety two percent buffaloes were infested with *Haematopinus* spp., 6% with *Damalinia* spp. and 2% with *Linognathus* spp. The relationship between sex of animal and different lice was also determined. It was 94.1% in females for *Haematopinus* spp., 5.8% for *Damalinia* spp. and 2.35% for *Linognathus* spp., while in males it was 80, 6.66 and 0 percent, respectively.

Corn *et al.* (2009) examined small mammals, birds, white-tailed deer, *Odocoileus virginianus* (Zimmermann), and feral cattle, *Bos taurus* L., at nine premises, in mountainous rain forest, and in surrounding areas in western St. Croix. They found that small Asian mongooses, *Herpestes javanicus* (E′. Geoffroy Saint-Hilaire), yielded 1,566 ectoparasite species, and including larvae of a soft tick, *Carios puertoricensis* (Fox); the tropical horse tick, *Anocentor nitens* (Neumann); and the southern cattle tick, *Rhipicephalus* (*Boophilus*) *microplus* (Canestrini); black rats, *Rattus rattus* L., yielded 144 specimens, representing six ectoparasite species, including *C. puertoricensis*.

Tanasak *et al.* (2009) surveyed the ectoparasites on domestic animals in the Royal Thai Army areas of operation along the Thai-Myanmar Border, Tak Province, Thailand, and found eleven different ectoparasites as following: two species of hard ticks (Ixodidae), three species of fleas (Siphonaptera) and 6 species of sucking or chewing lice (2 species each in the suborders Anoplura, Ischnocera and Amblycera). Domestic dogs (*Canis lupus familiaris*) (*n*=94) were found infested with 2 species of flea *Ctenocephalides felis orientis* (86.2%) and *Echidnophaga gallinacea* (1.1%), one species of tick, *Rhipicephalus sanguineus* (21.3%), and one louse species, *Heterodoxus spiniger* (7.4%).

Rodents Ectoparasites

Maher Ali *et al.* (1974) found that there is a direct relationship between fleas density in burrows and on rats.

Abdel-Gawad and Maher Ali (1982) recorded four species of mites (i.e. *Ornithonyssus bacoyi, Echinolaelaps echidninus, Dermanyssus gallinae and Phipicephalus sp.*) associated with the rodent species in the cultivated and semi-arid areas in Assiut Governorate.

Baker *et al.* (1995) collected four species of mites, *Ornithonyssus bacoti, Laelapsnuttalli, Dermanssus gallinae, and Allodermanyssus sanguincus* from commensally rodent *M. musculus, R. r. alexandrinus and R. norvegicus* in many Egyptian Governorates.

El-kady *et al.* (1995) recorded four species of mites *Eulaelaps stabularis, Laelaps nuttalii, Ornithonyssus bacoti,* and *Dermancyssus gallinae* from *Rattus norvegicus, R. r. alexandrinus,* and *R. r. frugivorus,* in Ismailia Governorate.

Baker *et al.* (1996) collected four species of fleas *Xenopsylla cheopis, Xenopsylla ramesis, Pulex irritans* and *Leptopsylla segnis,* from *Mus musculus, Rattus rattus, R. norvegicus* in some Egyptian Governorates.

Zahedi *et al.* (1996) studied the ectoparasites of the common house rat, *Ratrus ratrus diardii* from Kuala Lumpur city, Malaysia for over a period of one year. they found that 73'% of the rats harboured the flea *Xenopsylla cheopis,* followed by mites *Laelaps eckidninlrs* 64%**,** *L.nuttalli* 31% and lice *Polyplax spinulosa* 21%. It was noted that rats from semi-urban areas were mostly infested with mites; 50% were infested with *L. nuttalli* and 38% with *L. echidninus.* In addition, 55% were infested with the lice *P.spinulosa* and 12% with *Hoplopleura pucifica,* as well as 22% of the rats were infested with the flea *Xcheopis.*

Embarak (1997) recorded 16 species of mites, two species of ticks, two species of lice (*Polyplax spinulosa* and *Haplopleura oenorydis*) and two species of fleas (*Xenopsylla cheopis* and *Pulex irritans*) during study the ectoparasites of rodents in Assiut Governorate.

Battesti *et al.* (1998) collected sixteen ectoparasite species from 50 wild rodents, from August 1990 to August 1991, in an area of Araucaria augustifolia forest, in the municipality of Tijucas do Sul, State of Paraná, Brazil. Ectoparasites infested 98% of the rodents, with the highest indices of infestation found in the drycool season. Ectoparasite/host associations were significant ($p<0.01$) for *Gigantolaelaps wolffsohni/Oryzomys nigripes, Polygenis pradoi/Oxymycterus* sp. and *Amblyopinus* sp./*Oxymycterus* sp. The following represent new host records: *Polygenis (Polygenis) tripus* from *Akodon serrensis* and *Hoplopleura sciuricola* from *Sciurus aestuans.*

El-kady *et al.* (1998) found three ectoparasite species, *Polyplax spinulosa* (lice), *Allodermanyssus saguineus* (mites), *Xenopsylla dipodilli* (fleas) in *Acomys cahirinus* from saint cathrine area, Egypt.

El-Deeb *et al.* (1999) collected three species of ectoparasites fleas *Xenopsylla cheopis, Leptopsylla segins, Echidonphaga gallinacea,* and three lice species namely *Polyplax cheopis,polyplax vacillata, P. spinulosa* and four mite species *Ornithonyssus bacoti, Laelps nuttalli, Echinolaelaps echidnius* , and *Haemolaelps glasgwi* from three rodent species *Rattus r. frugivorus, Meriones shaw* and *Mus musculus* in new reclaimed areas of Egypt.

Wilamowski (1999) considered the oriental rat flea, *Xenopsylla cheopis,* as a parasite of the two rat species, *Rattus norvegicus* and *Rattus rattus,* in Israel.

Bochkov *et al.* (2000) identified sex mites of the family myobiidae, *Austromybia persics* sp., *Austromyobia merioni bochkov, Rodofordia acomys, Rodofordia affinis, Graphiurobia dyromys,* and *Myobia murismusculi,* in Iran on the rodents *Gerbillus cheesmani, Meriones libycus, Acomys cahirinus,* and *Mus musculus.*

Durden *et al.* (2000) recorded that one species of fleas *Polygenis gawyni,* and two of ticks *Dermacentor variabilis, Ixodes scapularis* from *Rattus rattus rattus* in the two locations in north western Florida, USA.

Lance *et al.* (2000) recorded 19 species of ectoparasitic arthropods (2 sucking lice, 4 fleas, 4 ticks, 2 mesostigmatid mites, 5 chiggers, 2 fur mites) from 106 rodents belonging to 5 species (cotton mouse, *Peromyscus gossypinus,* n=64; cotton rat, *Sigmodon hispidus,* n=23; eastern woodrat, *Neotoma floridana,* n=9; golden mouse, *Ochrotomys nuttalli,* n=9; eastern gray squirrel, *Sciurus carolinensis,* n=1) at Tall Timbers Research Station, Leon County, Florida. During the same period, 13 species of ectoparasites (2 sucking lice, 1 flea, 3 ticks, 3 mesostigmatid mites, 2 chiggers, 2 fur mites) were recovered from 57 rodents belonging to 3 species (*S. hispidus,* n=40; black rat, *Rattus rattus,* n=16; *S. carolinensis,* n=1) from Panama City, Bay County, Florida. Noteworthy ectoparasite records include Ixodes minor from both sites, which extends.

Soliman *et al.* (2001) found three mites *Ornithonyssus bacoti, Radfordia ensiifera* and *Laelaps nuttalli* and three fleas, *Echidnophaga gallinacea, Leptopsylla segnis* and *Xenopsylla cheopis,* on *Rattus rattus* and *R. norvegicus* in Sharkiya Governorate, Egypt.

Nava *et al.* (2003) collected 1,022 ectoparasites and recorded three new ectoparasite-host associations from Fifty-five rodents were captured from January 2000 to March 2001 in northeastern Buenos Aires Province, Argentina; ectoparasites were mites, ticks and fleas.

Khokhlova *et al.* (2004) collected two different flea species, *Xenopsylla conformis mycerini* and *Xenopsylla ramesis,* from *Meriones crassus.*

Stojcevic *et al.* (2004) collected three species of lices *Poliplax spinulosa* 14.5%, *Trimenopon jennings* and *Gyropus ovalis* 4.7%, and two species of fleas *Leptopsylla segnis* and *Ceratophylus fasciatus* 13.3% of rats trapped in rural regions of Croatia.

Beldomenico *et al.* (2005) found that *Ixodes loricatus* has long been considered with strict-total specificity to New World Marsupials. However, frequent findings of its immature stages on rodents suggest that these vertebrates play an important role in the tick's life cycle. Aspects dealing with the ecology of Sigmodontinae rodents infestation by *I. loricatus* are unknown. To contribute to the knowledge of the ecology of this tick species, environmental factors, as well as host species, sex and age, were evaluated to find associations of immature *I. loricatus* infestation of the most abundant wild rodent species from riparian locations of Buenos Aires province (Argentina).

Shaya and Rafinejad (2006) collected 218 ectoparasites belonging to 3 orders, 6 families, 6 genera, and 7 species from 24 localities in six major land-resource areas in Korram-Abad, Lurestan Province, Iran during the year of 2002-2003. Fleas with 3 species had the most number of species, mites and lice allocated the most (64.67%) and the least (3.21%) frequency of ectoparasites, respectively. Ectoparasites were more prevalent in Zagheh area (38.99%). *Haemolaelaps glasgowi* (42.2%) was the most common ectoparasite while, *Nosopsyllus irranus* only constituted approximately 0.91% of specimens.

Reeves *et al.* (2007) collected 616 tropical rat mites (*Ornithonyssus bacoti* (Hirst)) from rats (*Rattus norvegicus* (Berkenhout) and *R. rattus* (Linnaeus)) throughout 14 governorates in Egypt.

Telmadarraiy *et al.* (2007) in a plateu and mountanous areas in Iran, collected 9 species of ectoparasites including 3 fleas (*Pulex irritans, Xenopsylla buxtoni* and *Nosopsyllus medus*), one sucking lice (*Polyplax spinolosa*), two ticks (*Rhipicephalus* sp. and *Hyalomma* sp.), and 3 mites (*Lealaps nuttalli, Dermanysus sanguineus* and *Ornithonussus bacoti*), from *Microtus socialis, Mus musculus, Rattus rattus, Nesokia indica, Meriones persicus* and *Tatera indica*.

Matthee and Ueckermann (2008) described *Androlaelaps rhabdomysi* as a new species from the pelage of the endemic rodent *Rhabdomys pumilio* (Sparrman) in the Western Cape Province, South Africa.

Kia *et al.* (2009) found that, flea and lice had the most and the least frequency, respectively, among all collected arthropods. Nearly all rodent species were infested with *Xenopsylla*.

Matthee and Krasnov (2009) found that seven ectoparasite species (fleas *Chiastopsylla rossi* and *Dynopsyllus ellobius*, a louse *Polyplax arvicanthis*, mites *Androlaelaps fahrenholzi* and *Laelaps giganteus* and two ticks *Haemaphysalis elliptica* and *Hyalomma truncatum*) were exploiting the same populations of the rodent host *Rhabdomys pumilio* in South Africa.

Omudu and Ati (2010) found that the ectoparasites, collected from *Rattus rattus, M. natalensis, M. musculus* and *R. norvegicus* from residential buildings in Makurdi, Nigeria, comprised ticks *Haemophysalis* and *R. sanguineus* species (74.3%), fleas *Xenopsylla* species (31.3%), lice *Polyplax* species (69.3%) and mites *Dermanyssus* and *Myocoptes* species (71.9%).

Control Studies

Control of Animal Ectoparasites

Thomas and Niels (1990) found that several formulations of Permethrin are effective acaricides against ectoparasites of rodents and other animals, in the wild or in laboratory and commercial settings. Many of the features of this acaricide, including its low degree of toxicity to the animals and their caretakers, make it more advantageous than other products and methods for controlling fur mites.

Wichai and Ching (1991) studied the insecticidal activity of Ivermectin compared with coumaphos against lice (*Haematopinus* spp.). Both display the same activity with regards to the ability to get rid of the external parasites. Parasite count results showed more significant reduction of ectoparasite in coumaphos and Ivermectin groups than the control. Ivermectin had more prolonged effect than comaphos.

Abo Elmaged (1998) found that spraying with Diazinon (2ml/L) and injection with ivermectin (200mg/kg) were more effective in curing sheeps and buffaloes mange. The mean time of recovery for infested sheep and buffaloes with mange ranged between 23-37 days, respectively.

Hussain *et al.* (2005) studied a variety of chemicals including trichlorophon (Neguvon), deltamethrin, flumethrin, ivermectin, doramectin, moxidectin, eprinomectin, abamectin, malathion, chlorinated hydrocarbons, cyhalothrin, cypermethrin, neguvon and tiguvon to control lice in cattle and buffaloes. Among these insecticides and antiparasiticides, ivermectin had been found to have maximum control over the infestation.

Sargison (2005) found that Sheep scab is a highly contagious and rapidly progressive disease of sheep of all ages, caused by infestation with the non-burrowing mite *Psoroptes ovis*.

Makeri *et al.* (2007) studied the effect of topical application of neem seed extract against the tick *Ablyomma variegatum* on sheep. The seed extract showed acaricidal activity at 5.0, 2.5 and 1.0% concentration *in vitro*. The extract had no acaricidal activity *in vivo*. However, it showed a repellant activity against ticks at 5.0 and 2.5% concentration.

Wall (2007) found that Synthetic neurotoxic insecticides have provided over 50 years of potent parasite control; they are highly effective, easy to apply and relatively inexpensive.

Leemon and Jonsson (2008) bioassayed thirty-one isolates of *Metarhizium anisopliae* against the cattle tick *Boophilus microplus*. More than half of these isolates showed a high degree of virulence to ticks.

Ramzan *et al.* (2008) evaluate and compare the efficacy of ivermectin, doramectin and *Azadirachta indica* (neem) leaves against tick infestation in cattle in Dera Ghazi Khan (Pakistan). They found that the efficacy of ivermectin, doramectin and *Azadirachta indica* (neem) against ecto parasites was 100%, 60% and 0%, respectively. From this study it was concluded that ivermectin is drug of choice against ecto-parasites of cattle.

Hosking and George (2009) in Australia, studied the efficacy of CLiK® Spray-On (50 g/L dicyclanil) in protecting unmulesed sheep from naturally occurring blowfly strike. Unmulesed sheep were treated on day 0 and inspected for fly strike at defined intervals thereafter. They found that CLiK Spray-On protected unmulesed Merino and cross-breed sheep of various ages and wool lengths for the Australian registered protection period of 18-24 weeks, which had been previously determined using only mulesed animals.

Khater *et al.* (2009). Studied the effects of five essential oils against the buffalo louse, *Haematopinus tuberculatus*, and flies infesting water buffaloes in Qalyubia Governorate, Egypt. They found that all treated lice were killed after 0.5– 2 min, whereas with d-phenothrin, 100% mortality was reached only after 120 min. The number of lice infesting buffaloes was significantly reduced 3, 6, 4, 6 and 9 days after treatment with camphor, peppermint, chamomile, onion, and d-phenothrin, respectively. Moreover, the oils and d-phenothrin significantly repelled flies, *Musca domestica, Stomoxys calcitrans, Haematobia irritans* and *Hippobosca equina*, for 6 and 3 days post-treatment, respectively.

Natala and Ochoje (2009) questioned people about the pesticides, which used to control ectoparasites of farm animals in Zaria and Kaduna towns and their environs in Kaduna State, Northern Nigeria. Information was gathered from a total of 22 veterinary drug stores, 14 farms and 8 veterinary clinics were visited. A total of 28 different pesticides were encountered in veterinary drug stores, with synthetic pyrethroids (50%) being predominant. On the farms and veterinary clinics, 19 different pesticides were encountered, with organophoshates (42.1%) being the most widely used. The most popular method of application of pesticides was dipping.

Rodent Control

Attractant and Repellent Baits

Jacobson (1986) stated that *Azadirachta indica* has been used for a long time in many fields, and showed many benefits for agricultural and industrial application. In agriculture, neem extracts of the seeds, kernels and cake have a potential role in controlling pests. They are natural resources, which are effective against a broad spectrum of insect pests. They act as a repellent, phago-deterrent and antifeedant.

Burwash *et al.* (1998) evaluated eight synthetic predator odors and mongoose *(Herpestes auropunctatus)* feces for eliciting avoidance responses and/or reduced feeding by wild captured Hawaiian roof rats *(Rattus rattus).* They found that rats displayed a response to the predator odors in terms of increased elapsed time before initial arena entry and initial eating bout, a lower number of eating bouts, and less food consumption than in the respective control groups.

Dielenberg and McGregor (1999) studied the efficacy of predatory odors avoidance for rodents. Results showed that rats exposed to the cat collar displayed a robust avoidance response, spending about 70% of a 20-min session in the hide box compared to 25% in control rats. This avoidance response was completely reversed in rats given a low dose (0.375mg/kg) of midazolam. During the test phase, rats exposed to the cat odor on the previous day showed elevated levels of hiding when returned to the test apparatus without the cat odor present.

Khan *et al.* (2000) studied field trials on four field rodents *viz.*, *Bandicota bengalensis, Millardia meltada, Mus musculus* and *Nesokia indica* to control their populations in rice crop by improving poison bait acceptance using the additives *viz.*, minced meat, egg-yolk, egg-shell and yeast.

Boeke *et al.* (2004) found that the neem tree, Azadirachta indica, provides many useful compounds that are used as pesticides and could be applied to protect stored seeds against pests.

Witmer *et al.* (2008) investigated 18 commercially available materials for their attractiveness to wild Norway rats in a pen study. The most promising candidate attractants, based on the number of station visits, were anise, almond, ginger, and lemon extracts.

Rodenticides

Abdel-Gawad and Farghal (1982) in the central hospital in Assiut of Egypt, found that *A. niloticus* was more susceptible to Warfarin (0.04%) than *R. norvegicus* in all maturity stages (early, medium and mature).

Helal and Zedan (1982), in Assiut Governorate of Egypt, used Difenacoum at 0.005% against *R. norvegicus* and *R.r. alexandrinus*. They found that the LT_{50} and LT_{95} values were 5.5 days and 21 days.

Ali (1991) in Sohag Governorate of Egypt, studied efficacy of anticoagulant rodenticides using multiple feeding for 6 days under field condition. He found in multiple doses that Racumin and Matikus have the highest percentage of rodents control success 98.5% and 95% consequently.

Asran *et al.* (1992) evaluated the efficacy of 6 anticoagulant rodenticides against Nile grass rat, *A. niloticus*. Results indicated that 0.005% Flocoummafen, 0.005% Brodifacoum anticoagulants were the most effective ones followed by 0.005% Diphacinone, 0.006% Chlorophacinone, 019% Sulphaquinoxaline, 0.005% Bromadiolone and 0.05% Warfarin. The reduction caused by the above mentioned six rodenticides were 91.2%, 85.4%, 82.8%, 76.8% and 64.2%, respectively.

Gill (1992) in UK, determined the toxicity of the anticoagulant Flocoumafen to three universal commensal rodent pest species, *R. norvegicus, R. rattus* and *Mus domesticus* and four tropical rodent species not native to UK, *Meriones shawi, Acomys cahirinus, A. niloticus* and *Mesocricetus auratus*. In the 1-day no-choice tests, Flocoumafen gave 97.5% mortality of Warfarin-resistant laboratory rats, 100% mortality of Difenacoum-resistant rats, 92% mortality of *R. rattus*, 75% mortality of warfarin-resistant *M. domesticus* Linn., and 100% mortality of *A. niloticus*.

Parshad and Malhi (1995) in India, studied the efficacy of Racumin to three species of South Asian rodents, *Bandicota bengalensis, Tatera indica* and *Rattus rattus* in laboratory and field experiments. Species-specific differences occurred between the efficacy of 0.75% Racumin tracking powder (RTP) used for contact poisoning, and 0.0187, 0.0375 and 0.075% Racumin baits (RB), prepared by mixing the concentrate with cracked wheat, powdered sugar and peanut oil (96:2:2), used for poison baiting. *B. bengalensis* was most susceptible to the toxic effects of Racumin as both RTP and RB caused 80–100% mortality after short exposures (15 min and 3 h) to a floor/runway treated with 1 g/rat of RTP in forced contact and simulated runway techniques and 1–2 days of choice feeding of 0.0187 and 0.0375% RB in feeding tests. These treatments were less effective against *T. indica* and least effective against *R. rattus*. In pen experiments, in which the runway was treated with 2g of RTP, 100 and 60% mortality from groups of 5 rats each of *B. bengalensis* and *T. indica* occurred, respectively.

Vaziri and Farid (1995) in Iran, studied the efficacy of the rodenticides, Bromadiolone 0.005%, Chlorophacinone 0.006% plus Sulphaguinoxaline 0,019% against *Rattus norvegicus* and *Nesokia indica* under field conditions. The results showed that Bromadiolone gave 88.4% mortality of *Nesokia indica* in Karaji and 90.13% mortality in Djiroft. However, Chlorophacinone plus sulfaquinoxaline gave 86 and 85.15% mortality, respectively, in these areas.

Chander-sheikher *et al.* (1996) tested the rodenticide baits containing Zinc phosphide 2.5%, Bromadiolone 0.005%, Flucoumafen 0.00% and Cholecalciferol 0.075. Results indicated that the above mentioned rodenticides were most effective when applied through burrow baiting, leading to a 61.11, 83.64 ,84.61 and 36.36% reduction in the number of active burrows, respectively.

Khan *et al.* (1998) used both acute and anticoagulant baits against *Bandicota bengalensis* and *Nesokia indica*. The results showed that the efficacy of three formulations of 2% zinc phosphide in reducing rodent activities were 97.5%, 96.7% and 95.2% for wax coated cake, grain, and plain cake respectively. Meanwhile, the treatments with wax blocks of 0.005% Brodifacoum and 0.037 % coumatetraly gave 98.8% and 98.95% mortality, respectively.

Moran (1999) used wheat grain bait, treated with sodium fluoroacetate, and is used to control field rodents in Israel

Hygnstrom *et al.* (2000) in USA, studied the efficacy of in- furrow applications of 2% Zinc phosphide at planting for control of rodent damage in no-till corn, in three independent field. The population in the most severely damage fields ranged from 104 to138 active colonies/ha. Zinc phosphide reduced yield loss in the three studied areas by 7-34%.

Farghal *et al.* (2000) in Qena Governorate studied the toxicity of three anticoagulant i.e. Farobaid, Caid and Supercaid against *A. niloticus* under field conditions. Farobaid gave complete control to *A. niloticus* inhabited tomato field after 20 days of treatment. The LT50 and LT95 values were 3.1 and 21 days. Supercaid reduced 77.3% of *A. niloticus* population in sugarcane field after 21days of treatment, with LT50 and LT95 values of 8.2 and 43 days. Caid gave 59% reduction in *A. niloticus* inhabited sugarcane after 20 days of treatment. The LT50 and LT95 values were 16 and 100 days. The acute rodenticides, Quintox reduced 70% of *A. niloticus* population in corn field after 20 days of treatment. The LT50 and LT95 values of 10 and 82 days. Storm completely eradicated *R. norvegicus* after 6 days of offering poisoned baits. The LT50 and LT95 values were 4.4 –6.0 days in 1995 and 4.0 – 5.8 days in 1996.

Shehab *et al.* (2000) in Syria, studied the efficacy of the poisoned bites prepared by mixing 95.5g bite base (water added until 40% moisture) + 2g vegetable oil + 2.5% Zinc phosphide. The results showed that the reduction in the active burrows, after 24 hour of treatment, were: 83.97% and 81.86% for grains of wheat and corn, However, the other bite bases were 74.95%, 65.13%, 58.78%, respectively.

Abdel-Gawad (2001a) in Assiut Governorate of Egypt, studied the rodent control in the student buildings of Assiut University during ten successive years from 1991 to 2000. Zinc phosphide 3% was used through July as quick acting poison outside the buildings one time during the first year to reduce the high density of rodents. The anticoagulant rodenticide, Retak (Difenacoum0.005%) followed the treatment of Zinc phosphide twice a year one during February and the other through July month, outside and inside the building.The reduction in rodent population after the treatment with Zinc phosphide was 76.8% from the initial population. The decrease in rodent density during the years of study which treated with anticoagulant rodentcide was about 69.8% during 1994, 80.7% in 1995 and 1998.

Oconnor and Booth (2001) in New Zealand, studied the sensitivity of four rodent species include *Ratus norvegicus, R. rattus, R. exulans* and *Mus musculus* Linn., to brodifacoum. Results indicated that the LD_{50} in rodents ranged from 0.17 mg/kg to 0.52 mg /kg.

Twigg *et al.* (2002) used 2.5% Zinc phosphide wheat bait in dry storage against house mice in the canola in the central wheat belt region of western Australia.

Donlan *et al.* (2003) tested brodifacoum and two less toxic rodenticides, diphacinone and cholecalciferol, in eradicating *Rattus rattus* from three small islands in the northern Gulf of California, Mexico. All three rodenticides were successful in eradicating rats, suggesting that the less toxic diphacinone and cholecalciferol may be useful alternatives to brodifacoum for some island eradication programs.

Eisemann *et al.* (2003) in USA, studied the utilizing of Zinc phosphide as population control against the Norway rat, roof rat and house mouse. The efficacy of Zinc phosphate under laboratory and field condition have been conducted against the three species of mice, *Peromyscus mainiculatus, Acomys cahirinus, Mus musculus* Linn. The efficacy rate for mouse control using ZP was higher than 70% in all studies.

Moran (2003) in Israel, tested Cholecalciferol whole wheat bait in no-choice laboratory experiments as rodenticides for the field rodent species Microtus guentheri and Meriones tristrami. The LT50 was 40.86 and 32. 17 days for both species, respectively.

Shriprakash *et al.* (2003) studied the efficacy of baits formulated with two acute rodenticides, Uoroacetamide and Zinc phosphide and two second generation anticoagulants, Bromodialone and Difethialone at diferent concentrations against laboratory-bred wild type rats, *Rattus rattus* (Linn.). The mortality data clearly indicated that Uoroacetamide was more effective than Zinc phosphide at all three concentrations and produced complete mortality at 2% and 3%. In contrast, the Zinc phosphide bait did not show appreciable mortality and caused lower bait acceptance and palatability. The mortality patterns were significantly different and there were decrease in mortality caused at some concentrations. Bromodialone admixed cereal-based bait did not cause any deference mortality pattern among rats. However, the mortality pattern was inurned by concentration and duration of exposure. Bromodialone at the higher concentration (0.0075%) showed less effectiveness than at 0.005%, which caused 100 % mortality after 96 h exposure.

Prakash *et al.* (2003) evaluated the bio-efficacy of cereal-based bait formulated with two acute rodenticides, fluoroacetamide and zinc phosphide and two second generation anticoagulants, bromodialone and difethialone at different concentrations against laboratory-bred wild type rats, *Rattus rattus*. Bait containing 2% fluoroacetamide and incorporating edible green colour 0.025% and human feeding deterrent denatonium benzoate 0.001% produced complete mortality in 6 days and was considered to be the most effective.

Johnston *et al.* (2005) in California found that efficacy of zinc phosphide-coated baits and sugar-enhanced rolled oat based zinc phosphid bait with pre-baiting gave 100 and 60% mortality, respectively.

Kaur and Parshad (2005) in South Asia studied the efficacy of 0.0375% Racumin to control the lesser bandicoot rat, *Bandicota bengalensis*. The results showed high success in rice and wheat cropping.

Ahmed (2006) in Assiut Governorate of Egypt found that the application of Zinc Phosphide singly was the superior in controlling rodents, while supercaid only had lowest effect. Whereas, using both rodenticide together achieved a moderate effect.

Baghdadi (2006) found that the Bromadilone 0.005% was more effective than Brodifacoum 0.004%in controlling *Arvicanthus niloticus*.

El-Saady (2009) found that zinc phosphide surpassed racumin and tomorin in killing *rattus rattus alexandrinus*. This rodenticide was faster, whereas the highest reduction of density was observed within one day after application giving a mean value of 78.8% reduction. The bait consumption disappeared in the 3rd day of application with zinc phosphate while with racumin and tomorin the bait consumption gradually reduced and the completely nonconsumption was attained after 18 and 21 days of application , respectively, more than 50% reduction in rat density was observed in the 6th and 12th days from application with racumin and tomorin, respectively. The estimated LT_{50} was less than one day with zinc phosphide. The LT_{50} with rocumin were 5.20 days, and Tomorin came in last whereas the LT_{50} was 7.98 days.

Investigation Protocol and Control Methods

The present study was conducted in the farm animals of the Faculty of Agriculture, Assiut University, during three years, starting from December 2007. This farm consisted of about five feddans, including the buildings of animal- sheds and animal food storages. This farm contains buffaloes, cattle and sheep. The present survey of ectoparasites included both ectoparasites associated with animals and rodent species in addition to the pests collected from animals manure in the ground of the farm, during the study period. The present work was done to study the following topics:

GENERAL SURVEY OF PESTS INHABITING FARM ANIMALS IN THE AREA OF STUDY

Rodents

Twenty wire-box traps were baited and distributed twice every week at 6 pm and collected at 7 am. The captured rodents were classified and recorded. The percentage of each species was estimated during the survey period.

Flies

Flies were collected by using a sweeping net (handle, 80cm long, hoop 28 cm in diameter, Egyptian white cloth bag 80 cm depth). Samples were taken twice each week through fly activity inside and outside door. Flies were anaesthetized by chloroform and transferred to the laboratory for identification.

Mosquitoes

A 100-150 ml of water was taken weekly at a depth of 10 cm of the pool, and put in plastic containers, then transferred to the laboratory for further identification.

SURVEY AND POPULATION DENSITY OF ANIMAL ECTOPARASITES

Animals Ectoparasites

Samples were taken once weekly from five regions of the animal body chosen to the study. Samples were individually anaesthetized in a jar containing a cotton pad moistened with chloroform, then brushed in a deep white plate using a relatively hard brush. Collected ectoparasites were preserved in plastic tubes containing 70% ethyl alcohol and labeled with necessary information for identification.

Animal Manure Pests

Samples were taken ten times each month during two successive seasons, 2008 to 2010 from soil of rodent burrows, cattle and sheep at Experimental Farm of Assiut University. Soil samples were preserved in plastic bags labeled with necessary information and then transferred to the laboratory for extraction and identification. Extraction was carried out using the modified Berlese's extractor apparatus. After extraction of the whole fauna in the samples, arthropods were isolated in small vials then counted by using a stereoscopic binocular microscope. Clearing of collected specimen was done using lactic acid and higher technique was used for mounting of mites. Mites were mounted and left to dry by using a hot plate and prepared for microscopic examination. Identification of mites and ticks was done using different keys constructed by **Hoogstraal and Kaiser (1958), Zaher (1986a and b) and Evans (1992).**

Associated Rodents in Animal-farm

Rodents were collected alive and classified to species and subspecies, male and female of each as well as the distribution frequency of each species (%) was estimated. For collection of ectoparasites, rodents were individually anaesthetized in a jar containing a cotton pad moistened with chloroform then brushed in a deep white plate using a relatively hard brush. After collecting the ectoparasites, they were preserved in plastic tubes containing 70% ethyl alcohol and labeled with necessary information. The ectoparasites were classified as fleas, lice, mites and ticks. From the whole fauna in the sample, mites were isolated in small vials using a Camel's hair brush to avoid destruction and counted using stereoscopic binocular microscope. Clearing of collected specimens was done using lactic acid. Mites were mounted in Hoyer's media and left to dry by using a hot plate and prepared for microscopic examination. Identification of mites was done using different keys constructed by **Karg (1971), Hughes (1961 and 1976) and Krantz (1978).**

CONTROL OF ECTOPARASITES IN FARM ANIMAL

In Animals

Sheep Fleas

Animal was virtually divided into five groups. The infested group was isolated in special places to prevent spreading of the ectoparasites and was divided into equal subgroups; one was treated with Diazinon 60% EC spray, Vertimec 1.8% EC, Butox 5% EC at the concentration of 1cm/liter, and the second group was treated by Radiant 12% SC at the concentration of 4, 6 and 8 ml/liter. Treatments were compared with the control group; the results were taken after 1, 3, 5, 7, 10, 15, 20, 25, 30 and 45 days.

Buffalo Lice and Cattle Ticks

Animal was virtually divided into five groups. The infested group was isolated in special places to prevent spreading of the infestation and divided into equal subgroups; first group was treated with Diazinon 60% EC spray, Vertimec 1.8% EC, and Butox 5% EC at concentration of 1, 1.5 and 2 ml/ liter .The second group was treated by Radiant 12% SC at the concentration of 4, 6, 8 and 12 ml/ liter. Results of aforementioned compounds were compared with Ivermectin 1% injection, 1 ml / 50 kg of animal as a control agent of ectoparasites in the farm. Treatments were compared with the control group; the results were taken after 1, 3, 5, 7, 10, 15, 20, 30 and 45 days.

Buffalo and Sheep Mange

Infested spots with *Sarcoptes* were sprayed with Diazinon 60% EC spray, Vertemic 1.8% EC and Butox 5% EC at the concentration of 1 cm/liter, Radiant 12% SC 6 cm/liter. Tincture iodine 4% and Sulfur with vaseline 10% were evaluated during the study along with Ivermectin 1 ml injection / 50 kg of animal to control scabies in the farm. The results were taken after 1, 3, 5, 7, 10, 15, 20, 30 and 45 days.

Animal Manure:

Mechanical Control

Five samples were taken after each treatment of cleaning and burning of sheep soil. Soil of the experiment was covered with Quicklime, which was turned to be $Ca(oH)_2$. Fleas were recorded and compared with which in the control samples of sheep soil. The results were taken after 1, 3, 5, 7, 10, 15, 20, 25, 30 and 45 days.

Chemical Control

Each pesticide was sprayed on five regions of manure infested with fleas larvae in sheep farm and then compared with the control group. Pesticides were: Diazinon 60% EC spray, Vertimec 1.8% EC, and Butox 5% EC at the concentration of 2 cm/liter and Radiant 12% EC 4 ml /1 liter. The results were taken after 1, 3, 5, 7, 10, 15, 20, 25, 30 and 45 days.

Flies larvae

Each pesticide was sprayed on five regions of manure contained flies larvae in farm animal and then compared with the control regions. The pesticides were: Diazinon60% EC, Vertimec1.8% EC, and Butox 5% EC at the concentration of 1cm/1liter water and the second region was treated by Radiant 12% EC 4cm/1liter water and Quicklime. The results were taken after 1, 3, 5, 7, 10, 15, 20, 25 and 30 days.

The percentage of reduction in the population density of animal parasites were computed according to the formula given by **Henderson and Tilton (1955).**

% Reduction = 1-[(C1/T1) × (T2/C2)] × 100

Where,

C1 = pre-treatment population density in control habitat.

C2 = post treatment population density in control habitat.

T1 = pre-treatment population density in treated units.

T2 = post treatment population density in treated units.

RODENT CONTROL

Under Laboratory Condition

Attractant and Repellent Baits

Rodents were trapped and transferred to the laboratory; healthy mature males and females of *Arvicanthis niloticus* (120-150g), *Rattus rattus frugivorus* (180-200g) and *Rattus rattus alexandrinus*(160-190g) were chosen for these tests. The animals were singly caged and suitably accommodated in the laboratory for two weeks, then provided with crushed maize bait and water. Ten animals (5 from each sex) of rodent species were selected for study.

Four kinds of foods used in the preference test, which were Cumin, coriander, anise and yeast. For all experiments, 50 grams of each were mixed with crushed maize and provided in each food, and free crushed maize introduced to the control group. The consumption was recorded daily for each animal and each kind of food on five days period. The position of the cups inside the cage was changed daily to avoid baits of position preference.

The same method was carried out with black pepper, jojoba seed, oshar leaf powder and neem leaf powder as repellents.

Toxicity of two-anticoagulant Rodenticides to Certain Rodent Species

Rodents were trapped and transferred to the laboratory, healthy mature males and females of *Arvicanthis niloticus* (120-150g), *Rattus rattus frugivorus*

(180-200g) and *Rattus rattus alexandrinus*(160-190g) were chosen for the tests. Animals were singly caged and suitably accommoded in the laboratory for ten days and provided with enough wheat bait and water. For each of the two tested rodenticides (Supercaid 0.004% and Caid 0.005%), five males and five females were selected; the consumption was recorded daily for each animal and for each kind of food on five days period. The daily poison bait consumed for each animal was recorded. The poison bait was replaced by bait in cages.

Under Field Conditions

Toxicity of Rodenticides

Three areas of farm animal were selected to conduct chemical control. The first area was treated with the common anticoagulant rodenticide, Supercaid 0.004% with crushed maize by distributing 10-paper bait stations containing 200g poison bait. The second area has 10-paper bait stations from Caid 0.005% with crushed maize. The reduction of rodents was estimated by trapping methods and compared with the control group (third area), the experimental lasted for 11days.

Acceptability of Rodent Species for Two Attractive Baits

The field trial was carried out in the experimental faculty farm in three areas. In each, replicate 5 paper bait stations for Supercaid 0.004%. Supercaid 0.004% with vanilla and Supercaid 0.004% with yeast, each station treated with 200 gm poison bait. The position of the baits stations was daily changed to avoid the shyness. The consumption of baits was daily estimated in each station to the nearest gram, the experiment lasted for 6 days.

Toxicity by Aluminum Phosphide 33%

Aluminum phosphide was evaluated against rodents under field conditions based on reduction in the active burrows. In three areas for each treatment, 20 active burrows were marked. A distance of 200 m was left between each treatment and the others. The fumigation tablets were distributed into the active burrows. On the other hand, 20 active burrows were marked as a control; the percentage of rodent active burrows was recorded two times every week. The experimental lasted for one month.

DATA TREATMENT AND STATISTICAL BY ANALYZED

Simple correlation was conducted between ectoparasite populations and weather factors to identify the role of those factors in distributing the population.

Data were analyzed using analyses of variance **(MSTAT-C 1988)** and means were separated using the least significant differences method (LSD) at 5% probability level **(Steel and Torrie, 1984),** only when a significant "F" test was obtained. The percentage of reduction was calculated by **Henderson and**

Tilton (1955). All percent mortality data were arcsin transformed to suit the analysis.

6. PESTICIDES

The common names, chemical group and chemical structures of the rodenticides used in the toxicological and control studies are:

1. **Diazinon 15 % and 60% EC**

   Common name (diazinon)

   Chemical group: Organophosphate

   Used method: Spraying

   Chemical structure

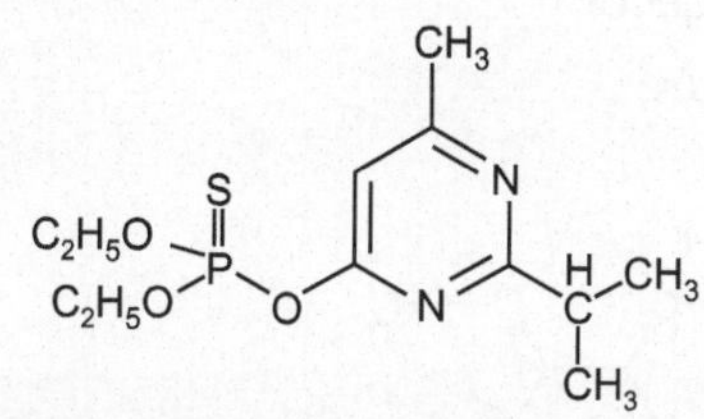

2. **Vertimec 1.8% EC**

   Common name (abamectin)

   Chemical group: macrocyclic lactone (Avermectins)

   Used method: Spraying

   Chemical structure

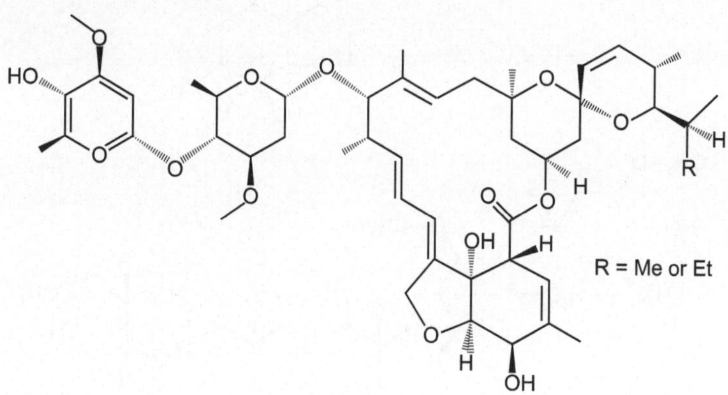

3. **Butox 5%EC**

   Common name (deltamethrin)

   Chemical group: Synthetic Pyrethroid

   Used method: Spraying

   Chemical structure

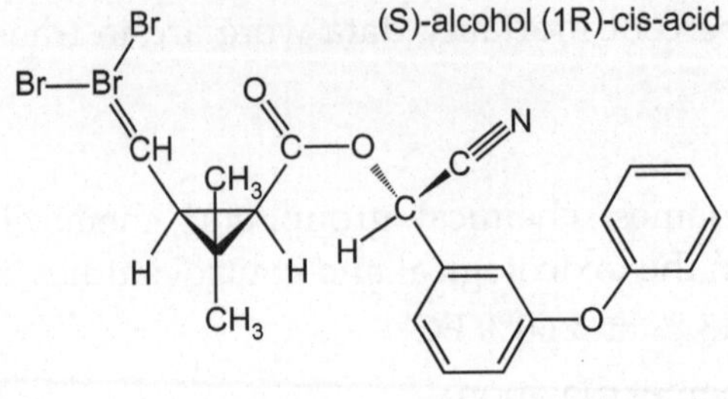

4. Ivomec 1% L

Common name (ivermectin)

Chemical group: macrocyclic lactone (Avermectins)

Used method: Injection

Chemical structure

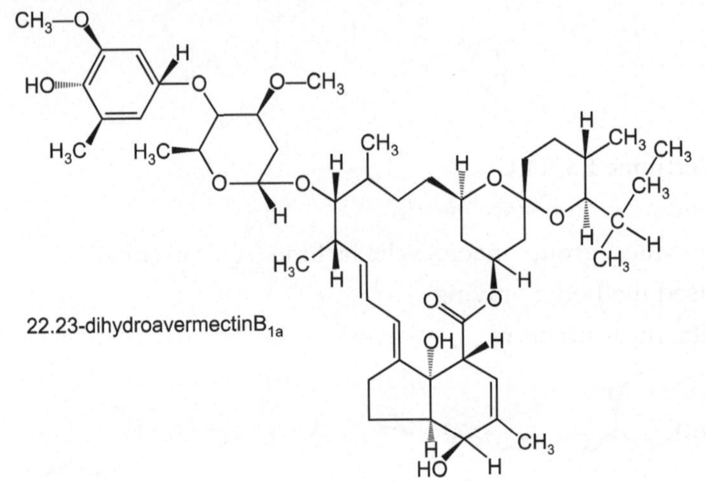

22.23-dihydroavermectinB_{1a}

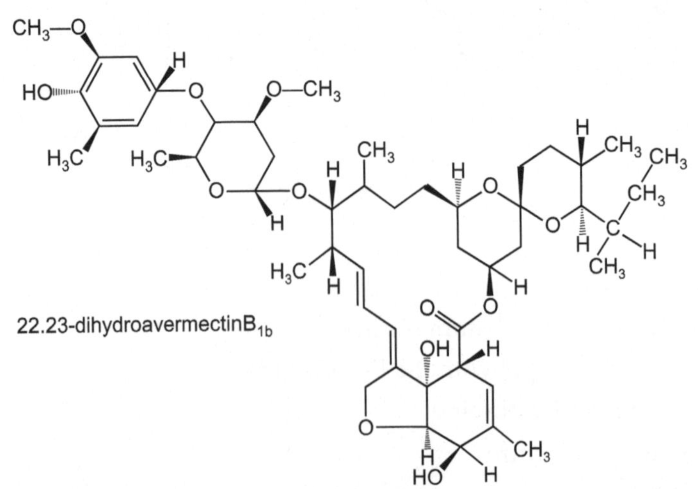

22.23-dihydroavermectinB_{1b}

5. **Radiant 12% SC**

   Common name (spinotrame)

   Chemical group: Synthetic pyrethroid

   Used method: Spraying

   Chemical structure

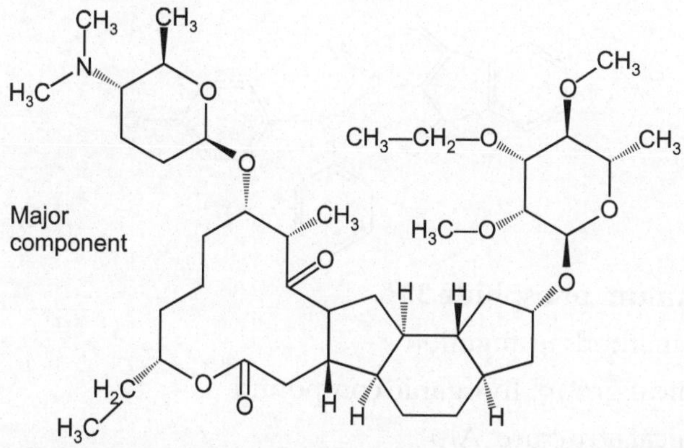

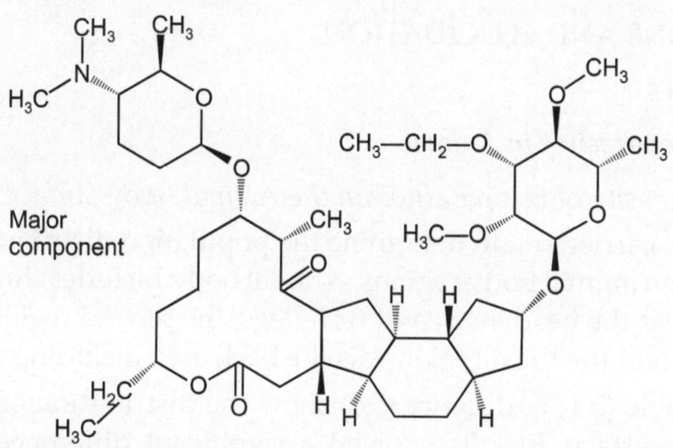

6. **Supercaid 0.004%**

   Common name (bromodialone)

   Chemical group: Coumarine

   Used method: Bait

   Chemical structure

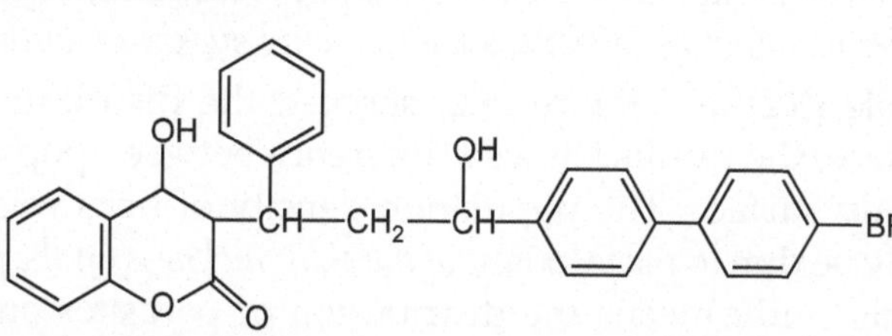

7. **Caid 0.005%**
   Common name (chlorophacinone)
   Chemical group: Indandione
   Used method: Bait
   Chemical structure

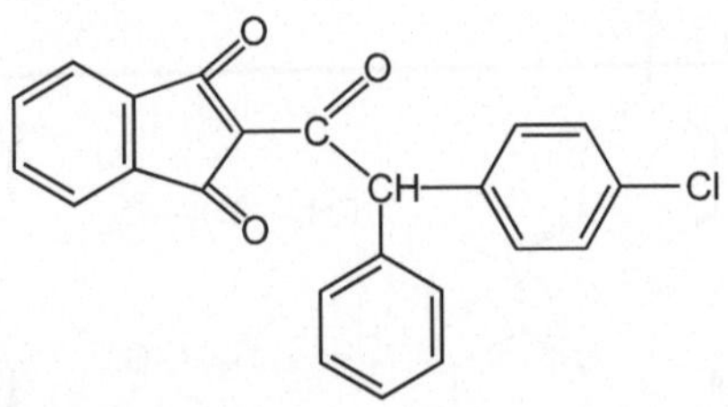

8. **Aluminum phosphide 33%**
   Used method: fumigation
   Chemical group: Inorganic compound
   Chemical structure: Alp

OBSERVATIONS AND ELUCIDATION

Control Studies

Control of Ectoparasites in Animal

Localization Density of Ectoparasites on the Animal Body Surface

This work was carried out to determine the population distribution of various ectoparasites on animal body regions. Animal body includes three regions, the front region was the head, neck and front legs, the second region was the area between legs, and the third region was the back area including the back legs.

Data in Table (5.1) and figure (5.1) show the distribution of lice stages on buffalo body surface. Results showed a significant difference between lice (eggs, nymph and adults) on buffalo body regions. The population density of eggs was higher than other stages in front region, the population density of adult was higher than eggs and nymphs in medium region, but the population of nymphs were higher than eggs and adults in back region. This may be due to nature of buffalo skin and *increasing the length* of *hairs in the front region, also increasing the nymphs in the back region* may be *due to the smooth skin in this region, this makes it easier for nymphs with the small piercing sucking mouth parts* **to** *feed.*

Data in Table (5.2) and figure (5.2) showed the distribution of ticks on cattle body surface, the results showed difference between population of ticks on cattle for body surface. The population density of ticks was high in back region. This may be due to *the weakness of the skin thickness on the posterior region of the animal*.This study means the distribution of parasites on animal body (surface and abdomen) during day periods such as (morning period, noon period and evening period), This may be due to to escape of parasites from the hot period of the day .

Data in Table (5.3) and figures (5.3 and 5.4) showed the distribution of buffalo lice and cattle ticks on body region during day time. Results showed significant difference between the distributions of buffalo lice. The population density of lice was high in the morning period on surface region but for abdomen region it was in noon period. Whereas the population density of cattle ticks on body region during daytime, show also a significant difference between cattle tick populations. The population density of ticks was in high numbers in abdomen body Milnes *et al.*, (2003). This may be because of the farness from the temperature that concentrated in the posterior abdominal *prefering the back and side abdominal* region *especially for easy absorption of blood.* Hussain *et al.*, (2005) found that there are several factors related to environment and host, which contribute to lice infestation (e.g., poor nutrition, intensity of sunlight, temperature, humidity, crowding, management conditions, host-skin reaction, hair condition, hair length and shedding, animal grooming, licking, physiological resistance, breeds, etc.).

Table 5.1: Distribution of Lice on Buffalo Body Surface

Body region	Front region Medium region			Medium region			Back region		
Stages	Stages			Stages			Stages		
	Egg	Nymph	Adult	Egg	Nymph	Adult	Egg	Nymph	Adult
Mean	49.60 a	10.80f	42.20b	21.20d		34.80c	5.00g	22.80d	15.80ef

Table 5.2: Distribution of ticks on cattle body surface

Region Rep.	Front region	Medium region	Back region
1	6	4	28
2	7	3	31
3	5	9	30
Mean	6A	5.33A	29.67 B

Table 5.3: Distribution of Lice and Ticks on the Animal Body Surface During the Day Time

ParasitesPeriods	Buffaloes lice		Cattle ticks	
	Surface region	Abdomen region	Surface region	Abdomen region
	1	2	1	2
Morning	63 a	10.33 e	9 e	38 bc
Noon	30 cd	37 bc	7.33 e	36.67 bc
Evening	44.33 b	21.67 d	5 e	34 c

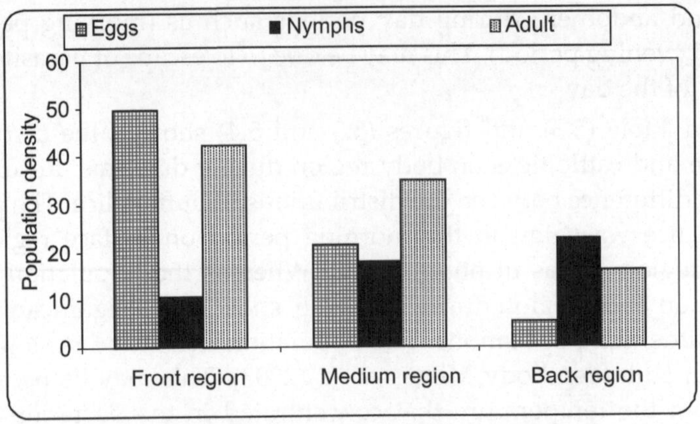

Fig. 5.1: Distribution of lice on buffalo body surface

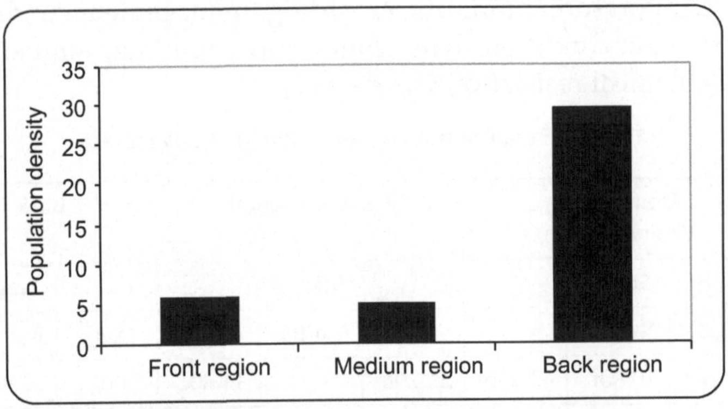

Fig. 5.2: Distribution of ticks on cattle body surface

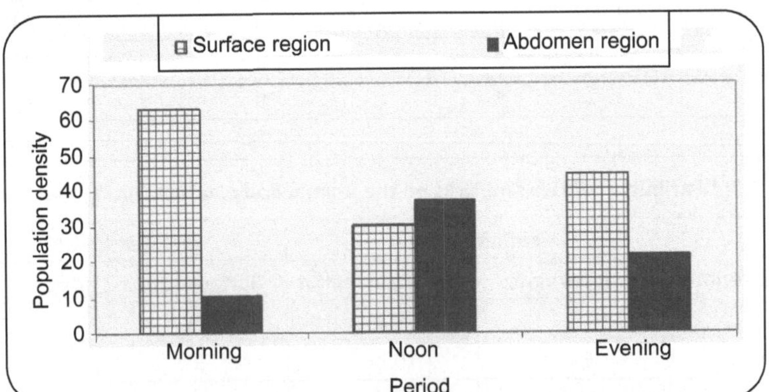

Fig. 5.3: Distribution of lice on buffalo body surface during the day time

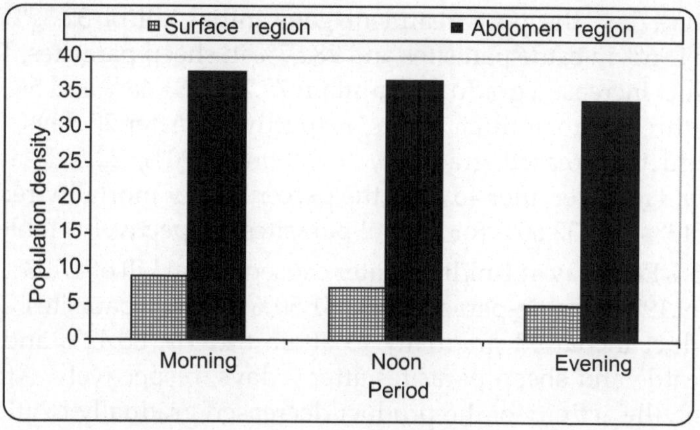

Fig. 5.4: Distribution of ticks on cattle body surface during the day time

In Animals

Data in Tables (5.4 and 5.5) and figures (5.5 and 5.6) represented the percentage of mortality in animal ectoparasites after one to 45 days from applications with Diazinon 15% EC spray at 1 ml/liter water. Results showed that after one day, the post treatment gave an initial kill of 34.78%, 25.87%, and 10% in buffaloes, cattle and sheep-parasites, respectively. The activity of the product increased gradually to attain 50.37%, 55.95% and 23.08%, respectively after 5 days from treatment. By time the activity of the product decreased gradually to attain 26.18%, 18.59% and 10.31%, after 20 days for the above mentioned three animals, respectively. However after 45 days, the mortality percentage of ectoparasites reduced to be 10.19%, 3.43% and 1.86%, respectively (Table 5.4).

Diazinon 60% EC spray at 1ml/liter water, gave an initial kill of 40.58%, 36.46% and 22.85% after 24 hrs in buffalo, cattle and sheep parasites, the activity of the product increased gradually to attain 80.52%, 55.31% and 64.12% in buffalo, cattle and sheep-parasites after 7 days respectively. The activity of the product decreased gradually to attain 63.76%, 33.92% and 49.06% after 20 days, respectively. However after 45 days the percentage of mortality reduced to be 20.38%, 11.65% and 30.40% for the three animals parasites, respectively (Table 5.28 and figure 5.6).

In general the Diazinon product showed variable toxicity to animals parasites. According to the percentage of mortality recorded after 24hrs and 45 days, Diazinon 60% EC showed the highest toxicity, followed by Diazinon 15% EC, this may be due to the increasing of active ingredient in Diazinon 60% EC, the same results were obtained with Abo Elmaged (1998) and Rajput *et al.*, (2006).

Data in Tables (5.6 and 5.7) and figures (5.7 and 5.8) represented the percentage of mortality in animal ectoparasites after one to 45 days from applications with Vertimec 1.8% EC spray at 1ml/liter water. Results showed that after one day, the post treatment gave initial kill of 32.35% in buffalo parasites, 55.96% in cattle parasites and 28.57% in sheep parasites. The activity of the product increased gradually to attain 78.77%, 81.48% and 56.94% for the parasite of three animals after 7 days, respectively. After 20 days, the activity of the product decreased gradually to attain 59.90%, 52.46% and 56.13%, respectively. However after 45 days the percentage of mortality reduced to be 39.03%, 36.13% and 32.60% for animal parasites, respectively (Table 5.6).

Butox 5% EC spray at 1ml/liter water caused initial kill of 47.33% in buffalo-parasites, 59.19% in cattle-parasites and 51.50% in sheep parasites. The activity of the product increased gradually to attain 84.93%, 85.42% and 76.59% in buffaloes, cattle and sheep parasites after 7 days, respectively. After 20 days of treatment, the activity of the product decreased gradually to attain 71.88%, 58.03% and 62.50% for the parasites of the animals respectively. However, after 45 days the percentage of mortality reduced to be 42.24%, 34.46% and 43.92% for the three animals-parasites, respectively (Table 5.7 and figure 5.8). The present results agreed with those obtained by Mehlhorn *et al.*, (2010).

In general the Butox5% product showed variable toxicity to animal parasites. According to the percentage of mortality recorded after 24 h and 45 days, Butox5% EC showed the highest toxicity, followed by Vertimec 1.8% EC and Diazinon 60% EC.

Ivermectin 1% (Injection) at 1 ml/50 kg caused initial kill to 63.77%, 67.89% and 12.69% in buffalo, cattle in sheep parasites after 24 hrs. The activity of the product increased gradually to attain 98.05%, 97.22% and 77.21% in buffalo, cattle and sheep parasites after 7 days, after so the activity of the product decreased gradually to attain 78.53%, 64.76% and 37.50% after 20 days, respectively. However, after 45 days the percentage of mortality reduced to be 35.03%, 34.20% and 13.08% for the three animals parasites, respectively (Table 5.31 and figure 5.9).

In general the Ivermectin 1% injection product showed variable toxicity to animals parasites .According to the percentage of mortality recorded after 24 h to 45 days, Ivermectin 1% injection showed the highest toxicity, followed by Vertimec 1.8% EC, the results were in agreement with the finding of Hussain *et al.*, (2005) and Ramzan *et al.*, (2008).

Table 5.4: Reduction Ratios of Animal Ectoparasites after Spraying with Diazinon 15% EC (1ml/L) under Field Conditions, in Farm Animals, Faculty of Agriculture, Assiut University, during, 2009-2010

Days	Mean ±SE (%)		
	Buffalo parasites	Cattle parasites	Sheep parasites
1	34.78± 1.28 ef	25.87 ±2.08 gh	10.00 ± 1.18 o-q
3	46.51 ± 1.37 bc	41.46 ± 2.15 cd	20.12 ± 1.14 i-l
5	50.37 ±3.29 ab	55.95 ± 3.21 a	23.08 ± 1.13 h-j

7	48.70± 2.38 b	44.68 ± 2.17 bc	17.88± 0.99 k-m
10	37.25± 1.16 de	26.67 ± 1.96 gh	13.68 ± 0.54 m-o
15	29.61 ±2.42 fg	24.26 ± 1.71 g-i	11.98 ± 0.53 n-q
20	26.18± 2.46 gh	18.59 ± 2.39 j-l	10.31 ± 0.91 o-q
25	21.98 ±1.63 h-k	12.50 ± 2.94 n-p	9.40± 0.87 p-r
30	15.68 ±2.01 l-n	8.15 ± 0.75 qr	6.03 ± 0.51 r
45	10.19 ±1.13 o-q	3.43 ± 1.21 s	1.86 ± 0.78 s
Mean	32.13 A	26.16 B	12.43 C

- Means followed by the same letter are insignificantly different.

Table 5.5: Reduction Ratios of Animal Ectoparasites after Spraying with Diazinon 60% EC (1ml/L) under Field Conditions, in Farm-animals, Faculty of Agriculture, Assiut University, during, 2009-2010

Days	Mean ±SE(%)		
	Buffalo parasites	Cattle parasites	Sheep parasites
1	40.58 ± 0.74 jk	36.46 ± 2.08 kl	22.85 ± 1.01 n
3	50.39 ± 2.09 gh	53.65 ± 3.29 fg	38.15 ± 0.91 j-l
5	66.67 ± 1.31 bc	66.67 ± 1.21b	46.00 ± 0.88 hi
7	80.52 ± 1.15 a	55.31 ± 1.88 ef	64.12± 1.69 cd
10	79.10 ± 1.76a	40.00 ± 1.96jk	69.81 ± 0.48 b
15	69.74 ± 0.67b	34.95 ± 2.62kl	61.06 ± 0.85 d
20	63.76 ± 1.18 cd	33.92 ± 0.91 lm	49.06 ±0.83 gh
25	59.86 ± 0.69 de	22.50 ±1.47 n	42.25 ± 0.83 ij
30	39.56 ± 1.32 jk	17.04 ± 0.75o	36.44± 0.48 kl
45	20.38 ± 2.83 no	11.65 ± 1.21p	30.40 ±1.19 m
Mean	57.06 A	37.22 C	46.01 B

-Means followed by the same letter are insignificantly different.

Table 5.6: Reduction ratios of animal ectoparasites after spraying with Vertimec 1.8% EC (1ml/L) under field conditions, in farm-animals, Faculty of Agriculture, Assiut University, during, 2009-2010

Days	Mean ±SE (%)		
	Buffalo parasites	Cattle parasites	Sheep parasites
1	32.35± 2.82 mn	55.96 ± 1.62 fg	28.57 ± 2.10 n
3	41.35 ± 1.33 k	69.70± 1.78 bc	42.27 ± 1.39 jk
5	65.76 ± 1.85 cd	73.07 ± 1.93 b	50.00 ± 1.35 hi
7	78.77 ± 1.85 a	81.48 ± 0.94 a	56.94 ± 0.85 fg
10	80.43 ± 0.96 a	67.33 ± 1.75 de	62.26 ± 1.27 de

15	70.39 ± 1.14 b	57.14 ± 1.68 fg	71.15 ± 0.85 b
20	59.90 ± 2.31 ef	52.46 ± 2.21 gh	56.13 ± 0.83 fg
25	50.58 ± 2.34 hi	46.45 ± 2.12 ij	43.66 ± 0.83 jk
30	41.77 ± 2.08 jk	42.36 ± 3.08 jk	39.72 ± 0.83 kl
45	39.03 ± 1.89 kl	36.13 ± 2.28 lm	32.60 ± 0.78 mn
Mean	56.03 b	58.21 a	48.33 c

-Means followed by the same letter are insignificantly different.

Table 5.7: Reduction ratios of animal ectoparasites after spraying with Butox 5% EC, (1ml/L) under field conditions, in farm-animals, Faculty of Agriculture, Assiut University, during, 2009-2010

Days	Mean ±SE(%)		
	Buffalo parasites	Cattle parasites	Sheep parasites
1	47.33 ± 1.35 mn	59.19± 1.04 i-k	51.50 ± 2.01 lm
3	63.91± 2.65 h	76.34± 1.10 de	62.41 ± 1.91 h-j
5	76.71 ± 0.70 de	83.33± 1.96 bc	68.92 ± 1.82 g
7	84.93 ±1.85 ab	85.42 ±1.06 ab	76.59 ± 0.65 de
10	86.96 ± 0.96 a	75.51 ± 1.80 ef	81.48 ± 1.09 c
15	79.89 ± 2.61 cd	61.39 ±1.75 h-j	70.25 ± 2.33 g
20	71.88 ±0.92 fg	58.03 ± 0.91 jk	62.50 ± 1.05 h-j
25	62.64 ± 1.55 hi	48.72 ± 1.51 m	55.74 ± 0.96 kl
30	48.83 ± 1.04 m	37.84 ± 1.59 pq	49.29 ± 1.28 m
45	42.24 ± 0.94 op	34.46 ± 1.48 q	43.92 ± 0.82 no
Mean	66.53 a	62.02 b	62.26 b

- Means followed by the same letter are insignificantly different.

Table 5.8: Reduction Ratios of Animal Ectoparasites after Ivermectin 1%, (1m/50kg, Injection) under Field Conditions, Farm-animals, Faculty of Agriculture, Assiut University during, 2009-2010

Days	Mean ±SE(%)		
	Buffalo parasites	Cattle parasites	Sheep parasites
1	63.77± 1.95 jk	67.89 ± 2.47 h-j	12.69 ± 2.63 s
3	82.17 ± 2.09 ef	74.75 ± 2.72 gh	25.53 ± 2.50 r
5	93.33 ± 2.61 bc	88.01 ± 1.76 de	73.65 ± 2.39 g-i
7	98.05 ± 1.15 a	97.22 ± 1.64 a	77.21 ± 2.23 fg
10	94.12± 1.15 b	89.01± 2.69 cd	68.52 ± 1.09 h-j
15	88.82 ± 2.42 d	78.10 ± 2.57 fg	52.53 ± 1.11 lm
20	78.53 ± 2.46 fg	64.76 ± 2.21 j	37.50 ± 1.05 n-p

25	66.67 ± 1.83 ij	58.26 ± 2.12 kl	28.42 ± 1.47 qr
30	44.03 ± 1.31 mn	43.05 ±1.87 no	21.32 ± 1.28 r
45	35.03± 1.12 o-q	34.20 ± 1.14 pq	13.08 1.65 s
Mean	74.45 a	69.53 b	41.05 c

- Means followed by the same letter are insignificantly different.

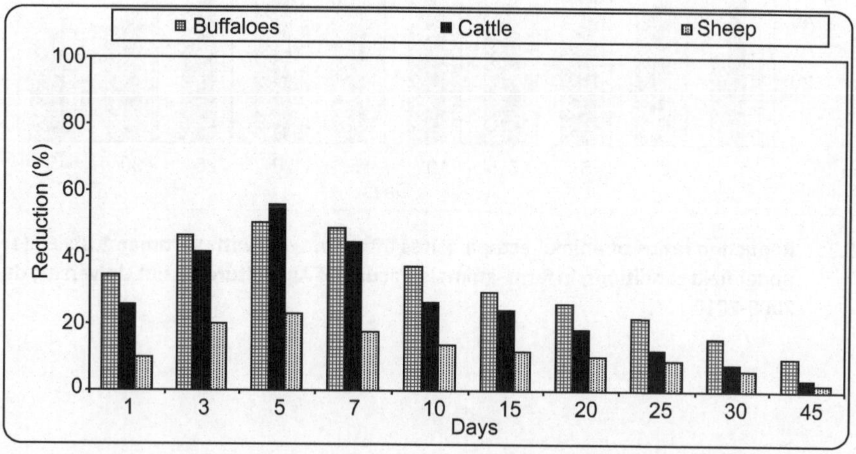

Fig. 5.5: Reduction ratios of animal ectoparasites after spraying with Diazinon 15% EC (1ml/L) under field conditions, in farm-animals, Faculty of Agriculture, Assiut University, during, 2009-2010

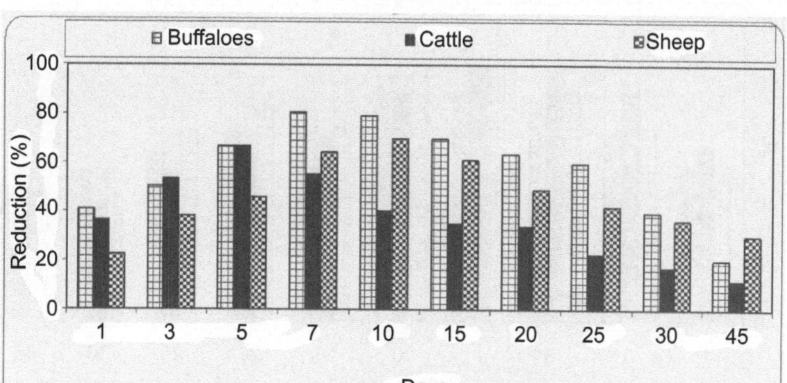

Fig. 5.6: Reduction ratios of animal ectoparasites after spraying with Diazinon 60% EC (1ml/L) under field conditions, in farm- animals, Faculty of Agriculture, Assiut University, during, 2009-2010

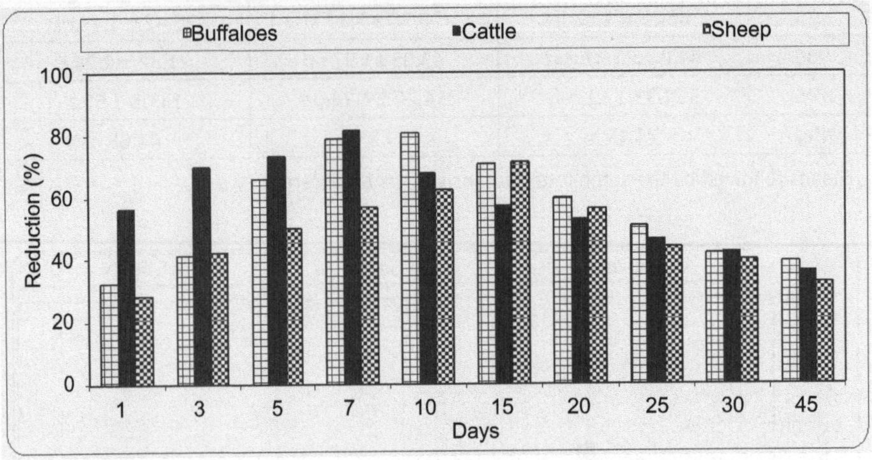

Fig. 5.7: Reduction ratios of animal ectoparasites after spraying with Vertimec 1.8% EC (1ml/L) under field conditions, in farm- animals, Faculty of Agriculture, Assiut University, during, 2009-2010

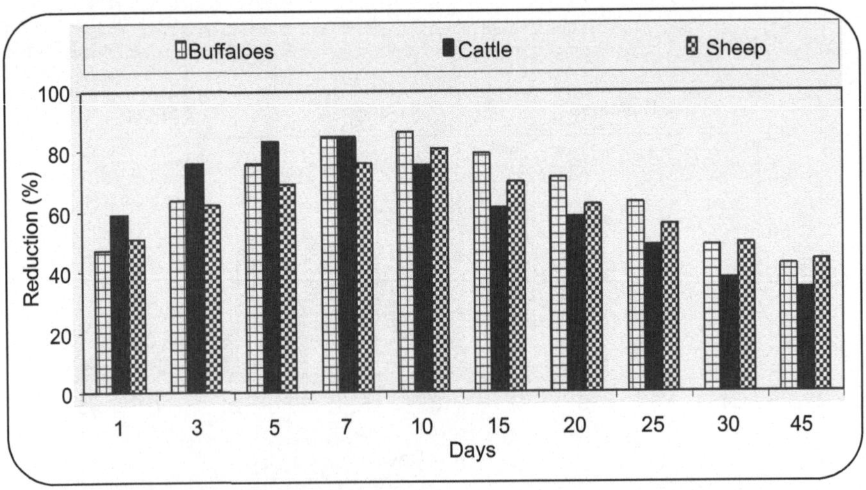

Fig. 5.8: Reduction ratios of animal ectoparasites after spraying with Butox 5% EC (1ml/L) under field conditions in farm-animals, Faculty of Agriculture, Assiut University, during, 2009-2010

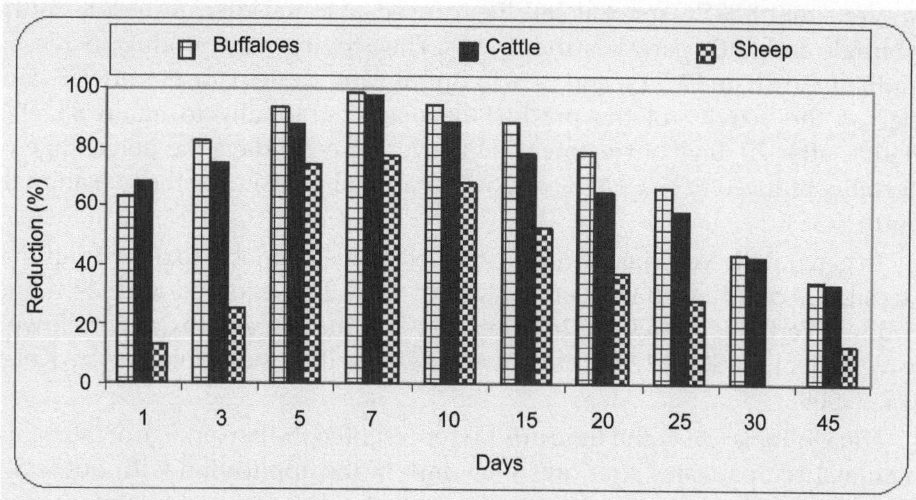

Fig. 5.9: Reduction ratios of animal ectoparasites after Ivermectin 1%, (1m/50kg, injection) under field conditions in farm-animals, Faculty of Agriculture, Assiut University, during, 2009-2010.

Data in Table (5.9) and figure (5.10) represented the percentage of mortality to animal ectoparasites after one to 45 days after applications of Diazinon 60% EC spray at 1.5 ml/liter. Results showed that after one day, the post treatment gave an initial kill of 43.75% and 54.43% in buffalo and cattle parasites. The activity of the product increased gradually after 7days to attain 84.40% and 82.91% in buffalo and cattle parasites. The activity of the product decreased gradually to attain 54.61%, 56.63% after 20 days, respectively. However after 45 days the percentages of mortality reduced to be 38.51%, 26.19% for buffalo and cattle, respectively.

Diazinon 60% EC spray at 2 ml/liter water, caused an initial kill of 51.12% and 64% in buffaloes and cattle parasites. The activity of the product increased gradually to attain 87.13% and 88% in buffalo and cattle parasites after 7 days, after so the activity of the product decreased gradually to attain 77.63%, 74.22% after 20 days, respectively. However after 45 days the percentages of mortality reduced to be 51.67%, 43.88% for the two animals parasites, respectively (Table 5.9 and figure 5.11).

Data in Table (5.10) and figure (5.12) represented the percentage of mortality in animal ectoparasites after one to 45 days of applications with Vertimec 1.8% EC spray at 1.5ml/liter, caused an initial kill of 54.17% and 63.71% in buffalo and cattle parasites after 24 hrs. The activity of the product increased gradually to attain 89.82% and 85.47% in buffalo and cattle parasites after 7days, after so the activity of the product decreased gradually to attain 68.42% and 61.45%, after 20 days. However, after 45 days the percentage of mortality reduced to be 44.90%, 33.33% for the two animals parasites, respectively.

Vertemic1.8 % EC spray at 2ml/liter caused an initial kill of 64.66% and 70% in buffalo and cattle parasites after 24 hrs. The activity of the product increased gradually to attain 94.74% and 90% in buffalo and cattle parasites after 7days, after so the activity of the product decreased gradually to attain 88.59%, 78.91%, after 20 days of treatment. However, after 45 days the percentage of mortality reduced to be 69.45%, 50.36% for animal parasites of the two animals (figure 5.13).

In general the Vertimec1.8% EC product showed variable toxicity to animal parasites .According to the percentages of mortality recorded after 24 h and 45 days, Vertimec1.8%EC at 2ml/liter showed the highest toxicity, followed by Vertimec1.8%EC at 1.5ml/liter, in according with results obtained by Kolar *et al.,* (2008).

Data in Table (5.11) and figure (5.14) represented the percentage of mortality to animal ectoparasites after one to 45 days of the application with Butox 5% EC spray at 1.5 ml/liter, results showed that after one day post treatment gave an initial kill of 61.46% and 66.30% in buffalo and cattle parasites. The activity of the product increased gradually to attain 86.24% and 85.31% in buffalo and cattle parasites after 7 days, after so the activity of the product decreased gradually to attain 72.18% and 67.82%, after 20 days. However, after 45 days the percentage of mortality reduced to be 47.29%, 39.53% for the two animals parasites, as similar as Bossche and Mudenge (1999).

Butox 5% EC spray at 2ml/liter caused an initial kill of 73.38% and 72.92% in buffalo and cattle parasites. The activity of the product increased gradually to attain 91.89% and 93.46% in buffalo and cattle parasites after 7days, after so the activity of the product decreased gradually to attain 93.13%, 81.85%, after 20 days. However, after 45 days the percentage of mortality reduced to be 67.86% and 55.96% for the two animals parasites. The obtained results are in agreement with the finding of Mehlhorn *et al.,* (2009) who found that, the Deltamethrin containing product of Butox® protected sheep and cattle against midges, which suck blood at the legs or at the belly for at least 4 weeks, even if the animal becomes wet several times during these 4–5 weeks, (Figure 5.15)

In general the Butox5% EC product showed variable toxicity to animal parasites. According to the percentage of mortality recorded after 24h and 45 days, Butox5% EC at 2ml/liter water showed the highest toxicity, followed by Butox 5% EC at 1.5ml/liter.

Data in Table (5.12) and figure (5.16) represented the percentage of mortality in sheep-ectoparasites after one to 30 days from the application with Butox 5% at 1ml/liter on woolly and fleeced-sheep. Results show that, the one day post treatment gave an initial kill of 91.51% for fleas on fleeced-sheep and 51.50% on woolly sheep. The activity of the product increased gradually to attain 100% and 76.59% for fleas on the former sheep after 7 days, after so the activity of the product decreased gradually to attain 79.5% and 62.50% after 20 days. However, after 30 days the percentage of mortality reduced to be 70.43% and 55.74% for fleas on fleeced and woolly sheep.

In general, according to the percentage of mortality recorded after 24h and 30 days, the fleas on fleeced-sheep showed the highest toxicity, followed by fleas on woolly sheep when used Butox 5% EC at 1ml/liter.

Data in Table (5.13) and figure (5.17) represented the percentage of mortality in animal ectoparasites after one to 30 days from the application with Radiant 12% SC spray at 4ml/liter water. Results showed that, after one day post treatment gave an initial kill of 22.50% and 14.10% in buffalo and sheep-parasites. The activity of the product increased gradually to attain 54.62% and 22.92% in buffalo and sheep-parasites after 5 days .However after 30 days the percentage of mortality reduced to be 57.14%, 15.42% for buffalo and sheep-parasites.

Radiant 12% SC spray at 6 ml/liter, caused an initial kill 35.83% and 21.47% after 24 hrs in buffalo and sheep parasites. The activity of the product increased gradually to attain 62.8% and 28.02% in the two animals parasites. After so, the activity of the product decreased gradually to attain 65.18% and 39.61%, after 30 days (Figure 5.18).

In general the Radiant 12% SC 6ml/liter showed variable toxicity to animal parasites. According to the percentage of mortality recorded after 24h and 30 days, Radiant 12% SC at 6ml/liter water showed the highest toxicity, followed by Radiant1 2% SC at 4ml/liter.

The results of using Radiant 12 % SC spray at 8ml/liter, showed that, after one day post treatment the compound gave an initial kill of 45.83%, 29.99% and 30.06% in buffalo, cattle and sheep parasites respectively. The activity of the product increased gradually to attain 81.08%, 64.71% and 55.41% in buffalo, cattle and sheep parasites after 5 days respectively, after so the activity of the product decreased gradually to attain 75.89%, 35.25%, and 69.57 after 30 days, respectively (Table 5.17 and figure 5.13). In general, Radiant 12%SC at 8cm/liter showed the highest toxicity, followed by Radiant 12% at 6cm/liter.

Data in Table (5.18) represented the percentage of mortality for hard ticks on cattle from one to 30 days after applications of Radiant 12 % SC spray at 6, 8 and 12 ml/liter water. Results showed that, the one day post treatment the compound gave an initial kill of 15.99%, 29.99% and 40.99% with Radiant12% SC sprayed at 6, 8 and12ml/L. The activity of the product increased gradually to attain 48.04, 64.71 and 66.67% for ticks on cattle parasites after 5days, respectively. Then the activity of the product decreased gradually to attain 13.12%, 35.25%, and 55.74% after 30 days respectively. These results agreed with those obtained by El Kady *et al.,* (2007). In general, Radiant12% SC at

12ml/liter showed the highest toxicity, followed by Radiant 12% at 6 and 8 ml/liter for control of ticks infested cattle.

Diazinon 60% EC spray and or in contact methods at 1 ml/liter caused an initial kill of 39.13% and 56.52% in control of buffalo parasites and 37.61% and 50.45% in control of cattle ones, after 24 hrs. The activity of the product increased gradually to attain 78.57% and 86.36% after 7 days with spray and contact method in buffaloes parasites, also 68% after 5 days with spray method and 80.56% after 7 days with contact method in cattle parasites, after so the activity of the product decreased gradually to attain 59.73%, 77.85%, 34.43% and 65.58% after 20 days, respectively. However after 45 days the percentage of mortality reduced to be 31.21%, 43.31%, 16.78% and 43.92% for animal parasites, respectively (Table 5.19 and figure 5.20). In general, contact method was the best produced high toxicity, followed by spray method for the control of animal parasites control.

Table 5.9: Reduction Ratios of Animal Ectoparasites after Spraying with Diazinon 60% EC (1.5 and 2ml/L) under Field Conditions, in Farm Animals, Faculty of Agriculture, Assiut University during, 2009-2010

Days	Mean ±SE (%)			
	1.5 ml/L		2 ml/L	
	Buffalo parasites	Cattle parasites	Buffalo parasites	Cattle parasites
1	43.75 ± 1.84 k	54.43 ± 1.49 ij	51.12 ± 2.02 j	64.00 ± 1.76 h
3	56.88 ±1.87 i	73.33± 1.57 ef	69.50 ± 0.72 g	75.79 ± 1.07 f
5	78.38 ± 1.59 cd	80.49 ± 1.44 bc	82.47 ± 1.14 cd	82.35 ± 1.73 cd
7	84.40 ± 1.87 a	82.91± 0.87 ab	87.13 ± 1.58 ab	88.00± 1.76 ab
10	75.22 ±0.90 de	69.44± 1.63 fg	89.76 ± 0.61 a	88.57 ± 1.68 bc
15	62.30 ± 2.07 h	65.85 ± 1.44 gh	85.88 ± 1.04 b	80.33 ± 1.45 de
20	54.61 ± 2.08 ij	56.63 ± 1.42 ij	77.63 ± 0.60 ef	74.22 ± 1.38 f
25	51.70 ± 1.83 j	45.24 ± 1.40 kl	68.85 ± 0.96 g	60.00 ± 1.47 hi
30	46.10 ± 2.60 k	36.59 ±1.43 m	63.10 ± 0.94 h	56.82 ±1.34 i
45	38.51 ±1.82 lm	26.19 ± 1.40n	51.67 ± 0.98 j	43.88 ± 1.27 k
Mean	59.19 a	59.11a	72.71 a	71.40 b

- In the same concentration, means followed tby the same letter are insignificantly different.

Table 5.10: Reduction Ratios of Animal Ectoparasites after Spraying with Vertimec 1.8% EC (1.5 and 2ml/L) under field conditions, in farm animals, Faculty of Agriculture, Assiut University during, 2009-2010

Days	Mean ±SE (%)			
	1.5ml/L		2ml/L	
	Buffalo parasites	Cattle parasites	Buffalo parasites	Cattle parasites
1	54.17± 2.81 ij	63.71± 2.28 gh	64.66 ± 1.53 j	70.00 ± 1.76 h-j
3	71.79 ± 0.93 ef	78.67 ± 1.57 cd	73.76 ± 1.91 g-i	75.79 ± 2.84 gh

5	82.88 ± 2.43 bc	83.74 ± 0.83 b	88.31 ±1.15 cd	87.26 ± 1.00 de
7	89.82 ± 0.84 a	85.47± 0.87 b	94.74 ±1.03 b	90.00 ± 1.02 cd
10	85.85 ± 0.91ab	74.07± 0.94 d-f	96.97 ± 1.63 a	91.43 ± 1.68 bc
15	76.15 ±0.78 de	70.73± 1.44 de	97.65 ± 0.60 a	87.71 ± 1.44 cd
20	68.42 ± 1.33 fg	61.45 ± 1.42 h	88.59 ± 0.96 cd	78.91 ± 1.38 fg
25	59.18 ±1.20 hi	50.00 ±1.40 jk	82.52 ± 0.56 ef	67.50 ± 1.47 j
30	53.90 ± 1.91 ij	41.46 ± 1.44 l	75.93 ± 0.94 gh	65.91 ± 1.34 j
45	44.90 ± 2.40 kl	33.33 ± 1.40 m	69.45 ± 1.50 ij	50.36 ± 1.27 k
Mean	68.71 a	64.26 b	83.26 a	76.49 b

- In the same concentration, means followed by the same letter are insignificantly different

Table 5.11: Reduction ratios of animal ectoparasites after spraying with Butox5% (1.5 and 2ml/L) under field conditions, in farm animals, Faculty of Agriculture, Assiut University during, 2009-2010.

Days	Mean ±SE (%)			
	1.5ml/L		2ml/L	
	Buffalo parasites	Cattle parasites	Buffalo parasites	Cattle parasites
1	61.46 ± 2.81 gh	66.30 ± 1.11 fg	73.38 ± 1.42 g	72.92 ± 1.06 g
3	75.23 ±1.62 de	75.26 ± 1.82 de	82.35 ± 1.30 f	81.82 ± 1.78 f
5	81.98 ± 2.43 bc	81.00 ± 1.02 b-d	88.46 ± 1.36 d	92.38 ± 0.97 c
7	86.24 ± 1.62 ab	85.31 ± 1.74 ab	91.89 ± 1.62 c	93.46 ± 0.95 c
10	89.28 ± 1.57 a	88.89 ± 1.64 a	94.45 ± 0.81 bc	96.16 ± 0.98 ab
15	79.23 ± 1.36 cd	75.68 ± 1.59 c-e	97.03 ± 0.67 a	87.18 ± 1.51 de
20	72.18 ± 2.03 ef	67.82 ± 2.34 fg	93.13 ± 1.35 c	81.85 ± 0.86 f
25	63.27 ± 1.20 gh	56.67 ± 3.06 fg	84.09 ± 1.34 ef	76.52 ± 1.54 g
30	56.03 ± 1.45 h	47.15 ± 2.19 i	75.37 ± 1.31 g	64.22 ±1.62 h
45	47.29 ± 1.19 i	39.53 ± 1.37 i	67.86 ± 1.26 h	55.96 ± 1.62 i
Mean	71.22	68.36	84.80 a	80.25 b

- In the same concentration, means followed by the same letter are insignificantly different

Table 5.12: Reduction Ratios of Fleas on Sheep after Spraying with Butox 5%EC (1ml/L) with Woolly and Fleeced Sheep under Field Conditions, in Farm Animals, Faculty of Agriculture, Assiut University during, 2009-2010

Days	Mean ±SE (%)	
	Fleeced sheep	Woolly sheep
1	91.51 ± 1.66 c	51.50 ± 2.01 j
3	100.00 ±0 a	62.41 ± 1.91 hi
5	100.00 ± 0 a	68.92 ± 1.82 gh
7	100.00 ±0 a	76.59 ± 0.65 ef
10	97.27 ± 1.60 b	81.48 ± 1.09 de

15	85.56 ±1.05 d	70.25 ± 2.33 fg
20	79.05 ± 2.57 e	62.50 ± 1.05 hi
30	70.43 ±2.35 fg	55.74 ± 0.96 ij
Mean	90.48 a	66.17 b

- Means followed by the same letter are insignificantly different.

Table 5.13: Reduction Ratios of Animal Ectoparasites after Spraying with Radiant 12% SC (4 and 6ml/L) under Field Conditions, in Farm Animals, Faculty of Agriculture, Assiut University during, 2009-2010

Days	Mean ±SE (%)			
	4ml/L		6ml/L	
	Buffaloes	Sheep	Buffaloes	Sheep
1	22.50 ± 1.47 e	14.10 ± 1.65 hi	35.83 ± 2.25 gh	21.47± 1.66 k
3	39.44 ±1.62 c	19.26 ± 1.67 e-g	44.95 ± 1.62 ef	23.70 ± 1.18 jk
5	54.62 ± 2.70 b	22.92 ±0.65 e	62.28 ± 2.37 c	28.02 ± 1.72 ij
10	66.07 ± 2.40 a	19.47 ± 0.93 ef	72.32 ± 0.91 b	50.00 ± 1.07 de
15	67.59 ± 2.49 a	16.92 ± 0.91 f-h	77.78 ± 1.64 a	46.67 ± 1.38 e
30	57.14 ± 1.58 b	15.42 ±1.00 g-i	65.18 ± 1.57 c	39.61 ± 1.30 fg
Mean	39.99 a	13.46 b	59.72 a	34.91 b

- In the same concentration, means followed by the same letter are insignificantly different.

Table 5.14: Reduction Ratios of Animal Ectoparasites after Spraying with Radiant 12% SC (8ml/L) under Field Conditions, in Farm Animals, Faculty of Agriculture, Assiut University during, 2009-2010

Days	Mean ±SE (%)		
	Buffaloes parasites	Cattle parasites	Sheep parasites
1	45.83 ± 2.25 g	29.99 ± 2.70 h	30.06 ± 1.08 h
3	58.71 ± 1.62 e	47.04 ± 2.92 fg	34.79 ± 1.10 h
5	81.08 ±1.59 b	64.71 ± 1.73 de	55.41 ± 1.72 ef
10	87.50 ± 0.91 a	69.00 ±1.02 cd	68.95 ± 1.42 cd
15	89.82 ± 0.94 a	47.62 ±2.57 fg	77.95 ± 0.52 b
30	75.89 ± 1.58 bc	35.25 ± 1.67 g	69.57 ± 0.85 c
Mean	73.14 a	48.94 c	56.12 b

Means followed by the same letter are insignificantly different.

Table 5.15: Reduction Ratios of Ticks on Cattle after Spraying with Radiant 12% SC using (6,8 and 12ml/L) under Field Conditions, in Farm Animals, Faculty of Agriculture, Assiut University during, 2009-2010

Days	Mean ±SE (%)		
	Radiant 12%SC		
	6ml/L	8ml/L	12ml/L
1	15.99± 1.76 i	29.99 ± 2.70 h	40.99 ± 3.67 fg
3	35.80 ± 2.84 gh	47.04 ± 2.92 ef	55.79 ± 1.86 de
5	48.04 ± 2.64 f	64.71 ±1.73 cd	66.67 ± 2.00 bc
10	55.00 ± 1.76 de	69.00 ± 1.02 bc	82.00 ± 1.76 a
15	31.43 ± 3.36 h	47.62 ± 2.57 fe	71.43 ± 1.68 b
30	13.12 ± 2.21 i	35.25 ± 1.67 f	55.74 ±1.45 de
Mean	33.23 c	48.94 b	62.10 a

- Means followed by the same letter are insignificantly different.

Table 5.16: Reduction Ratios on Animal Ectoparasites by using Washing and Spraying Method with Diazinon 60% EC at (1ml/L) under Field Conditions in Farm Animals, Faculty of Agriculture, Assiut University during, 2009-2010

Days	Mean ±SE (%)			
	Buffalo parasites		Cattle parasites	
	Spraying method	Contact method	Spraying method	Contact method
1	39.13± 1.28 no	56.52± 1.28 h-j	37.61± 0.93 op	50.45± 1.62 lm
3	51.16± 1.37 k-m	67.44± 1.37 f	54.55 ±1.78 i-l	63.64± 1.78 fg
5	64.44± 1.31 gh	77.78± 1.31 cd	68.00 ±1.21 f	73.27± 1.75 e
7	78.57± 1.15 c	86.36± 1.15 ab	58.33 ± 1.63 hi	80.56± 1.63 c
10	74.51± 1.15 de	88.24 ± 1.16 a	49.04 ±1.76 m	85.15 ± 1.75 ab
15	64.48± 1.16 f	84.21± 1.16 b	40.00 ±1.68 no	74.29 ±1.68 de
20	59.73± 1.19 gh	77.85± 1.19 cd	34.43 ± 2.21 pq	65.58± 1.45 f
25	51.02± 1.20 k-m	67.35± 1.20 f	26.77 ±1.39 r	52.75± 1.39 j-m
30	39.56± 1.32 no	55.23± 1.32 h-k	20.83 ± 1.23 s	41.67 ± 1.23 no
45	31.21± 1.13 q	43.31 ± 1.72 n	16.78 ± 1.14 t	32.91± 1.74 q
Mean	55.38 c	70.43 a	40.63 d	62.03 b

Means followed by the same letter are insignificantly different

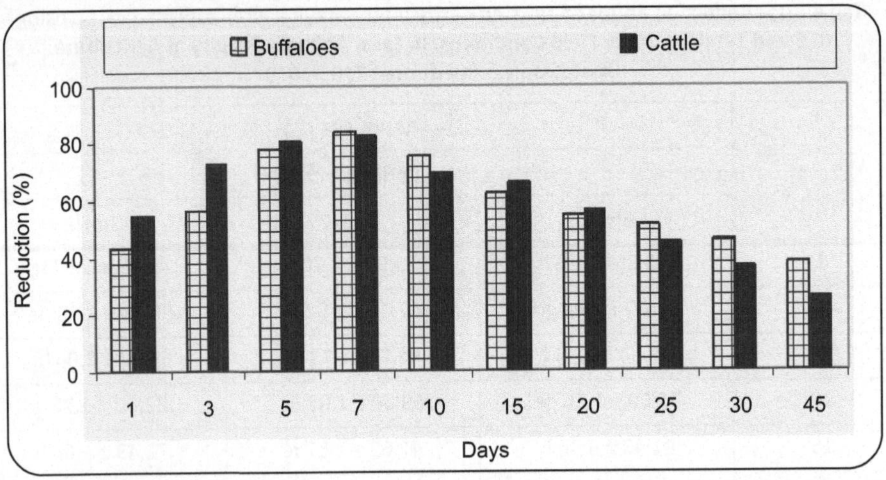

Fig. 5.10: Reduction ratios of animal ectoparasites after spraying with Diazinon 60% EC (1.5 ml/L) under field conditions in farm-animals, Faculty of Agriculture, Assiut University during, 2009-2010.

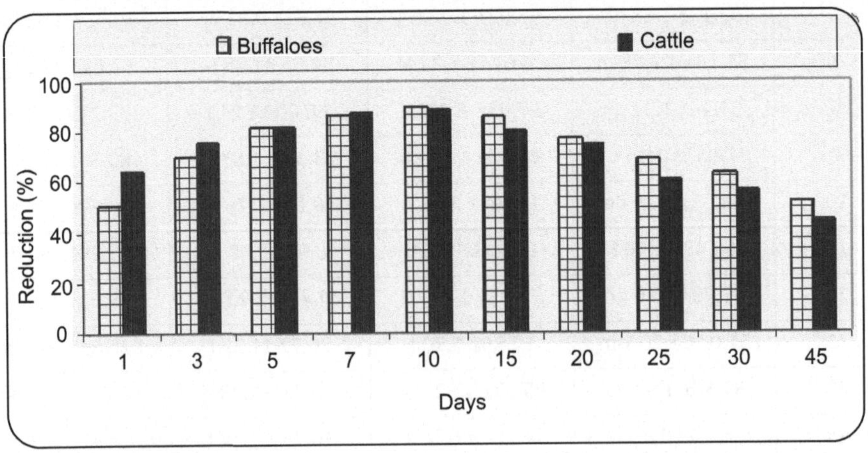

Fig. 5.11: Reduction ratios of animal ectoparasites after spraying with Diazinon 60% EC (2 ml/L) under field conditions, in farm-animals, Faculty of Agriculture, Assiut University during, 2009-2010.

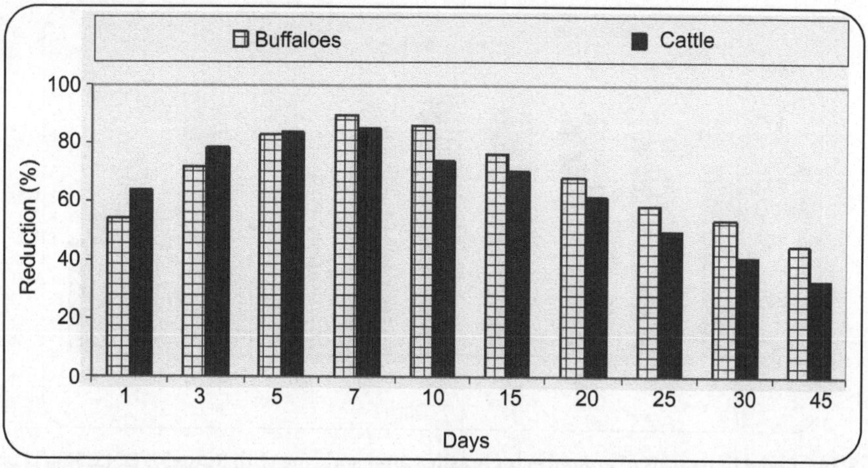

Fig. 5.12: Reduction ratios of animal ectoparasites after spraying with Vertimec 1.8% EC (1.5 ml/L) under field conditions, in farm- animals, Faculty of Agriculture, Assiut University during, 2009-2010.

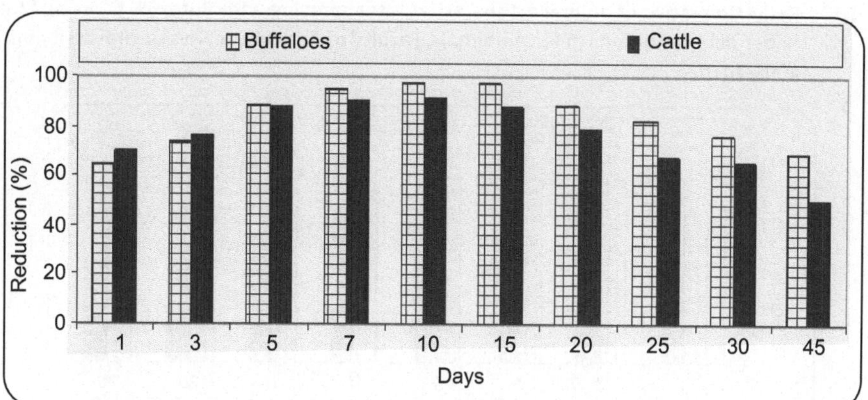

Fig. 5.13: Reduction ratios of animal ectoparasites after spraying with Vertimec 1.8% EC (2ml/L) under field conditions, in farm- animals, Faculty of Agriculture, Assiut University during, 2009-2010.

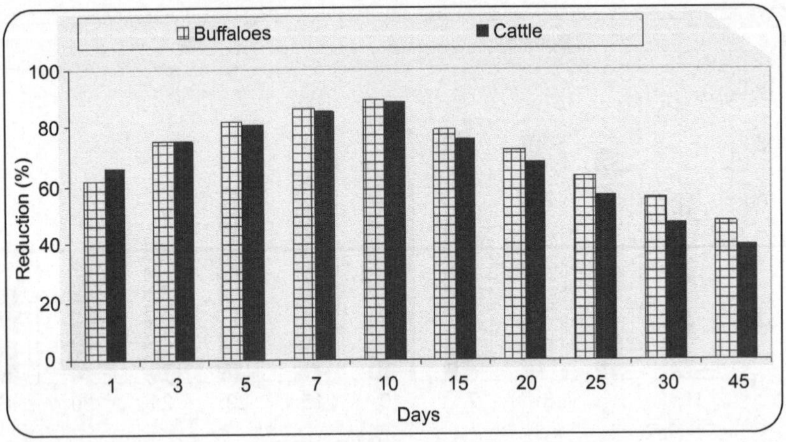

Fig. 5.14: Reduction ratios of animal ectoparasites after spraying with Butox5% EC (1.5ml/L) under field conditions, in farm-animals, Faculty of Agriculture, Assiut University during, 2009-2010.

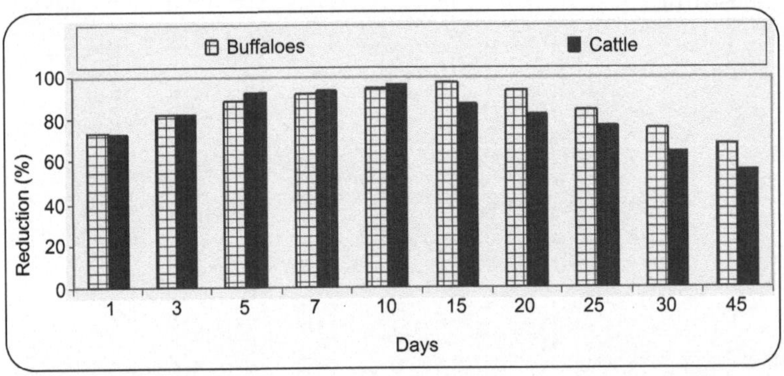

Fig. 5.15: Reduction ratios of animal ectoparasites after spraying with Butox5% EC using (2ml/L) under field conditions in farm-animals, Faculty of Agriculture, Assiut University during, 2009-2010.

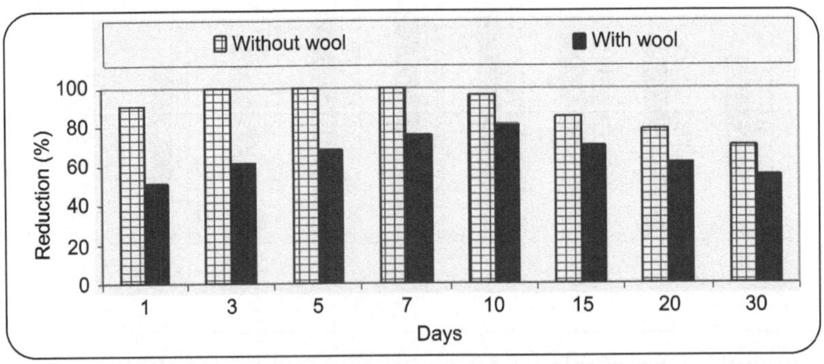

Fig. 5.16: Reduction ratios of fleas on sheep after spraying with Butox (1ml/L) with and without wool on sheep under field conditions, farm-animals, Faculty of Agriculture, Assiut University during, 2009-2010.

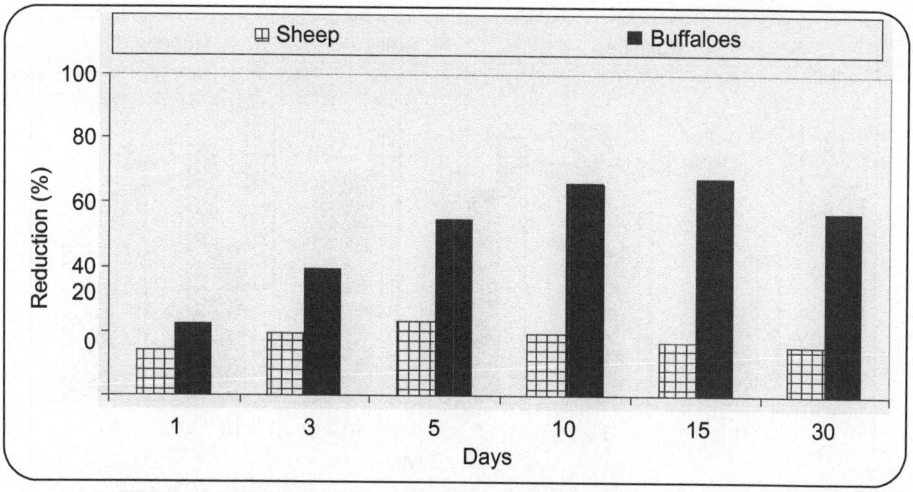

Fig. 5.17: Reduction ratios of animal ectoparasites after spraying with Radiant 12% SC using (4ml/L) under field conditions, in farm- animals, Faculty of Agriculture, Assiut University during, 2009-2010.

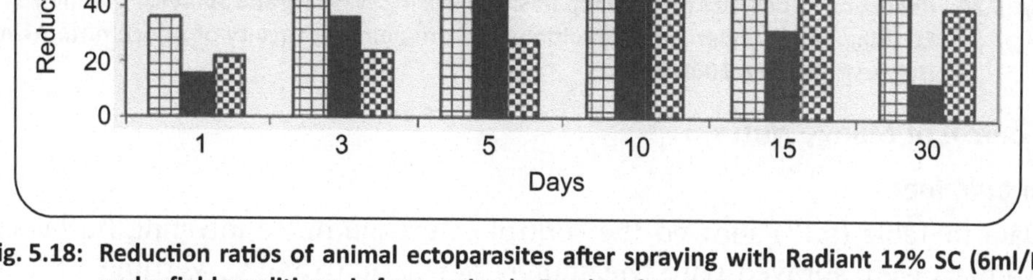

Fig. 5.18: Reduction ratios of animal ectoparasites after spraying with Radiant 12% SC (6ml/L) under field conditions, in farm- animals, Faculty of Agriculture, Assiut University during, 2009-2010.

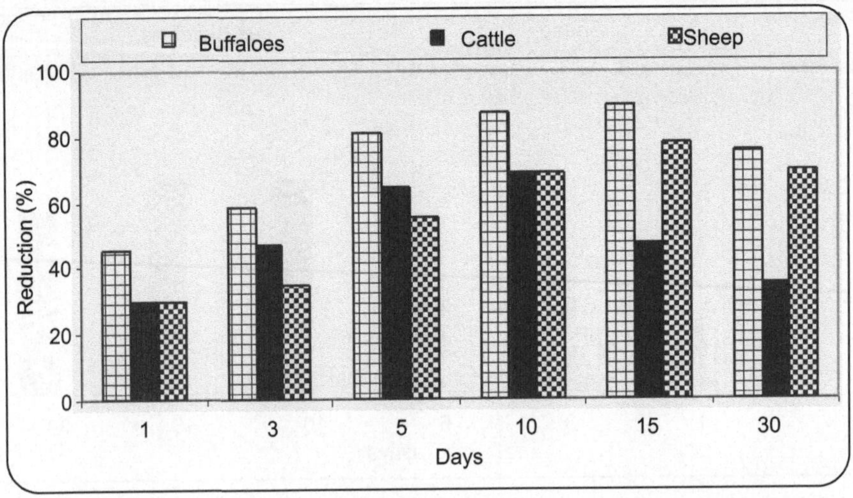

Fig. 5.19: Reduction ratios of animal ectoparasites after spraying with Radiant 12% SC (8ml/L) under field conditions, farm-animals, Faculty of Agriculture, Assiut University during, 2009-2010.

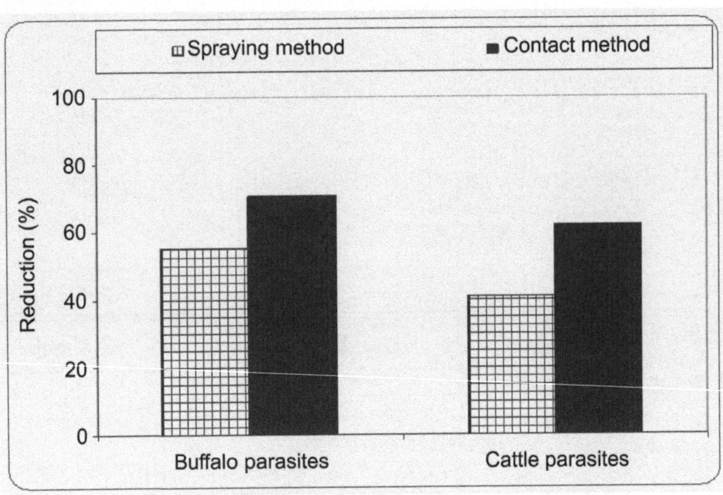

Fig. 5.20: Reduction Ratios on Animal Ectoparasites by using Washing and Spraying Diazinon 60% EC using 1ml/L under Field Conditions in Farm-animals, Faculty of Agriculture, Assiut University during, 2009-2010.

Control of Mange Mites

In buffaloes

Data in Table (5.17) showed the control of mange mites infesting buffaloes. Animals were sprayed with Diazinon 60% EC, Butox5%EC, Vertimec1.8%EC at 1ml/L, Radiant 12% SC 6ml/L and Ivermectin 1% (injection). The results showed that, treated animals with Diazinon 60% EC began to respond after

30 days, 35-45days with Vertimec1.8%EC, 25-30 days by Butox5% EC and after 20-35 days by Ivermectin1% (injection). All buffaloes returned to normal conditions (normal skin) after an average of 45-55 days (Table 5.17). It might be concluded that spraying with Butox5% EC and Ivermectin 1% (injection) gave a good results in curing buffaloes mange. These results coincided with those obtained by Abo Elmaged (1998) and Mehlhorn *et al.,* (2010).

The treated animals with sulfur began to respond after 45-55 days, 20-30 days for Ivermectin 1% (injection) and sulfur, 25- 30 days for Ivermectin1% (injection) and Butox5% EC spray and 20-35 days for Ivermectin 1% (injection) twice a month. All buffaloes returned to normal conditions (normal skin) after an average of 25-40 days, (Table 5.18).

In general Butox spray and Ivermectin injection gave a good results in curing buffaloes mange. All animals showed a slight improvement in the clinical picture of the disease by using Ivermectin one time in month, but gave satisfactory results when used fortnightly. It might be concluded that, the subcutaneous injection with Ivermectin eliminates *Sarcoptes scabiei* from buffaloes. The present results on buffaloes agreed with those obtained by Abo Elmaged (1998).

In sheep

Table (5.19) showed the results of control mange mites infesting sheep. The spray with Diazinon 60% EC, Butox5% EC, Vertimec1.8% EC at 1 ml/L, Ivermectin 1% (injection) and Ivermectin with Diazinon 60% EC revealed that the treated animals with Diazinon 60%EC began to respond after 25-30 days, 20-35 for Vertimec1.8% EC, Butox5% EC 20-30, Ivermectin 1% (injection) 15-30 days and 15-25 days for Ivermectin with Diazinon 60% EC. All sheep returned to normal conditions (normal skin) after an average of 30-45. It might be concluded that spraying with Diazinon 60% EC, Butox5% EC and Ivermectin 1% injection gave satisfactory results in curing buffaloes mange. These results coincided with those obtained by Ibrahim (1994), when used Diazinon and Ivermectin on infested sheep, he found that the mean time for recovery was 26.4 days in animals treated with Diazinon and 28.4 days in Ivermectin treatments. In general, sheep treated with Ivermectin take less time to recover than in Diazinon treatment. Cozma *et al.,* (2010) in a study of three acaricides, Doramectin (Dectomax, Pfizer) used at a single dose of 300 μg/kg b.w. given intramuscularly showed a high efficacy (95%) against *Psoroptes ovis,* in naturally infected sheep. All Doramectin treated animals were clinically normal and all skin scrapings were negative for mites 50 days after treatment. At the end of experiment (70 days) only 5% of the animals showed skin lesions and a low infestation score (1+), compared to 10% for Ivermectin.

Table (5.20) emphasized the results on sheep with infested sarcoptes and treated with tincture iodine 4%, sulfur with vaseline 10%, Ivermectin 1%

(injection) with sulfur and Ivermectin with Butox5% EC. The results showed that the treatment individuals with iodine began to respond after 45-55 days, 35-45 days for sulfur, Ivermectin with sulfur 15-25 days and 15-25 days for Ivermectin with Butox 5% EC. It might be concluded that spraying with Butox5% EC and injection with Ivermectin gave satisfactory results in curing sheep mange, wholly in agreement with Hagawane *et al.*, (2010).

In general treated sheep for controlling scabies took less time to recovery than in case of buffaloes scabies. The best results in controlling scabies were obtained when used Ivermectin injection mixed with sulfur or tested pesticide spray on body surface of buffalo and sheep mange. *Ivermectin injection is the best way to control animals mange and using spraying on animals,* Also *Injection can be used only twice a month is better than a one-time* usage (Table 5.21). The results were obtained by (Witmer *et al.,* 1995).

Table 5.17: Effect of Diazinon 60% EC, Vertimec 1.8% EC and Butox 5% EC at 1 ml/L, Radiant at 6 ml/L and Ivermectin1%injection 1 ml/50 kg on Buffalo Mange Mites under Field Conditions on Farm-animals, Faculty of Agriculture, Assiut University during, 2009-2010

Pesticide	Diazinon 60% EC			Vertimec 1.8% EC			Butox 5% EC			Radiant 12% SC			Ivermectin 1% L		
Days	1	2	3	1	2	3	1	2	3	1	2	3	1	2	3
1	+	+++	++	+++	++	+	++	+++	++	++	++	+	+++	++	+
3	+	+++	++	+++	++	+	++	+++	++	++	++	+	+++	++	+
5	+	++	++	++	++	+	++	+++	++	++	++	+	++	+	+
7	+	++	++	++	+	+	++	+++	++	++	++	+	+	+	+
10	+	+	+	+	+	+	+	++	+	++	++	+	+	+	+
15	+	+	+	+	+	+	+	+	+	++	++	+	+	+	-
20	+	-	+	+	+	+	-	+	-	+	+	+	-	-	-
30	-	-	-	+	+	-	-	-	-	+	+	+	-	-	-
45	N	-	-	-	-	-	N	N	-	+	+	-	-	N	N

+++ = heavily infested animals with scabies
++ = moderately infested animals with scabies
+ = slightly infested animals with scabies
- = no infested and the wool started to grow
N = normal skin and wool

Table 5.18: Effect of using Ivermectin 1% 1ml/50kg (injection) with Sulfur with Vaseline, Ivermectin1% (injection) and Butox 5% EC spray, Ivermectin 1% and Diazinon 60% EC Spray and Ivermectin Twice on Buffalo Mange Mites under Field Conditions on Farm-animals, Faculty of Agriculture, Assiut University during, 2009- 2010

Treated Days	Ivermectin 1% and (Sulfur with vaseline)			Sulfur with vaseline 10%			Ivermectin 1%and Butox 5% EC*			Ivermectin 1% and Diazinon 60% EC*			Ivermectin (twice)		
	1	2	3	1	2	3	1	2	3	1	2	3	1	2	3
1		++	+			++	++	+		++		++		++	
3		++	+			++	++	+		++	++	++	++	++	++

5	+	+	+	++		++	++	+	++	++	++	++	++	+	++
7	+	+	+	++	++	++	+	+	+	+	+	++	+	+	+
10	-	-	+	+	++	+	+	+	+	+	+	+	+	+	+
15	-	-	-	+	++	+	+	-	+	-	+	+	+	-	-
20	N	-	-	+	++	+	-	-	-	-	-	-	N	-	-
30	N	N	-	+	+	+	N	N	N	N	N	-	N	-	N
45	N	N	N	+	-	-	N	N	N	N	N	N	N	N	N

*1ml/liter

+++ = heavily infested animals with scabies

++ = moderately infested animals with scabies

+ = slightly infested animals with scabies

- = no infested and the wool started to grow

N = normal skin and wool

Table 5.19: Effect of Vertemic 1.8% EC ,Butox5% EC, Daizinon60% EC at 1ml/liter, Ivermectin1% injection 1ml / 50 kg and Radiant 12% SC at 6ml/L on Sheep Mange under Field Conditions on Farm-animals, Faculty of Agriculture, Assiut University during, 2009-2010

Pesticide Days	Vertimec 1.8% EC			Ivermectin 1% L			Butox 5% EC			Diazinon 60% EC			Radiant 12% SC		
	1	2	3	1	2	3	1	2	3	1	2	3	1	2	3
1		+	++	++	++		++		+	++		+	++	++	+
3	++	+	++	++	++	+	++	++	+	++	+	+	++	++	+
5	++	+	++	+	+	+	+	++	+	++	++	+	++	++	+
7	+	+	+	+	+	+	+	++	+	++	++	+	++	++	+
10	+	+	+	+	+	-	+	+	+	+	+	+	++	++	+
15	+	+	+	-	-	-	+	-	-	+	+	+	++	++	+
20	-	-	-	-	-	N	-	-	-	-	-	-	+	+	+
30	-	-	-	N	-	N	-	-	N	-	-	-	-	-	-
45	N	N	-	N	N	N	N	N	N	N	-	N	-	-	-

+++ = heavily infested animals with scabies

++ = moderately infested animals with scabies

+ = slightly infested animals with scabies

- = no infested and the wool started to grow

N = normal skin and wool

Table 5.20: Effect of Tincture iodine 4% , Sulfur with Vaseline10% , Ivermectin1% and (Sulfur with vaseline), Ivermectin and Butox 5% EC and Ivermectin and Diazinon60% EC on Sheep Mange under Field Conditions on Farm-animals, Faculty of Agriculture, Assiut University during, 2009- 2010

Pesticides Days	Tincture iodine 4%			Sulfur with vaseline10%			Ivermectin and (Sulfur with vaseline)			Ivermectin and Butox*			Ivermectin and Diazinon*		
	1	2	3	1	2	3	1	2	3	1	2	3	1	2	3
1	++	+++	+	++	+	+++	+++	++	+	++	+	++	+++	++	+
3	++	+++	+	++	+	+++	+	++	+	++	+	++	+++	++	+
5	++	+++	+	++	+	+++	+	+	+	++	+	+	++	+	+
7	++	++	+	+	+	++	-	-	-	+	-	+	+	+	-
10	++	++	+	+	+	++	-	-	-	-	-	-	+	-	-
15	++	++	+	+	+	+	-	N	-	-	-	N	-	-	-
20	+	+	+	+	+	+	N	N	-	N	N	N	-	-	-
30	+	-	+	+	-	+	N	N	N	N	N	N	-	N	N
45	-	-	-	-	-	-	N	N	N	N	N	N	N	N	N

* 1ml/liter
+++ = heavily infested animals with scabies
++ = moderately infested animals with scabies
+ = slightly infested animals with scabies
- = no infested and the wool started to grow
N = normal skin and wool

Table 5.21: Mean Time in Days for Treated Buffalo and Sheep by Some Chemicals to Recover from Scabies during 2009-2010

AnimalsTreatment	Mean time of recovering (days)	
	Buffalo mange	Sheep mange
Vertimec 1.8% EC at 1ml/L	>45	40-45
Ivermecin 1% (injection) twice	25	-
Ivermecin1% 1 time	45	25-30
Butox 5% EC at 1ml/L	40	30 40
Diazinon 60% EC at 1ml/L	45-50	40 45
Radiant 12% SC at 1ml/L	> 45	45
Tincture iodine 4%	-	>45
Sulfur with Vaseline 10%	>45	>45
Sulfur with Ivermecin	30	15-20
Ivermectin and Diazinon	30	30
Ivermectin and Butox	30	20

Control of Manure Ectoparasites

Mechanical Control

Data in Table (5.22) and figure (5.21) represented the percentage of mortality in sheep-sheds ectoparasites after one to 45 days after applications of cleaning, burning and quicklime methods, caused initial kill of 92.56%, 99.17% and 99.17% with cleaning, burning and quicklime. The activity of the method increased gradually, after so the activity of the method decreased gradually to attain 72.73%, 51.52% and 76.52% after 20 days, respectively. However, after 45 days, the percentages of mortality were reduced to be 54.60%, 18.40% and 53.37% for sheep-sheds parasites, respectively.

In general, quicklime and cleaning methods showed the highest reduction, followed by burning method. *Mechanical methods* can be used to *avoid fleas resistance by insecticides in sheep-sheds and the best way is the use of quicklime and extinguished* it *in the soil.* Also *the best of these methods is cleaning or disposal of soil containing fleas and larvae from the sheep farm,* and *these methods are found to be safed without using pesticides.*

Chemical Control

Data in Table (5.23) and figure (5.22) represented the percentage of mortality in sheep-sheds ectoparasites after one to 45 days after applications with Diazinon 60% EC, Vertimec 1.8% EC and Butox 5% EC spray at 2ml/liter water. Results showed that, the one day post treatment gave an initial kill of 93.43%, 88.35% and 95.45 Diazinon 60% EC, Vertimec 1.8% EC and Butox 5% EC. The activity of the product increased gradually to attain 99.13%, 100% and 99.57% after 7days respectively, after so, the activity of the product decreased gradually to attain 82.41%, 82.40% and 88.84% after 20 days, respectively. However after 45 days the percentage of mortality reduced to be 66.67%, 62.24% and 69.58% for sheep-sheds parasites, respectively. *The results showed that, the effect of biocides was slow but still a long time and recommend the using of biocides are for its safe to the environment.* *The bio-insecticide gave long residual effect* and with using low concentration *(2%) in the control of animals ectoparasites,* in agreement with Kolar *et al.,* (2008).

Table 5.22: Reduction Ratios on Animal Ectoparasites by using Mechanical Control on Fleas in Sheep-sheds under Field Conditions, Farm Animals, Faculty of Agriculture, Assiut University during, 2009-2010

Days	Mean ±SE (%)		
	Cleaning method	Burning method	Quicklime
1	92.56 ±1.46 c-e	99.17 ± 0.84 ab	99.17 ± 0.84 ab
3	95.20 ±1.41 cd	98.40 ± 1.63 ab	100.00 ± 0 a
5	99.16 ± 0.86 ab	78.15 ± 2.26 gh	98.32 ± 1.71 ab
7	95.69 ± 3.16 bc	68.11 ± 2.32 hi	94.83 ±1.52 cd

10	86.67 ± 0.85 e-g	63.33 ± 2.25 j-l	90.83 ± 1.70 de
15	80.95 ±1.40 f-h	57.14 ± 1.40 k-m	88.10 ± 1.40 ef
20	72.73 ± 2.67 h-j	51.52 ± 2.04 m	76.52 ± 2.04 hi
25	66.67 ± 0.77 i-k	39.39 ± 3.36 n	67.42 ± 0.77 i-k
30	58.44 ± 1.75 k-m	27.92 ± 2.29 o	62.98 ± 1.14 j-l
45	54.60 ± 1.66 lm	18.40 ± 2.72 p	53.37 ± 2.73 lm
Mean	80.27 b	60.15 c	83.15 a

- Means followed by the same letter are insignificantly different.

Table 5.23: Reduction Ratios on Animal Ectoparasites by using Diazinon 60% EC, Vertimec 1.8% EC , and Butox 5% EC using (2cm/liter) on Fleas in Sheep-sheds under Field Conditions in Farm Animals, Faculty of Agriculture, Assiut University during, 2009-2010

Days	Mean ±SE (%)		
	Diazinon 60% EC	Vertimec 1.8% EC	Butox 5% EC
1	93.43 ± 1.86 fg	88.35 ± 1.39 hi	95.45 ± 0.89 r
3	97.03 ± 0.87 de	93.94 ± 0.89 fg	100.00 ± 0 a
5	99.55 ± 0.46 ab	100.00 ±0 a	100.00 ±0 a
7	99.13 ± 0.44 bc	100.00 ±0 a	99.57 ± 0.44 ab
10	90.95 ± 1.52 gh	98.71 ± 0.76 bc	97.84 ± 1.16 cd
15	84.58 ± 1.19 ij	95.49 ± 0.96 ef	93.83 ± 1.19 fg
20	82.41 ± 1.16 jk	82.40 ±0.87 jk	88.84 ± 1.16 hi
25	78.07 ± 1.12 k-m	76.05 ± 0.74 l -n	85.29 ±1.13 ij
30	73.44 ± 1.12 m-o	70.95 ± 0.42 n-p	81.33 ± 0.73 j-l
45	66.67 ± 1.12 pq	62.24 ± 1.12 q	69.58 ± 1.12 op
Mean	86.53 c	86.81 b	91.17 a

- Means followed by the same letter are insignificantly different.

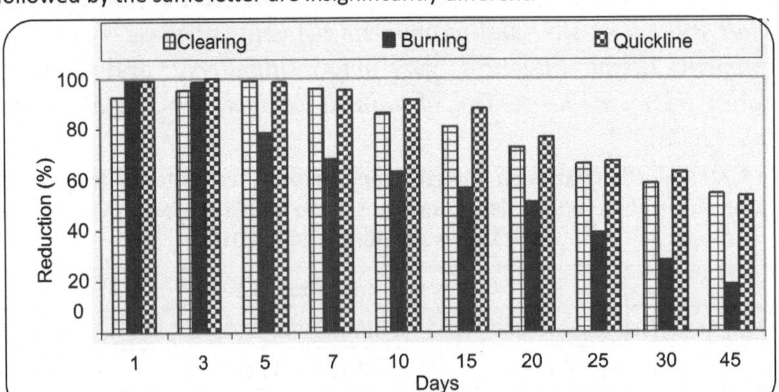

Fig. 5.21: Reduction ratios on animal ectoparasites by using mechanical control on sheep fleas in sheds under field conditions, in farm animals, Faculty of Agriculture, Assiut University during, 2009-2010.

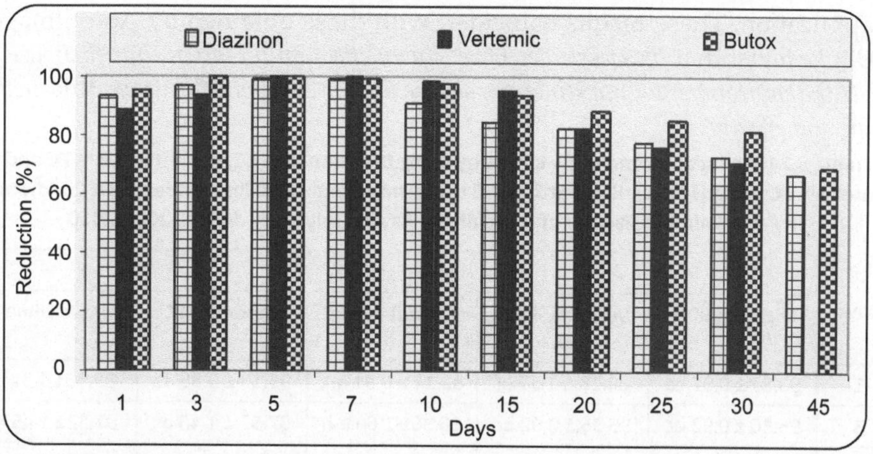

Fig. 5.22: Reduction ratios on animal ectoparasites by using Diazinon 60% EC, Vertimec 1.8% EC, and Butox 5% EC (2cm/liter) on fleas in sheep-sheds under field conditions, in farm animals, Faculty Agriculture, Assiut University during, 2009-2010.

Fly larvae

Data in Table (5.24) and figure (5.23) represented the percentage of mortality for fly larvae in animal manure after one to 30 days after applications with Diazinon 60% EC, Vertimec 1.8% EC spray at 1cm/liter and Radiant 12% SC at 4cm/liter. Results showed that, the one day post treatment gave an initial kill of 93.85%, 89.28% and 82.14% when treated with Diazinon 60% EC, Vertimec1.8% EC and Radiant 12% SC, respectively. The activity of the product increased gradually to attain 100%, 100% and 96.83% after 7 days, respectively. The activity of the product decreased gradually to attain 85.27%, 96.90% and 78.52% after 20 days, respectively. However after 30 days the percentage of mortality reduced to 79.22%, 84.41% and 69.48% for fly larvae in animal-manure, respectively.

The percentages of mortality for fly larvae in animal manure after one to 30 days after applications of Quicklime at dust and Butox 5% EC spray at 1cm/liter were presented (Table 47). Results showed that the one day post treatment gave an initial kill of 93.10% and 89.66% with Butox 5% EC and Quicklime. The activity of the product increased gradually to attain 100% after 7 days when used Butox 5% EC and Quicklime after so, the activity of the product decreased gradually to attain 89.44% n 91.44% after 20 days respectively. However, after 30 days the percentage of mortality reduced to be 83.83% and 74.85% for fly larvae in animal-manure, respectively (Grabovac and Petriæ, 2003 and Mehlhorn *et al.,* 2010) .

In general, Vertimec 1.8% EC showed the highest toxicity for fly larvae followed by Diazinon 60% EC and Radiant 12% SC. The Butox 5% SC showed the highest toxicity for fly larvae followed by Quicklime regardless of the rate of application. These results coincided with those obtained by Abo Elmaged, (1998) *he found* that *bio-pesticides have slowly effect on fly larvae, but their use are safe to the environment. Quicklime can also be used to eliminate fly larvae,* this *method is safe and effective.*

Table 5.24: Reduction ratio of fly larvae by using Diazinon 60% EC, Vertimec 1.8 % EC and Butox 5% EC using (1ml/L), Radiant 12% SC using 4ml/L and Quicklime under Field Conditions in Farm Animals, Faculty of Agriculture, Assiut University during, 2009-2010

Days	Mean ±SE (%)				
	Diazinon 60% EC	Vertimec 1.8% EC	Radiant 12%SC	Butox 5% EC	Quicklime
1	93.85 ± 0.97 cd	89.28 ± 1.57 ef	82.14 ± 0.91 h-k	93.10 ± 0.88 de	89.66± 1.52 ef
3	96.36 ± 0.92 bc	96.36 ± 0.92 bc	86.36± 1.60 e-h	97.52 ± 1.46 bc	97.52± 1.46 bc
5	100.00 ±0 a	100.00 ± 00 a	90.82± 0.93 de	100.00± 0 a	100.00± 0 a
7	100.00 ± 0 a	100.00± 00 a	96.83 ± 1.62 b	100.00 ± 0 a	100.00± 0 a
10	100.00 ± 0 a	100.00 ± 00 a	98.57 ± 1.46 a	98.46± 1.57 ab	98.46 ± 0.78 b
15	87.97 ± 2.03 e-g	100.00 ± 00 a	84.21 ±1.33 g-j	94.96± 1.48 cd	92.44 ± 1.48 de
20	85.27± 2.09 f-i	96.90 ± 00.79 b	78.52± 0.93 k	91.44 ± 1.15 de	89.44 ± 1.24 ef
25	80.88 ± 0.75 i-k	90.44± 1.98 de	71.32 ±1.30 l	90.00 ± 1.18 ef	84.00± 1.18 f-h
30	79.22± 0.66 jk	84.41 ±1.14 f-j	69.48± 1.32 l	83.83 ± 1.06 f-h	74.85 ± 2.11 i-k
Mean	91.51 b	95.27 a	84.25 c	94.37 a	91.82 b

- Means followed by the same letter are insignificantly different.

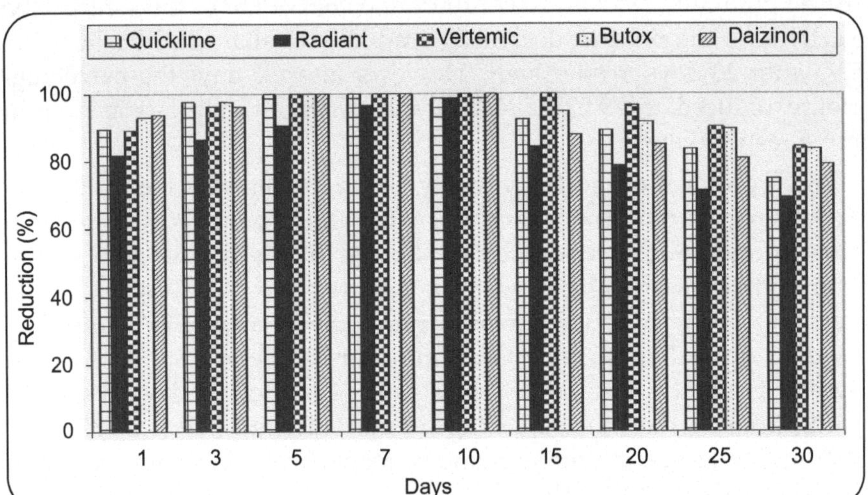

Fig. 5.23: Reduction ratios on fly larvae treated with Diazinon 60% EC, Vertimec 1.8% EC and Butox 5% EC (1ml/L), Radiant 12% SC 4ml/L and Quicklime under field conditions, farm animals, Faculty of Agriculture, Assiut University during, 2009-2010

RODENT CONTROL

Under Laboratory Conditions

Attractive Baits

Data in Table (5.25) and Figure (5.24) illustrated the food consumption of rodent (*R.r.frugivorus*) by using of 4 attractive baits mixed with crush maize (Cumin, coriander, anise, and yeast) as compare with control (crush maize) under laboratory conditions for 5 days. According to the mean consumption during 5 days, it was observed that the mean consumption was high in yeast bait (7.25 gm/rat), coriander (2.35 gm/rat) and anise (2.05 gm/rat) compare with control (0.9 gm/rat). It was found that there was a significant difference in the animal consumption of the four attractive baits tested for *R.r.frugivorus*. Also, there was a significant difference in food consumed by males and females.

In using the *R.r.alexandrinus* it was observed that, the mean consumption of yeast bait was 7.35 gm/rat, and anise (3.63 gm/rat) as compare with control (2 gm/rat). It was found that there was a significant difference in the animal consumption of the attractive baits tested for *R.r.alexandrinus*. In addition, there was a significant difference between males and females consumption of the four tested attractive baits.

For the *Arvicanthis niloticus* it was observed that, the consumption was high in yeast bait with crush maize was 4.75 gm/rat, as compared with control (1.83 gm/rat). There was a significant difference in the animal consumption of the four tested attractive baits for *Arvicanthis niloticus*, and there was a significant difference in males and females consumption of the four tested attractive baits. Baits preference tests should be done periodically to find out the proper bait for rodenticide formulation and to overcome the shyness of rodent baits (Table 5.48), the results are in accordance with Abd El-Rahman *et al.*, (1991), Shafi *et al.*, (1992) and Witmer *et al.*, (2008).

Generally, the above mentioned results emphasized the significant effect of attractive in bait of rodents. These results may be useful in preparation of rodenticides baits used in rodent control.

Repellent Baits

Data in Table (5.26) and Figure (5.25) illustrated the food consumption of rodent (*R.r.frugivorus*) for 4 repellents baits mixed with crush maize (black pepper, jejoba seed, and oshar powder leaf and neem powder leaf) as compared with control (crushed maize) under laboratory conditions for 5 days. According to the mean consumption during 5 days, it was observed that the consumption was low in black pepper bait with crush maize (0.32.5 gm/rat), jejoba seed with crush maize (1.15 gm/rat), while the control was 10.83 gm/rat. There was a significant difference in the *R.r.frugivorus* consumption of the four tested repellent baits. Also, there was a significant difference in food consumed by males and females.

In case of the *R.r.alexandrinus* it was observed that, the consumption was low in black pepper bait with crush maize (0.38 gm/rat), and powder leaf oshar with crush maize (0.85 gm/rat) as compared with control (7.05 gm/rat). It was found that there was a significant difference in the animal consumption of the repellent baits tested for *R.r.alexandrinus*. Also, there was a significant difference between males and females consumption of the four tested attractive baits.

The consumption was low in black pepper bait (0.83 gm/rat), powder leaf oshar (1.58 gm/rat) as compared with control (7.9 gm/rat) *Arvicanthis niloticus* .It was found that there was a significant difference in the animal consumption of the four repellent baits tested for *Arvicanthis niloticus*, and there was a significant difference in males and females consumption of the four tested attractive baits (Table 5.26).

Generally, the above mentioned results emphasized the significant effect of repellent in bait of rodents. These results may be useful in rodent control. in agreement with Boeke *et al.*, (2004) and Witmer *et al.*, (1995).

Evaluation of two Rodenticides

Data in Table (5.27) and figure (5.26) illustrated the food consumption of rodent (*R.r.frugivorus*) when used two rodenticde baits (Supercaid 0.004% and Caid 0.005%) under laboratory conditions for 5 days. According to the mean consumption during 5 days, in males, the consumption was scarce in Supercaid bait (56.40 gm) as compared with Caid (89 gm), but in females (61.80 gm, 78.20 gm) were counted for the two rodenticide baits. The dead period for Caid was longer than in the case of Supercaid. It was found that there was a significant difference in the animal consumption of the tested rodenticide baits for *R.r.frugivorus*. Also, insignificant difference in rodenticides consumed by males and females.

In *R.r. alexandrines* male, the consumption was scarce in Supercaid bait (43.40 gm) as compared with Caid (80.40 gm), but in females (34.60 gm, 74.80.20 gm) were observed. The dead period for Caid was longer than in Supercaid. It was found that there was a significant difference in the animal consumption of the tested rodenticide baits for *R.r. alexandrines*. Also, no significant difference was observed between males and females, the results are as similar as Abazaid (1990), Littin *et al.*,(2000) and Shooba, (2003).

In *Arvicanthis niloticus*, it was observed that the consumption of males was scarce in Supercaid bait (45.20 gm) as compared with Caid (64 gm), but in females 56.80 gm, 60.20 gm were recorded. The dead period for Caid was longer than supercaid. It was found that there was a significant difference in the animal consumption of the rodenticide baits tested for *R.r. alexandrines*.

Also, a significant difference was found in rodenticides consumed by males and females, in agreement with Ali (1991), Abazaid (1997), Jackson (2001), Abd El-Galil (2005) and Baghdadi (2006).

Under Field Conditions

Toxicity of Rodenticides

Data in Table (5.28) studied the two rodenticde bait (Supercaid0.004% and Caid0.005%) under field conditions for 11 days. the population density estimated by trap method. According to the mean of the population, the mean of caught rodents were in Caid (8.18%) higher than in Supercaid (2.18%) as compared with control (11.55%) during the study period. It was found that there was a significant difference in the number of animal catched when used the two rodenticide baits tested, the results agreement with Maher Ali (1972), Maher Ali and Abdel-Gawad (1982), Saied (1985), Abdel-Gawad (2001b), Ahmaed (2006), Baghdadi (2006) and Valchev *et al.*, (2008).

Acceptability of Rodent Species to two Attractive Baits

Data in Table (5.29) and Figure (5.27) summarized the consumption of rodent by Supercaid with two attractive (vanilla and yeast) under field conditions for 6 days. According to the mean consumption (in gm) during 6 days, it was observed that the mean of consumption bait was high in Supercaid with yeast bait (18.17 gm/day) and (11/gm/day) for Supercaid with vanilla compared with control (6.67gm/day). It was found that there was a significant difference in the animal consumption of the rodenticide with attractive baits tested in agreement with Khan *et al.*, (2000).

Toxicity by Aluminum Phosphide 33%

Data in Table (5.30) and figure (5.28) studied the Aluminum phosphate fumigation under field conditions for four weeks. The population density estimated by active burrows method. The rodent active burrows were less gradually after so, the activity of the rodent active burrow increased gradually to attain by mean 64.19% after month. Aluminum phosphate can be used in rodent control (Carl Snider, 1983). Aluminum phosphide is a new burrowing rodent fumigant in USA. It reacts with water vapor to produce hydrogen phosphide gas. Hydrogen phosphide is a very toxic gas, however, several characteristics of the product and use pattern give most commercial formulations a low user hazard when used by trained applicators in accordance with label instructions. It is efficacious when used in many situations against several burrowing rodent species, but will not be effective in all situations.

Several factors to consider are burrow temperature, burrow humidity, burrow length and configuration, soil porosity, wind speed and direction, and species specific behavior characteristics. It is particularly desirable to use as a clean-up after a baiting program. Also, it can be used throughout most of the year. The user should read the label carefully to determine all endangered species precautions. Hydrogen phosphide has no secondary hazard although burrow dwelling non-target animals will probably be killed.

In conclusion, the recommended procedure for rodent control is applying aluminum phosphate followed by anticoagulants twice annually seems to be satisfactory to apply within active burrows. However, it is rather important to give all possible attention to environmental sanitation. At the same time, type of applied anticoagulant should be changed upon appearance signs of resistance of rodents under control to such product.) Witmer *et al.,* (1995).

Table 5.25: Mean Daily Consumption (by gram) of Some Attractive Baits against three Rodent Species under Laboratory Conditions

Rat species	Baits/ Sex species	Cumin	Coriander	Anise	Yeast	Control
R. r. frugivorous	♂	0.80 c	1.85 b	1.95 b	7.60 a	1.00 bc
	♂	1.00 c	2.85 b	2.10 b	6.90 a	0.80 c
	Total	1.80 c	4.70 b	4.10 b	14.50 a	1.80c
R. r. alexandrinus		0.45 d	2.75 bc	3.70 b	7.75 a	2.05c
	♂	0.75 d	2.50 bc	3.55 b	6.95 a	1.95 c
	Total	1.20 d	5.25 c	7.25 b	14.70 a	4.00 c
A. niloticus	♂	1.05 c	1.45 c	1.55 c	4.70 as	2.55 b
	♂	0.75 c	1.60 b	1.65 b	4.80 a	1.15 b
	Total	1.80 c	3.05 b	3.20 b	9.50 a	3.65 b

- Means followed by the same letter, in the same row, are insignificant different

Table 5.26: Mean Daily Consumption (by gram) of Some Repellents against three Rodent Species under Laboratory Conditions

Rat species	Baits/ Sex species	Cumin	Coriander	Anise	Yeast	Control
R. r. frugivorous	♂	0.40 c	0.80 c	1.10 c	2.35 b	12.50 a
	♂	0.25 c	1.50 b	1.35 b	1.45 b	9.15 a
	Total	0.65 d	2.30 c	2.45 c	3.80 b	21.65 a
R. r. alexandrinus		0.60 c	1.40 c	0.85 c	2.35 b	6.65 a
	♂	0.15 d	1.05 c	0.85 cd	1.95 b	7.45 a
	Total	0.75 d	2.45 c	1.70 cd	4.30 b	14.10 a
A. niloticus	♂	1.10 c	2.25 b	1.85 bc	2.30 b	8.35 a
	♂	0.55 c	1.30 c	1.30 c	2.50 b	7.45 a
	Total	1.65 d	3.55 bc	3.15 c	4.80 b	15.80 a

- Means followed by the same letter, in the same row, are insignificant different

Table 5.27: Means of Daily Consumption and Dead period of two Rodenticides on three Rodent Species under Laboratory Conditions

Rat sp.	Species	Males		Females	
		Supercaid 0.004%	Caid 0.005%	Supercaid 0.004%	Caid 0.005%
R.r. frugivorus	Consumption bait	56.40±5.33b	89.00±5.45a	61.80±2.92b	78.20±3.71a
	Dead period	5.60±0.68a	7.20±0.58a	5.00±0.32b	8.20±0.66a
R.r. alexandrinus	Consumption bait	43.40±3.28b	80.40±3.46a	34.60±1.81b	74.80±2.84a
	Dead period	4.80±0.37c	8.00±0.71c	3.80±0.37c	7.40±0.51c
A. niloticus	Consumption bait	45.20±2.48b	64.00±6.49a	56.80±3.43a	60.20±5.20a
	Dead period	4.60±0.40a	6.60±0.51a	3.80±0.37a	7.80±0.58a

- Means followed by the same letter in the same row are insignificantly different

Table 5.28: Effect of two Rodenticides on Rodent Population under Field Conditions in Farm Animals, Faculty of Agriculture, Assiut University, during study period

Rodenticides / Days post treatment	Supercaid 0.004%	Caid 0.005%	Control
1	2	5	14
2	1	6	8
3	0	9	14
4	0	3	11
5	0	6	9
6	0	8	9
7	1	9	7
8	3	9	13
9	4	10	11
10	6	12	14
11	7	13	17
Total	24	90	127
Mean	2.18±0.76 c	8.18±0.90 b	11.55±0.94 a

Table 5.29: Daily consumption of Supercaid Mixed with Attractive Baits during 6 days, under Field conditions in Animal Farms, Faculty of Agriculture, Assiut University, during the Study Period

Baits Days	Rodenticide with Attractant baits		
	Supercaid	Supercaid with vanila	Supercaid with yeast
1	4.33±1.20gh	10.67±0.88 ef	20.00±1.16b
2	3.67±1.86h	14.33±2.96c-e	28.00±1.15a

3	3.00±1.53h	11.66±1.45ef	18.00±1.53bc
4	3.33±2.03h	9.00±2.08fg	13.66±1.20c-f
5	3.00±0.58h	11.33±1.33ef	12.33±2.40d-f
6	4.67±2.40gh	9.00±3.06fg	17.00±1.73b-d
Mean	3.67±0.61c	11±0.85b	18.17±1.35a

Table 5.30: Reduction Ratios of Rodent Active Burrow after using Aluminum Phosphate 33% (Fumigation) during one Month under Field Conditions in Animal-farm, Assiut University

Reduction (%)			
Area (3)	**Area (2)**	**Area (1)**	**Number**
1	44.44	50	33.33
2	46.67	60	53.33
3	64.29	71.43	71.43
4	78.57	85.71	78.57
5	100	92.31	84.62
6	83.33	75	83.33
7	66.67	41.67	66.67
8	45.45	9.09	54.55
Mean	66.18	60.65	65.73

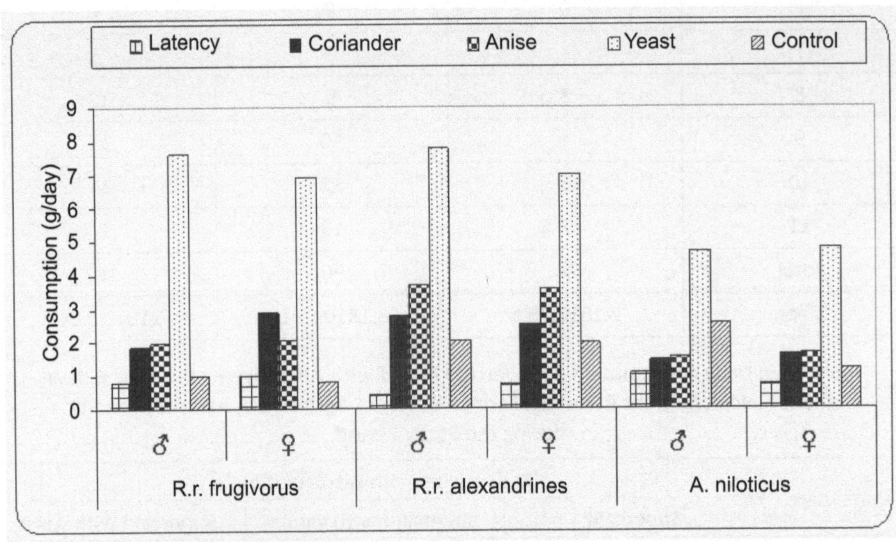

Fig. 5.24: Mean daily consumption (by gram) of some attractive baits against three rodent species under laboratory conditions

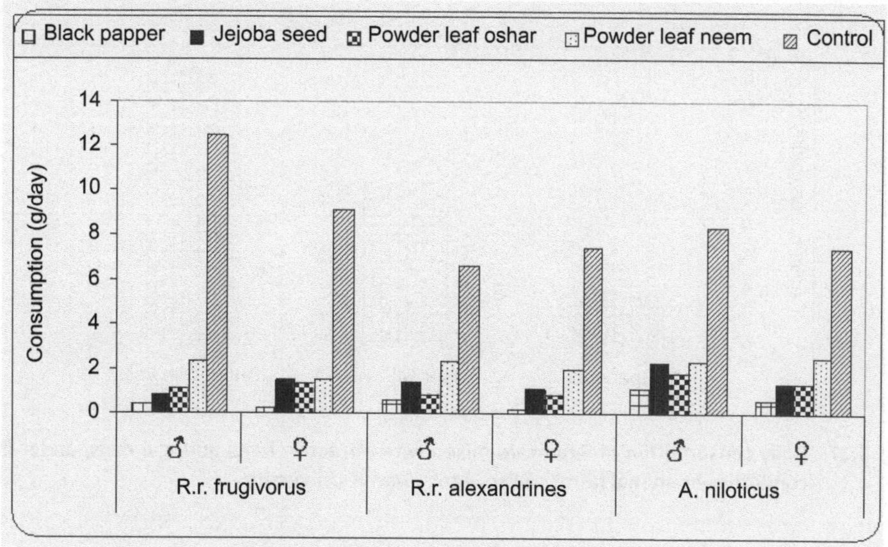

Fig. 5.25: Mean daily consumption (by gram) of some repellents against three rodents species under laboratory conditions

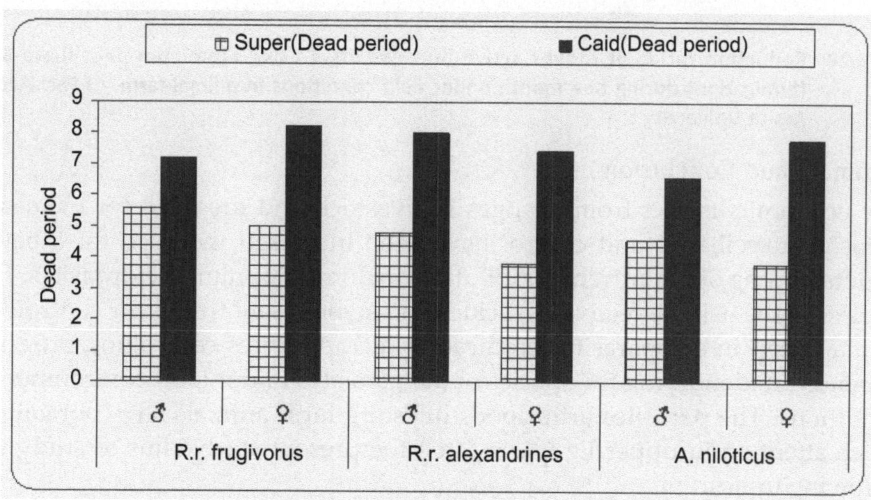

Fig. 5.26: Means of daily consumption and dead period of two rodenticides on three rodent species under laboratory conditions

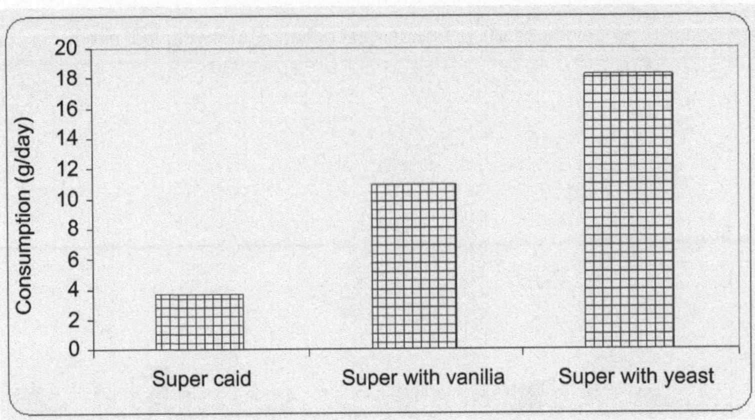

Fig. 5.27: Daily consumption of Supercaid mixed with attractive baits during 6 days, under field conditions in animal farms of Fac. Agric., Assiut University

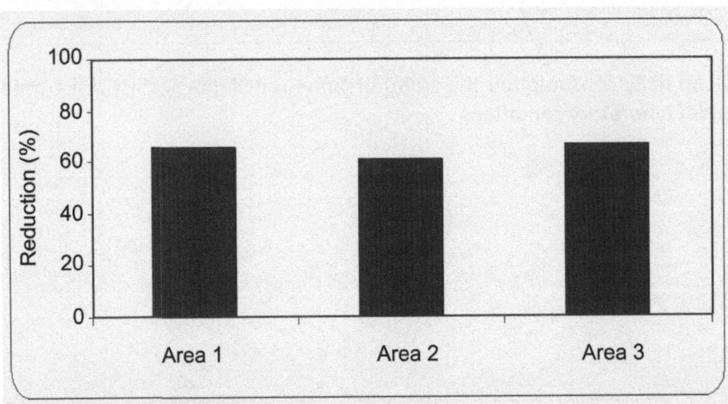

Fig. 5.28: Reduction ratios of rodent active burrows after using aluminum phosphate 33% (fumigation) during one month under field conditions in animal-farm, of Fac. Agric., Assiut University

Summary and Conclusion

The economic impact from changes in livestock and the need for increased parasite surveillance and control have been increased the need for a better understanding of the current distribution on domestic animal ectoprasites. The success in the using effective pesticides and some resent trends for controlling as main step in ectoparasites eradication. Ectoparasites controlling program depends on identifying the species of the parasites under local environmental conditions. The parasites arthropods infesting farm animals have not gained much attention in upper Egypt. So, that the present study aims to study the following topics.

- Survey the farm animal pests in addition to the farm animal ectoparasites.
- Survey the rodent species and their ectoparasites.

- Determining of population density of ectoparasites on their body surface and in the soil of the animal husbandry.
- Control the ectoparasites on the animal body and in the sheds.
- Control rodent in the animal husbandry using various methods.

GENERAL SURVEY OF PESTS INHABITING FARM ANIMALS IN THE AREA OF STUDY

Rodents

Rodents trapped from animal-farm, Assiut University during the period from 2007 to 2010 years. Recorded species were: the white bellied rat, *Rattus rattus frugivorus* (Linnaeus) represented by 52.86%, the grey-bellied rat, *Rattus rattus alexandrinus* (Linnaeus), 28.74% and the Nile grass rat, *Arvicanthis niloticus* (Desmarest), (18.40%).

Flies and Mosquitoes

Adult stages of fly and mesquite species, found in animal production farm during 2008-2010 at Assiut University, were: *Musca domestica* Macq, *Muscina canicularis* Wied, *Stomoxys calcitrans* L, *Tabania* sp. Merg, *Sarcophaga* sp. L and *Phormia regina* F. In addition to a single of mosquitoes, *Culex* sp.

SURVEY OF ECTOPARASITES

On Animal Body Surfaces

The animal body surfaces were suffered with infestation of certain pests (i.e., lice on buffaloes, fleas on sheep and ticks on cattle body surfaces.

In Manure of Animals

In soil of husbandry animals, the recorded ectoparasites were: *Amblyomma* sp., *Haemophysalis* sp., *Pullex irritans and Xenopsyllae cheopis* from cattle-sheds and *Sarcoptes* sp., the oriental flea *Xenopsyllae cheopis* and *Sarcoptes* sp., from sheep-sheds. Four species of mites were: *Amerosieus* sp., *Hypoaspis smithii, Glycyphagus* sp., and *Tarsonemus* sp., one species of hard tick, *Haemaphysalis* sp., a single species of fleas, *Xenopsylla cheopis* and a single species of lice, *polyplax spinulosa* were educed from rodent burrows.

On Rodent Species Body Surface

Eight species of mites (*Amerosieus* sp., *Hypoaspis smithii, Ornithonyssus bacoti, Rhizoglyphus echinopus, Glycyphagus* sp., *Myocoptes* sp., *Tarsonemus* sp. and *Cheyletus zaheri*): two species of hard ticks, *Amblyomma* sp. and *Haemaphysalis* sp.; three species of fleas *Xenopsylla cheopis, Leptopsylla segnis, Pulex irritans* and two species of lice, *Polyplax spinulosa, Haplopleura oenonydis* were also collected from the body surface of certain rodent species.

POPULATION DENSITY OF ECTOPARASITES

Ectoparasite on Animals

The population density of ectoparasit species occurred on animal bodies were studied of during the period 2008/2009. The dominant lice species infested buffaloes represented by 96.23% of the total number of buffalo ectoparasites, ticks on cattle by 97.31% and fleas on sheep by 78.47% of the parasites population .The highest density of ectoparasites in buffalo was recorded in spring (50.66%), and the lowest one was occurred in winter (3.39%). On cattle body surface, the highest density of ectoparasites was observed in spring (66.37%), the lowest population was recorded during winter representing by 2.69%. In sheep-farm, the highest density was observed in winter (67.83%) and the lowest was recorded during summer (5.19%). In 2009/2010, the lice were the dominant ectoparasites on buffaloes representing by 95.80% while ticks were the dominant ectoparsites on cattle representing by 94.81% and fleas on sheep represented by 94.32%.

The highest density of ectoparasites in buffalo-farm was observed in spring (58.12%), the lowest population was recorded during winter (4.12%), whereas on cattle high population was recorded during spring (60.99%) and the lowest population was recorded in winter (5.19%), whereas on sheep winter harbored high density (76.56%), in contrary summer exhibited only (1.68%) of ectoparasites.

Significant correlation coefficients between minimum and mean diurnal temperatures versus lice densities on buffaloes were 0.48* and 0.59*. (0.36* and 0.26*) were recorded between both temperatures versus ticks population on cattle. The effect of maximum and minimum relative humidity was also recorded (0.60*and 0.64*) on sheep fleas, significant correlation were obsereved during 2008/2009. In 2009/2010, r=0.48*was recorded between diurnal temp., of the density of lice on buffaloes, significant negative correlation (-0.71**and -0.69*) were found between max., and min., R.H. and the ticks population on cattle, (0.70and 0.65*) were recorded between max., and min., R.H. and fleas population sheep the study clearly indicated the temperature and relative humidity were determining factors in all husbandry animals ectoparasites and may explain the seasonal dynamics of these pests as well as the inhibition off-season.

Ectoparasites Collected from Animal Manure

The population of ectoparasite species in the animal soil during 2008/2009 showed that, ticks dominant species of parasites in cattle-sheds represented by 61.54% , while in sheep-sheds the fleas represented by 98.44% of the parasites population .In rodent active burrows, the mites were represented by 92.09%. High density of ectoparasites in cattle farm was observed in spring 42.31%, scarce in autumn. In sheep-sheds 74.98 % of ectoparasites were collected in winter. The lowest population was recorded during summer 3.54%. In rodent burrows the highest population was observed during spring 35.60 %, the lowest on was recorded during summer 13.63%. In 2009/2010, the highest population of ticks in cattle-sheds was 70.27% of the total parasites population. While in sheep-sheds, the fleas represented by 98.11% of the total parasites population and 89.97% in rodent active burrows.

The highest density of ectoparasites in cattle-sheds was observed in autumn (35.14%), the lowest was recorded during winter (14.41%). In sheep-sheds, the highest population was observed in winter (64.79%), the lowest one was recorded during summer (6.48 %). In rodent burrows, the highest population was observed in autumn (35.45%), the lowest population was recorded during summer (17.39 %).

The maximum and minimum relative humidity were significant positive correlations (0.65*and 0.65*) were recorded between max, and min., R.H. versus animal manure ectoparasites, significant negative correlations were recorded (-0.68*and -0.62*) between max., and min., R.H. versus fleas in rodent burrows.

Ectoparasites on Rodents

Ectoparasites Collected from Rattus r. rugivorus Body Surface

In 2007-2009, the study of rodent ectoparasites density showed that the high density of ectoparasites on *Rattus r. frugivorus* was observed in autumn (34.08%) followed by spring (27.99%) and summer (22.31%). The lowest population was recorded during winter (15.62%).

Males rodent were found to be harbored the highest density of ectoparasites in March and the lowest was in January. In female rodents, the highest density was recorded in October and the lowest was noticed in January. In 2009- 2010, high density of ectoparasites was observed in autumn (34.99%) followed by spring (30.20%) and winter (22.91%). The lowest population was recorded during summer (11.90%).

Males rodent were found to be harbored the highest density of ectoparasites in February and the lowest density in August, while in females rodents, the highest density of ectoparasites was recorded in October and the lowest was noticed in June. The comparative study between males and females showed that, there was an increase in the rate of infestation by females than males.

Significant correlation coefficients (0.43* and 0.59**) were noticed between the maximum and minimum of relative humidity versus mites on males. Also significant positive correlation were recorded between mites on females and the maximum temperature, the maximum and minimum relative humidity r= (0.034*, 0.46* and 0.42*) during the first year, respectively. The same results were obtained during the second year of study.

Ectoparasites Collected from Rattus r. alexandrines Body Surface

High density of ectoparasites was recorded during spring season followed by summer and autumn representing by 40.96%, 27.39% and 22.07%, respectively. The lowest density was observed during winter 9.58%. Male rodents were harbored the highest density of ectoparasites in June while the lowest density was in September, 2007-2009.

In the second year, high density of ectoparasites was recorded during spring season 45.63% followed by winter and summer representing by8.13% and 10.63% respectively. The lowest density was observed during winter representing 8.13%. Males rodent were harbuored the highest density of ectoparasites in April and October, the lowest one occurred in January. In females of rodent, the highest density was found in females of both rodent species.

Positive correlations were noticed between maximum temperature, minimum temperature, mean diurnal temperature and mean night temperature versus mites on rodent males (0.41*, 0.39*, 0.47* and 0.49*) respectively.

Ectoparasites Collected from Arvicanthis Niloticus Body Surface

The highest density of ectoparasites was recorded during summer and spring (31.37%, 29.81%). The lowest density was observed during winter by 11.49%. Males rodent were found to be harbored the highest density of ectoparasites in April, November and the lowest one in February, while in females rodent the highest density was found in both rodent species in June and July and the lowest one in January of 2009/2010.

Significant positive correlations were recorded between the maximum temperature, minimum temperature, mean diurnal temperature and mean night temperature versus mites on rodent males (0.45*, 0.39*, 0.44* and 0.48*) respectively and (0.51**, 0.61**, 0.56**and 0.58**) on rodent females respectively.

CONTROL STUDIES

Control of Ectoparasites in Animal

Ectoparasites on the Animal Body Surface Regions

Lice eggs were counted high numbers in animal front region,lice adult in medium region, nymph in back region. The population density of ticks on cattle in back region was higher than from front region.

In Animals

The mean of mortality percentages of lice on buffaloes, tick on cattle and fleas on sheep were recorded after 45 days from treatment with Diazinon 15% EC spray at 1ml/liter water 32.13%, 26.16% and 12.43%, respectively. However, by using Diazinon 60% EC spray at 1ml/liter these percentages were 57.06%,

37.22% and 46.01%, for lice on buffaloes, tick on cattle and fleas on sheep. The percentages of reduction after 45 days from treatment when used Vertiemec 1.8% EC spray at 1ml/liter water were 56.03%, 58.21% and 48.33% to lice on buffaloes, tick on cattle and fleas on sheep, but by using Butox 5% EC spray at 1ml/liter water these were 66.53%, 62.02% and 62.26%, respectively. The percentages of reduction after 45 days from treatment by using Ivermectin 1%, 1 m/50 kg injection were 74.45%, 69.53% and 41.05% for the same animals of parasites, respectively.

The mean mortality percentage to lice on buffaloes, tick on cattle, fleas on sheep after 45 days from treatment with Diazinon 60% EC spray at 1.5 and 2 ml/liter water, were recorded (59.19 and 59.11%) and (72.71 and 71.40) respectively, also (68.71% and 64.26%) ,(83.26 and 76.49) with Vertimec 1.8% EC spray at 1.5 and 2 ml/liter water and (71.22% and 68.36%), (84.40 and 80.25) with Butox 5% EC spray at 1.5 and 2 ml/liter water.

The mean mortality percentages to fleas on sheep after 30 days from treatment with Butox 5% EC spray at 1 ml/liter water on sheep with and without wool were recorded (90.48 and 66.17%).

The mean mortality percentage to lice on buffaloes, fleas on sheep were (39.99 and 13.46%), (59.72 and 34.91%) and (73.14 and 56.12%) after 30 days from treatment with Radiant 12% SC spray at 4,6 and 8 ml/liter water, respectively. But the percentage of reduction for tick on cattle was (33.23, 48.94 and 62.10%) after 30 days from treatment with Radiant 12% SC spray 6, 8 and12 ml/liter water, respectively.

The mean mortality percentage to lice on buffaloes and ticks on cattle were 55.38 and 70.43% on lice and 40.63 and 62.03%, on ticks after 30 days from treatment with Diazinon 60% EC spraying and contact method at 1 ml/liter water.

Control of Sarcoptic Mange

In Buffaloes

The results show that the treated individuals with sulfur began to respond after 45-55 days, 20-30 days for Ivermectin 1% 1 ml/50 kg (injection) with sulfur, Ivermectin with Butox 5% EC, 25- 30 days and Ivermectin 20-35. The spraying with Butox 5% EC and Ivermectin 1% injection gave satisfactory results in curing buffaloes mange.

In general, all husbandry animals showed a slight improvement in the clinical picture of the disease by using Ivermectin one time a month, but gave satisfactory results when used at two time month (20-30). It might be concluded that the subcutaneous injection with Ivermectin eliminates *Sarcoptes scabiei* from buffaloes after 20-30 days.

In Sheep

Sarcoptes were sprayed with Diazinon 60% EC, Butox 5% EC and, Vertemic 1.8% EC spray at 1 ml/L water, Ivermectin 1% 1 ml/50 kg (injection) and Ivermectin with Diazinon 60% EC, the results show that the treated individuals with Diazinon 60% EC began to respond after 25-30 days, 20-35 for Vertemic 1.8% EC, Butox 5% EC 20-30 , and Ivermectin 15-30 days and Ivermectin with Diazinon 60% EC 15-25 days all sheep returned to normal conditions (normal skin) after an average of 30-45. The spraying with Diazinon 60% EC, Butox 5% EC and Ivermectin injection gave satisfactory results in curing sheep mange.

The results show that the treated individuals with tincture iodine 4% began to respond after 45-55 days; 35-45 days for sulfur with vaseline 10%, Ivermectin with sulfur 15-25 days and Ivermectin with Butox 5% EC 15-25, the spraying with Butox 5% EC and Ivermectin injection gave good results in curing buffalo mange. It might be concluded that Ivermectin with sulfur or Butox 5% EC are effective in controlling mange mites in husbandry animals. Morever, *Injection treatment twice a month is better than a one-time use.*

Control of Manure Ectoparasites

Mechanical Control

The mean mortality percentage to fleas on sheep in soil were recorded 80.27, 60.15 and 83.15%, after 45 days from treatment with mechanical methods, Cleaning, Burning, and Quicklime methods, respectively.

Chemical Control

The mean mortality percentage to fleas on sheep in soil were recorded (86.53, 86.81 and 91.17%), after 45 days from treatment with Diazinon 60% EC, Vertimec 1.8% EC and Butox 5% EC spray at 2 ml/liter water, respectively.

Fly Larvae

The mean of mortality percentage to fly larvae in animal manure, were recorded (91.51 and 95.27%, 84.25, 94.37 and 91.82), after 30 days from treatment with Diazinon 60% EC, Vertimec 1.8% EC and Butox 5% EC (1ml/liter), Radiant 12% SC (4 ml/L) and quicklime, respectively.

The animal farm satisfactory, ventilation with periodical removal of animal manure and the renewal with the straw substrates, and the use of safer on the husbandry soil are recommended in order to control the immature stages of certain animal-ectoparasites such as flies and ticks.

RODENT CONTROL

Under Laboratory Conditions

Attractive Baits

The mean consumption of attractive baits was recorded. Yeast with crush maize (7.25 gm/rat) and coriander (2.35 gm/rat) are the most effective baits as compare with control treatment of (crush maize) only (0.9 gm/rat), for *R.r.frugivorus*. But in *R.r.alexandrinus*, it was observed that the mean consumption was high in yeast bait with crush maize (7.35 gm/rat), and anise (3.63 gm) as compare with control (2 gm/rat). In *Arvicanthis niloticus* the mean consumption was high in yeast bait (4.75 gm) as compared with the control bait (1.83 gm/rat). Baits preference tests should be done periodically to find out the proper bait for rodenticide formulation and to overcome the shyness of rodent baits.

Repellent Baits

The food consumption was less in black pepper bait with crush maize (0.32.5 gm/rat), jejoba seed (1.15 gm) as compared with control one (10.83 gm/rat) for *R.r. frugivorus*. In *R.r. alexandrinus* was observed that the consumption was less in black pepper bait (0.38 gm/rat), and oshar powder leaf (0.85 gm/rat) as compared with control (7.05 gm/rat). *A. niloticus* consumed scarce amount of black pepper bait (0.83 gm/rat) and powder leaf oshar (1.58 gm/rat) as compared with control (7.9 gm/rat) .Generally; these results may be satisfied in rodent control.

Evaluation of two Rodenticides

It was observed that the forced feeding of rodent males on Supercaid bait was (56.40 gm) as comparison with Caid (89 gm), but in females the numbers were: (61.80 gm, 78.20gm) in the feeding on Supercaid and Caid tell death.

In *R.r. alexandrines*, the males consumed less in Supercaid bait (43.40 gm) as comparison with Caid (80.40 gm),while the revere was observer in case females (34.60 gm, 74.80. gm), the same results were obtained when used *A. niloticus*.

Under Field Conditions

Toxicity of Rodenticides

Data show the mean of caught rodent individuals in field with baits satiations. Caid 0.005% was (8.18%) as compared by Supercaid 0.004% (2.18%). It was found that there was a significant difference between the caught animals of the tested rodenticide baits.

Acceptability of Rodent Species to two Attractive Baits

Data showed a significant difference in the animal consumptions of the rodenticide with different tested attractive baits. The consumption of attractive baits was 18.17 gm/day yeast with Supercaid as compared to vanilia with Supercaid, 11 gm/day.

Toxicity by Aluminum Phosphide 33%

The active burrows of rodent were decreased when used Aluminum phosphate fumigation (64.19%) after one month as compared to the normal burrows.

REFERENCES

Abazaid, A. A. (1990). Efficiency of Some Common and used Rodenticides and Some New Alternative against Rodents in Qena Governorate. M.Sc. Thesis, Fac. Agric., Assiut Univ., Assiut, Egypt. 93 pp.

Abazaid, A. A. (1997). Ecological and Toxicological Studies on Rodents in Qena Governorate, Ph.D. Thesis, Fac. Agric., Assiut Univ., Assiut, Egypt. 96 pp.

Abd El-Galil, Y. M. A. (2005). Comparative Studies on Rodenticides against Some Rodents. Ph.D. Thesis, Fac. Agric., Al-Azhar Univ. Egypt. 158 pp.

Abd El-Rahman, A.; A. Metwally and M. E. El-Naggar (1991). Rat Acceptance of Non-toxic Baits in Ryan Qatar State. Egypt J. Agric. Res., 69 (1): 257-261.

Abdel-Gawad, K. H. (2001a). Rodent Control in the Student Buildings at Assiut. 1st. Int. Conf. Safe Alternative of Pesticides for Pest Management Assiut Univ., Egypt. 421-429.

Abdel-Gawad, K. H. (2001b). Evaluation of Some Chemical and Mechanical Methods to Reduce Rodent Population in Maize fields. 1st. Int. Conf., Safe Alternatives of Pesticides for Pest Management Assiut Univ., Egypt. 413-420.

Abdel-Gawad, K. H. and Maher Ali, A. (1982). Population Density of Mites Associated with Rodent Species in Cultivated and Semi-arid Area. Assiut J. Agric. Sci., 13 (2): 39-44.

Abdel-Gawad, K. H. and A. I. Farghal (1982). Levels of Egypt Rodents Sensitivity to Warfarin. Assiut J. Agric. Sci., 13 (2): 145-152.

Abo Elmaged, T. M. (1998). Recent Trends for Controlling Some Harmful Arthropods in the Husbandry, M. Sc. Thesis, Fac. Agric., Assiut Univ., Assiut, Egypt.

Ahmed, H. S. K. (2006). Studies on Damage caused by Rodents on Some Field Crops and its Control in Upper Egypt (Assiut Area). M. Sc. Thesis, Fac.Agric., Al-Azhar Univ., Cairo, Egypt.

Alahmed, A. M. N. (1998). The Effect of Various Manure Suspensions (Camel, Cow and Sheep) on the Life Cycle of *Culex pipiens*. Saudi J. Bio. Sci., 5 (2):58-63.

Ali, M. K. (1985). Studies on Rodents and their Ectoparasites in Sohag Governorate. M. Sc. Thesis Fac. Agric., Assiut Univ., 82 PP.

Ali, M. K. (1991). Recent trends in Rodent Control and Efficacy of its Chemical agents. Ph.D. Sc. Thesis Fac. Agric., Assiut Univ., 137 pp.

Asran, A. A.; H. I. El-Deeb and M. A. El-Halfawy (1992). Field Trials on Certain Anticoagulant Rodenticides against the Field rat *Arvicanthis niloticus*. Egypt, J. Agric. Res., 70 (2): 461-467.

Baghdadi, S. A. S. (2006). Ecological Studies on Rodent Species on Al-Azhar University Farm in Assiut and its Control. M. Sc. Thesis Fac. Agric., Al-Azhar Univ., Egypt. 117 pp.

Baker, M. E.; T. A. Morsy; N. E. Nassef and M. A. El-Meligi (1995). Mites Infesting Commensal Rodents in Shebin El-Kom, Menoufia Gov. Egypt. J. Egypt. Soc. Parasitol. 25 (3): 853-859.

Baker, M. E.; T. A. Morsy; N. E. Nassef and M. A. El-Meligi (1996). Fleas Ectoparasites of Commensal Rodents in Shebin El-Kom, Menoufia Governorate, Egypt. J. Egypt. Soc. Parasitol, 26 (1): 39-52.

Battesti, D. M. B.; M. Arzua; P. M. Linardi; J. R. Botelho and I. J. Sbalqueiro (1998). Interrelationship between Ectoparasites and Wild Rodents from Tijucas do sul, State of Parana, Brazil. Mem. Inset. Oswaldo. Cruz, Rio de Janeiro, 93 (6): 719-725.

Bazarusanga, T ·; D. Geysen; J. Vercruysse and M. Madder (2007). An update on the Ecological Distribution of Ixodid ticks Infesting Cattle in Rwanda: Countrywide Cross-sectional Survey in the Wet and the Dry Season. Exp. Appl. Acarol., 43: 279–291.

Beldomenico, P. M.; M. lareschi; S. Nava; A. J. Mangold and A. A. Guglielmone (2005). The Parasitism of Immature Stages of Ixodes loricatus (Acari: Ixodidae) on Wild Rodents in Argentina, Exp. Appl. Acarol., 36: 139–148.

Bochkov, A.; M. Arbobi and V. Malikov (2000). Notes on Mites of the Family Myobiidae (Acari: Prostigmata) Parasitising Rodents (Mammalia: Rodentia) in Iran. Folia Parasitologica, 47: 73-77.

Boeke, S. J.; M. G. Boersma; G.M. Alink; J.A. van Loon; A. V. Huis ; M. Dicke ; and M.C.M. Rietjens (2004). Safety Evaluation of Neem (*Azadirachta indica*) Derived Pesticides. Journal of Ethnopharmacology 94: 25-41.

Bossche, P. V.; and D. Mudenge (1999). The Effect of Short-interval Deltamethrin Applications to Control Tsetse on the Seroprevalence of Babesiosis in Cattle. Tropical Animal Health and Production, 31: 215-222.

Burwash, M. D; M. E. Tobin; A. D. Woolhouse, and T. P. Sullivan (1998). Laboratory Evaluation of Predator Odors for Eliciting an Avoidance Response in Roof Rats *(rattus rattus)*. Journal of Chemical Ecology, 24 (1):49-66.

Byford, R. L.; M. E. Craig and B. L. Crosby (1992) A Review of on Ectoparasites and Their Effect Cattle Production. J. Anim. Sci. 70: 597-602.

Carl, S. (1983). Use of Aluminum Phosphide Fumigants For Burrowing Rodent Control. Wildlife Damage Management, Internet Center for Great Plains Wildlife Damage Control Workshop Proceedings. 57-59.

Chander-sheikher, C; S. D. Jain and C. Sheiker (1996). Mode of Application and Performance of Rodenticides in Vegetable Crops. Indian J. Agric. Sci .66 (7): 437-440.

Conraths, F. J.; M. Kramer and C. Freuling (2007). Bluetongue Disease in Germany. Clinical Aspects, Diagnosis and Epidemiology. Prakt Tierarzt 88:9–15.

Corn, j. L.; P. Berger and J. W. Mertins (2009). Surveys for Ectoparasites on Wildlife Associated with *Amblyomma variegatum* (Acari: Ixodidae)-Infested Livestock in St. Croix, U.S. Virgin Islands. Journal of Medical Entomology, 46 (6):1483-1489.

Cozma,V; E. ªuteu1; C. Gherman1; B. Losson (2010). Therapy with Avermectines and Diazinon of Psoroptic Mange in Sheep from Transylvania, Romania. Sci Parasitol., 11(2): 105-107.

Davoudi, J.; N. H. Rad and S. G. Adabi (2008). Ixodid Tick Species Infesting Cows and Buffaloes and their Seasonality in West Azerbaijan. Res. J. Parasitol., 3 (3): 98-103.

Deem, S. L.; F. Maisels; R. G. Robbins (2005). Necropsy and Parasitic Findings from an Adult Forest Buffalo (*Syncerus Caffer Nanus*) found Dead in the Republic of Congo. Eur. J. Wild Res., 51: 60-62.

Dettner, K. and W. Peters (2010). Lehrbuch der Entomologie. Heidelberg, Spektrum, 183 PP.

Dielenberg, R. A. and I. S. McGregor (1999). Habituation of the Hiding Response to Cat Odor in Rats (*Rattus norvegicus*). Journal of Comparative Psychology, Vol 113(4): 376-387.

Donlan, C. J.; G. R. Howalda; B. R. Tershya and D. A. Crolla (2003). Evaluating Alternative Rodenticides for Island Conservation: Roof Rat Eradication from the San Jorge Islands, Mexico. Biological Conservation, 114: 29–34.

Durden, L. A.; J. H. Oliver and J. E. Cilek (2000). Rodent Ectoparasites from two Location in Northwestern Florida. J. Vector Ecol., Dec; 25(2) 222-228.

Eckert, J.; K. T. Friedhoff; H. Zahner and P. Deplazes (2009). Lehrbuch der Parasitologie für die Tiermedizin, 2nd edn. Enke, Stuttgart, 2008.

Eisemann, J. D.; B. E. Petersen and K. A. Fagerstone (2003). Efficacy of Zinc Phosphide for Controlling Norway rat, Roof rat, house mise, *Peromyscus spp*, prairie Dogs and Squirrels. Proceedings of the 10th Wild Life, Damage Manage. Conf. Literature Review. 335-349.

El-Deeb, H. I.; Z. H. Zidan; N. El-Hawshy and A. A. Mourad (1999). Rodent Ectoparasites Relationship at New Reclaimed Areas of Egypt. Ann. Agric. Sci., 44 (2): 799-810.

El-Eraky, S. A and N. I. Shoker (1993). Description of two New Anoetid Mites (Acari: Anoetida) Collected from Different Habitats. Assiut J. of Agric. Sci., 24(2): 233-242.

El-kady, G. A.; A. Shoukry; D. A. Ragheb; A. M. El-Said; K. S. Habib and T. A. Morsy (1995). Mites (acari) Infesting Commensal Rats in Suez Canal zone, Egypt. J. Egypt Soc Parasitol. Aug; 25(2):417-425.

El-kady, G. A.; K. M. Makled; T. A. Morsy and Z. S. Morsy (1998). Rodents, their Seasonal Activity, ecto-and Blood- parasites in Saint Catherine area, South Sinai Governorate, Egypt. J. Egypt Soc. Parasitol., 28 (3): 815-826.

El Kady, G. A.; H. M. El Sharabasy, M. F. Mahmoud and I. M. Bahgat (2007). Toxicity of Two Potential Bio-insecticides Against Moveable Stages of *Tetranychus urticae* Koch. J., of Appli., Sci., Res., 3(11): 1315-1319.

El- Saady, M. A.(2009). Studies on Rodents and its Integrated Control in Minia region. PhD. Thesis, Fac. Agric., Minia Univ., Egypt.

Embarak, M. Z. (1997). Ecological and Control Studies on Rodents and their Ectoparasites in Cultivated and Newly-Reclaimed areas. M.Sc. Thesis, Fac. Agric., Assiut Univ., Assiut, Egypt.130 pp.

Evans, G.O. (1992): Principles of Acarology. C.A.B. International Walling Ford: 522 pp.

Farghal, A. I.; S. A. El-Eraky; K. H. Abdel-Gawad and A. A. Abazied (2000). Laboratory and Field Evaluation of some Rodenticides against Rodent Species in Upper Egypt. The 2nd Sci. Conf. Agric. Scie., Assiut, 531-536.

Förster, M., S. Klimpel and K. Sievert (2009). The House Fly (*Musca domestica*) as a Potential Vector of Metazoan Parasites caught in a Pig-pan in Germany. Vet. Parasitol. 160: 163–167.

Gill, J. E. (1992). Laboratory Evaluation of the Toxicity of Flocoumafen as a Single-feed Rodenticide to Seven Rodent Species. Int. Biodeterioration, 30: (1): 65-76.

Grabovac, S. and D. Petriæ, (2003). The fly fauna (Diptera: Cyclorrapha) on Animal Farms. Acta Entomologica Serbica, 8 (1/2): 63-72.

Hagawane, S. D.; G. R. Rajurkar and S. B. Shinde (2010). Ethno-Veterinary Drug Therapy for Ear Mange in Sheep. Veterinary World, 3 (6): 295-296.

Harris, R. l.; k. Onaga; R. R. Blume; J. P. Roth and J. W. Summerlin (1982). Survey of Beneficial Insects in Undisturbed Cattle Droppings on Oahu, Hawaii. Proceedings of Hawaiian Entomological Society, 24: 1.

Hawlena, H.; Z. Abramsky; B. R. Krasnov and D. Saltz (2007). Host Defense versus Intraspecific Competition in the Regulation of Infrapopulations of the Flea *Xenopsylla conformis* on its Rodent host *Meriones crassus*. International Journal of Parasitology, 37: 919–925.

Helal, T. Y. and M. Zedan (1982). Efficiency of Ratak in Rodent Control in Hospital in Assiut Region. Assiut J. Agric. Sci., 13 (2):137-143.

Henderson, C.F. and E. W. Tilton, (1955). Tests with Acaricides against the Brow wheat mite, J. Econ. Entomol. 48:157-161.

Hoffmann, B.; B. Bauer; H. J. Bätza and H .Mehlhorn (2009). Monitoring of Putative Vectors of the Bluetongue virus Serotype 8, Germany. Emerg Infect Dis. 15: 1481-1484.

Hoogstraal, H.; M.N. Kaiser (1958) The ticks (Ixodidae) of Egypt a Brief Review and keys.J.Egypt Rub.Health.Assoc.vol.33 (3):52-85.

Hosking, B.C.; A. J. George (2006). Efficacy of CLiK® Spray-On in Preventing Naturally Occuring Blowfly Strike When Applied to Unmulesed Sheep. Intern J. Appl. Res. Vet. Med .Vol. 7: (1).

Hughes, A.M. (1961): The Mites of Stored Food. Tech. Bull. Minist. Agric. Fisheries and Food.9:1-379.

Hughes, A.M. (1976): The Mites of Stored Food and Houses. Tech. Bull. Minist. Agric. Lodon.9:1-287.

Hussain, A. M.; M.N. Khan, Z. Iqbal and M. S. Sajid (2005). Prevalence and Chemotherapy of Lice Infestation in Bovines - Review. Int. J. Agri. Biol., 7: (4)694-697.

Hygnstrom, S. E.; K. C. V. Cauteren; R. A. Hines and C. W. Mansfield (2000). Efficacy of in-furrow Zinc Phosphide Pellets for Controlling Rodent Damage in on-till corn. Int. Biodeterioration, 43: 215-222.

Ibrahim, O.E (1994). Control of Skin Parasites among Sheep Flocks. M. Sc. Thesis, Fac. of Vet. Medicine, Cairo Univ., Cairo, Egypt, 70pp.

Jackson, W. B. (2001). Current Rodenticide Strategies. Int. Biodeterioration, 48: 127-136.

Jacobson, M. (1986) The Neem Tree: Natural Resistance par Excellence. American Chemical Society Symposium Series No. 296, 221-232.

Johnston, j. j.; D. L. Nolte; B. A. Kimball; K. R. Perry and J. C. Hurley (2005). Increasing Acceptance and efficacy of Zinc Phosphide Rodenticides Baits via Modification of the Carbohydrate Profile. Crop Protection, 24: 381- 385.

Kaal, J. F.; K. Baker and P. R. Torgerson (2006). Epidemiology of Flea Infestation of Ruminants in Libya. Veterinary Parasitology, 141: 313-318.

Kakar, M. N. and j. K. Kakarsulemankhel (2008). Prevalence of Endo (trematodes) and Ecto-parasites in Cows and Buffaloes of quetta, Pakistan. Pakistan Vet. J., 28 (1): 34-36.

Kakar, M. N. and j. K. Kakarsulemankhel (2009). Prevalence of Lice Species on Cows and Buffaloes of Quetta, Pakistan. Pakistan Vet. J., 29 (1): 49-50.

Karg, W. (1971): Acari (Acarina), Miben, Unterordnung Analinochaeta (Parasitiformes). Die freilebenden Gamasina (Gamasides). Jena Teil 59: 475 pp.

Kaur, H. and V. R. Parshad (2005). Laboratory and Field Evaluation of three Odorant compounds for Improving attraction of the Lesser Bandicoot rat, *Bandicota bengalensis* (Gray) to 0.0375% Coumatetraly bait. Int. Biodeterioration, 56: 135-142.

Khan, A. A.; S. Munir and A. R. Shakoor (1998). Development of under-ground Baiting Technique for Control of Rats in Rice Fields in Pakistan. Int. Biodeterioation, 42: 129-134 .

Khan, H. H.; A. Sohail and R. Yazdan (2000). Significance of Additives to Enhance Poison Baits Acceptance against Field Rats in Rice Paddy in Central Punjab, Pakistan . *Int. J. Agri. Biol., Vol. 2, No. 1-2.*

Khater, H. F.; M. Y. Ramadan and R. S. El-Madawy (2009). Lousicidal, Ovicidal and Repellent Efficacy of Some Essential Oils against lice and Flies Infesting Water Buffaloes in Egypt. Veterinary Parasitology, 164 : 257–266.

Khokhlova, I. S.; M. Spinu; B. R. Krasnov and A. A. Degen (2004). Immune Response to Fleas in a Wild Desert Rodent: Effect of Parasite Species, parasite burden, Sex of Host and Host Parasitological Experience. The Journal of Experimental Biology, 207: 2725-2733.

Kia, E. B; H. Moghddas-Sani; H. Hassanpoor; H. Vatandoost; F. Zahabiun; A. A. Akhavan, A. A. Hanafi-Bojd and Z. Telmadarraiy (2009). Ectoparasites of Rodents Captured in Bandar Abbas, Southern Iran. Iranian J. Arthropod-Borne Dis., 3 (2): 44-49.

Krantz, G.M. (1978). A manual of Acarology.2nd.edn. Oregon State University, Corvallis, Oregon: 509 pp.

Kolar, L.; N. K. Erzen; L. Hogerwerf and C. A. M. van Gestel (2008). Toxicity of Abamectin and Doramectin to Soil Invertebrates. Environmental Pollution, 151: 182-189.

Krasnov, B. R.; I. S. Khokhlova and G. I. Shenbrot (2003). Density-dependent Host Selection in Ectoparasites: An Application of Isodar Theory to Fleas Parasitizing Rodents. Oecologia, 134: 365–372.

Lance, A. D.; R. Hul; J. H. Oliver and J. E. Cilek (2000). Rodent Ectoparasites from two locations in Northwestern Florida. Journal of Vector Ecology, 25 (2): 222-228.

Leemon, D. M. and N. N. Jonsson (2008). Laboratory Studies on Australian Isolates of *Metarhizium anisopliae* as a Biopesticide for the Cattle tick *Boophilus microplus*. Journal of Invertebrate Pathology, 97: 40–49.

Littin, K.E.; C. E. O'connor and C.T. Eason (2000). Comparative Effects of Brodifacoum on Rats and Possums. New Zealand Plant Protection 53:310-315.

Maher Ali, A. and k. H. Abdel-Gawad (1982). On Some Practical Methods to Control the Nile grass rat, *A.niloticus* (Desm.) . 2nd Symposium on Rodent Control in Egypt. Assiut J. Agric. Sci., 13: 81-84.

Maher Ali, A.; M. A. Salit; I. Sheta and M. G. Mourad (1974). Ectoparasites on Rodent in the Nile Valley, Upper Egypt. J. Egypt. Public Health Assoc., 59 (1): 3-19.

Maher Ali, A. (1972). Planning for Rodent Control Field Experiment. 1stSymposium of Rodent and Their Control in Egypt, 241.

Makeri, H. K.; V. A. Maikai and J. A. Nok (2007). Effect of Topical Application of Neem Seed (*Azadiracta indica*) Extract on Sheep Infested with *Amblyomma variegatum*. African Journal of Biotechnology, 6 (20): 2324-2327.

Mamabolo, M. V.; L. Ntantiso; A. Latif; and P. A. O. Majiwa (2009). Natural Infection of Cattle and Tsetse Flies in South Africa with two Genotypic Groups of *Trypanosoma congolense*. Parasitology, 136: 425–431.

Matthee, S. and B. R. Krasnov (2009). Searching for Generality in the Patterns of Parasite Abundance and Distribution: Ectoparasites of a South African rodent, *Rhabdomys pumilio*. Int. J. for Parasito., 39: 781–788.

Matthee, S. and E. A. Ueckermann (2008). Ectoparasites of Rodents in Southern Africa: A New Species of Androlaelaps Berlese, 1903 (Acari: Parasitiformes: Laelapidae) from *Rhabdomys pumilio* (Sparrman) (Rodentia: Muridae). Syst Parasitol., 70: (3) 185–190.

Meerburg, B. G.; H. M. Vermeer and A. Kijlstra (2007). Controlling Risks of Pathogen Transmission by Flies on Organic Pig Farms. Outlook on Agriculture, 36 (3): 193–197.

Mehlhorn, H.; G. Schmahl; V. Walldorf, J. D'Haese and B . Schumacher (2008). Butox® 7.5 Pour on: a Deltamethrin Treatment of Sheep and Cattle. Parasitol. Res., 102: 515–518.

Mehlhorn, H.; K. A. S. Al-Rasheid; F. Abdel-Ghaffar; S. Klimpel and H. Pohle (2010). Life Cycle and Attacks of Ectoparasites on Ruminants during the year in Central Europe: Recommendations for Treatment with Insecticides (e.g., Butox®). Parasito. Res., 107(2): 425-431.

Mehlhorn, H.; V. Walldorf and S. Klimpel (2009). Bluetongue Disease in Germany: Monitoring of Entomological Aspects. Parasitol. Res., 105: 321–329.

Milnes, A. S.; C. J. O'Callaghan and L. E. Green (2003). A Longitudinal Study of a Natural lice Infestation in Growing Cattle over two winter periods. Veterinary Parasitology, 112: 307–323.

Moran, S. (1999). Rejection of Dyed Field Rodent baits by Feral Pigeons and Chukar Partridges. Phytoparasitica, 27 (1): 9-17.

Moran, S. (2003). Toxicity of Cholecalciferol Wheat Bait to the Field Rodents *Microtus guentheri* and *Meriones tristrami*. Crop Protection, 22: 341-345.

MSTAT-C. (1988). MSTAT-C, a Microcomputer Program for the Design, Arrangement, and Analysis of Agronomic Research Experiments. Michigan State University, East Lansing, USA.

Muhammad, G.; A. Naureen; S. Firyal1 and M. Saqib (2008). Tick Control Strategies in Dairy Production Medicine. Pakistan Vet. J., 28 (1): 43-50.

Natala, A. J. and O. S. Ochoje (2009). Survey of Pesticides used in the Control of Ectoparasites on Farm Animals in Kaduna State, Northern Nigeria. Journal of Animal & Plant Sciences, 4 (1): 276 - 280.

Nava, S.; M. Lareschi; D. Voglino (2003). Interrelationship between Ectoparasites and Wild Rodents from Northeastern Buenos Aires Province, Argentina. Mem. Inst. Oswaldo Cruz, Rio de Janeiro, 98: 1-5.

Oconnor, C. E.; L. H. Booth (2001). Palatability of Rodent Baits to Wild House Mice. Science for Conservation 184; 5-11.

Omer, L. T.; M. A. Kadir; U. Seitzer and J. S. Ahmed (2007). A Survey of Ticks (Acari:Ixodidae) on Cattle, Sheep and Goats in the Dohuk Governorate, Iraq. Parasitol. Res., 101 (Suppl 2): 179–181.

Omudu, E. A. and T. T. Ati (2010). A Survey of Rats Trapped in Residential Apartments and Their Ectoparasites in Makurdi, Nigeria. Research Journal of Agriculture and Biological Sciences, 6(2): 144-149.

Parshad, V. R.; and C. S. Malhi (1995). Comparative Efficacy of two Methods of Delivering an Anticoagulant Rodenticide to three Species of South Asian rodents. Int. Biodeterioration, 36 (1-2): 89-102.

Peter, R. J.; P. Van den Bossche; B. L. Penzhorn and B. Sharp (2006). Tick, fly, and Mosquito Control-Lessons from the Past, Solutions for the Future, Open UP (August 2006).

Prakash, S.; S. Kumara; V. Veer; N. Gopalan; K. S. Pandeyc and K. M. Raoa (2003). Laboratory Evaluation of Four Rodenticides Admixed in a Cereal-based bait against Commensal rat, *Rattus rattus* (L.) (Rodentia : Muridae : Murinae). Journal of Stored Products Research, 39: 141–147.

Raether, W. and A. Harder (2008). Chemotherapy In: Mehlhorn H. Encyclopedia of parasitology. Springer, New York.

Rahbari, S; S. Nabian; F. Nourolahi; F. Arabkhazaeli and E. Ebrahimzadeh (2008). Flea Infestation in Farm Animals and Its Health Implication, Iranian. J. Parasitol., 3 (2); 43-47.

Rajput, Z. I.; H. U Song-hua; C. Wan-jun; A. Abdullah and X. Chen-wen (2006). Importance of ticks and their Chemical and Immunological Control in Livestock. J. Zhejiang Univ. Science, B 7 (11):912-921.

Ramzan, M; M. S. Khan; M. Avais; J. A. Khan, K. Pervez and W. Shahzad (2008). Prevalence of Ectoparasites and Comparative Efficacy of different Drugs against tick Infestation in Cattle. J. Anim. Pl. Sci. 18 (1)17-19.

Reeves, W. K.; A. D. Loftis; D. E. Szumlas; M. M. Abbassy; I.M. Helmy; H. A. Hanafi and G. A. Dasch (2007). Rickettsial Pathogens in the Tropical Rat Mite *Ornithonyssus bacoti* (Acari: Macronyssidae) from Egyptian rats (*Rattus* spp.). Exp. Appl. Acarol., 41: 101–107.

Reeves, W. K.; D. E. Szumlas; J. R. Morlarity; A. D. Loftis; M. M. Abbassy; I. M. Helmy and G. A. Dasch (2006). Louse –borne Bacterial Pathogens in Lice (Phthiraptera) of Rodents and Cattle from Egypt. J. parasilto., 92 (2): 313-318.

Saied, A. A. M. (1985). Integrated Control of Rodents. PhD. Thesis Fac. Agric., Al-Azhar Univ., Egypt.

Sargison, N. (2005). Differential Diagnoses of Sheep Skin Conditions Part 1: Ectoparasitic Diseases. Uk Vet. 10: (3)1-8

Schnieder, T. (2008). Veterinärparasitologie. Parex, Berlin.

Shafi, M. M.; S. M. Ahmed; A. Pervez and S. Ahmad (1992). Enhancement of Poison Bait Acceptance through Taste Additives in *Rattusnorvegicus*. Journal of Stored Products Research, 28 (4): 239-243.

Shayan, A and J. Rafinejad (2006). Arthropod Parasites of Rodents in Khorram Abbad district, Lorestan Provincen of Iran. Iranian J. Publ. Health, 35 (3): 70-76.

Shehab, A.; F. Samara and A. Daoud (2000). The Effectiveness of different Bait Bases of Zinc Phosphide in Controlling Social Voles *Microtus socialis* in the Middle of Syria. The 2nd Scientific Conference of Agricultural Sciences, Assiut, Oct.

Shooba, K. M. I. (2003). Toxicological Studies of Chlorophacinone and Difenacoum as Anticoagulant Rodenticides in Albino Rat Male Rattus Norvegicus , Ph.D . thesis Fac. Agric., Cairo Univ., Egypt. 101 pp.

Shriprakash; S. Kumar; V. Veer; N. G. Purnanand; K. S. Pandeyc and K. M. Rao (2003). Laboratory Evaluation of Four Rodenticides Admixed in a Cereal-based bait against Commensal rat, *Rattus rattus* (L.) (Rodentia: Muridae: Murinae). Journal of Stored Products Research, 39: 141–147.

Soliman, S.; A. S. Marzouk; A. J. Main and A. A. Montasser (2001). Effect of six ,size, and age of Commensal Rat Hosts on the Infestation Parameters of their Ectoparasites in a Rural Area of Egypt. J. Parasitol. 87 (6): 1308-1316.

Steel, R. G. D and J. H. Torrie, (1984). Principles and Procedures of Statistics. McGraw Hill Book Co., Tokyo, Japan.

Stojcevic, D.; Z. Mihaljevic and A. Marinculic (2004). Parasitological Survey of Rats in Rural Regions of Croatia. Vet. Med. Czech, 49 (3): 70-74.

Tanasak C.; R. Buddhirongawatr; S. Suwanpakdee; J. Siengsanan; P. Yongyuttawichai; K. Cheewajorn; J. Jangjaras; C. Sangloung and P. Ratanakorn (2009). A Survey of Ectoparasitic Arthropods on Domestic Animals in tak Province, Thailand. Southeast Asian J. Trop. Med. Public Health, 40 (3):435-442.

Tasawar, Z.; I. Bano; C. S. Hayatl and M. H. Lashari (2008). Prevalence of lice on Buffaloes at Private Cattle Farm. Pakistan Vet. J., 28 (3): 147-149.

Tefera S. and W. Abebe (2007). A Study on Ectoparasites of Sheep and Goats in Eastern part of Amhara Region, Northeast Ethiopia. Small Ruminant Research, 69: (1) 62–67.

Telmadarraiy. Z; H. Vatandoost; S. Mohammadi; A. A. Akhavan; M. R. Abai; J. Rafinejad; E. B. Kia; F. Faghih Naini; M. Jedari; M .Aboulhasani (2007). Determination of Rodent Ectoparasite Fauna in Sarpole-Zahab District, Kermanshah Province, Iran, 2004-2005. Iranian J. Arthropod-Borne Dis., 1 (1): 58-62.

Thomas N. M. and C. G. L. Niels (1990). A New Insecticide Delivery Method for Control of Fur Mite Infestations in Laboratory Mice. Lab. Anim. Sci.; 34:260-262.

Twigg, L. E.; G. R. Martin and T. S. Stevens (2002). Effect of Lengthy Storage on the Palatability and Efficacy of Zinc Phosphide Wheat bait used for Controlling House Mice. Wildlife-Research, 29 (2): 141-149.

Valchev, I.; R. binev; V. Yordanova; Y. Nikolov (2008). Anticoagulant Rodenticide Intoxication in Animals - A Review. Turk. J. Vet. Anim. Sci.; 32 (4): 237-243.

Vaziri, A. S. and A. Farid (1995). The Comparative Efficacy of two Rodenticides against *Rattus norvegicus* Barkenhout and *Nesokia indica* Gray. Appl. Entomol. and Phytopathology 62) 1-2:(96-105.

Veneziano, V.; M. Santaniello; S. Carbone; S. Pennacchio; M. E. Morgoglione; M. Schioppi; R. Condoleo ; G. Cringoli (2007). Lice *(Haematopinus tuberculatus)* in Water Buffalo Farms from Central Italy. Ital. J. Anim. Sci., 6 (Suppl. 2): 926-927.

Wall, R. (2007). Ectoparasites: Future Challenges in a Changing World. Veterinary Parasitology, 148 : 62–74.

Wichai, S. and F. A. Ching (1991). A Field Trial on the Efficacy of ivermectin, Albendazole and Coumaphos against Parasites of Buffaloes. Kasetsart J. (Nat.Sci.), 25: 256-260.

Wilamowski, M. (1999). Fleas (Siphonaptera) Harmful to Man in Israel. Proceeding of the 3rd International Conference on Urban Pests. 281-287.

Witmer, G. W.; M. W. Fall and L. A. Fiedler (1995). Rodent Control, Research Needs, and Technology Transfer. International Wildlife Management Congress, 16-26.

Witmer, G.; P. Burke and S. Jojola (2008). An Evaluation of the Effectiveness of Potential Norway Rat Attractants. Proc. 23rd Vertebr. Pest Cont. (R. M. 11mm and M. B. Madon, Eds.) Published at Univ. of Calif., Davis. pp. 35-38.

Yakhchali, M and A. Hosseine (2006). Prevalence and Ectoparasites Fauna of Sheep and Goats Flocks in Urmia Suburb, Iran.Vet. arhiv. 76: 431-442.

Zahedi, M.; J. Jeffery; K. Krishnasamy and V. K. Bharat (1996). Ectoparasites of Rattus Rattus Diardii from Kuala Lumpur City Malaysia. Proceedings of the Second International Conference on Urban Pests. 437- 439.

Zaher, M. A. (1986a). Survey and Ecological Studies on Phytophagous, Predaceous and Soil Mites in Egypt. II-A: Predaceous and Non Predaceous mites in Egypt (Nile Vally and Delta): 567 pp.

Zaher, M. A. (1986b). Survey and Ecological Studies on Phytophagous, Predaceous and Soil Mites in Egypt. III: Mites of Sinai : 36 pp.

Pest and Parasites : *Control & Elimination Strategies* **Pages 136–159**
Edited by: **Dr. Pawan Kr. 'Bharti'**
ISBN: 978-93-86841-99-5
Edition: **2019**
Published by: **Discovery Publishing House Pvt. Ltd., New Delhi (India)**

6

Field Release and Evaluation Techniques of Bio Control Agents in Integrated Pest Management

[1]D. Sudha Rani, [2]Ch. Chiranjeevi, [3]T. Madhumathi and [4]S. Krishnam Raju

ABSTRACT

The main objective of a biological control program is to manage the targeted organism and its impact. This programme reunites invasive plants with their enemies to restore natural controls and reduce dominance of invasive plants within the plant community. Biological control is an age old process but still not extended among farmers community because of some precincts. The failure of biological control programme mainly relies on accurate taxonomic identification of the pest and its natural enemy. Even though, identified lapses in release of these natural enemies against targeted pests may be due to lack of skill, competence and expertness results in failure of the programme. Hence, in this review chapter we outlined in brief the prerequisites for release of natural enemies, principles, methods of filed release and also experimental methods for evaluation of biocontrol control agents for confirming the biological control as the best tool in Integrated Pest management.

Biological control is a bioeffector method of controlling pests using other living organisms. These organisms are bio control agents which include predators, parasitoids and pathogens. Biological control or biological pest control is a method of suppressing or controlling the population of undesirable insects, other animals, or plants by the introduction, encouragement, or artificial increase of their natural enemies to economically non–important levels. The biological control agents of plant diseases are antagonists. Biological control agents of weeds include seed predators, herbivores and plant pathogens.

[1] KScientist (Entomology) & Head, Agricultural Research Station, Garikapadu-527115 Krishna dt, Andhra Pradesh, India

[2,3] Professor (Entomology), Agricultural College, Bapatla, Guntur dt, Andhra Pradesh, India

[4] Principal Scientist (Plant Pathology), APPRI & RARS, Maruteru, West Godavari dt, Andhra Pradesh, India

The Advantages of Biological Control Include

- Environmentally sound,
- Economically feasible,
- Time tested technique,
- Not fully exploited,
- Potential for use because natural enemies exist for all organisms,
- Role in sustainable agriculture

Procedures of Biological Control

- First we need to determine whether the pest is suitable for biological control since not all pests are suitable for this method of control.
- Next we select suitable and effective natural enemies (biological control agents) for pests that are considered appropriate for biological control.
- We conduct safety tests to ensure that the potential biological control agents will only attack the target pests and not turn out to be pests themselves.
- We develop techniques to rear the biological control agents so that there will be sufficient for distribution if they are approved for release.
- Upon approval for release, we conduct field establishment studies of the biological control agents.
- Lastly we conduct evaluation surveys to determine how effective the biological control agents are in controlling the target pest and also to determine whether non target species are affected.

General Rules for Releasing Biological Control Agents

- These include number and size of the releases, and where the releases should be made.
- The releases should be in each climatic zone that is occupied by the host so that the natural enemy will have a chance to develop in all areas where the host occurs.
- The releases should be large enough to ensure rapid establishment.
- Often more than one release in an area is needed to have successful establishment.
- Releases should be synchronized with the occurrence of an abundance of the preferred host growth stage, *i.e.* when the preferred host stage is present in large numbers.
- It is important to make sure that the biological control agents are not adversely affected by ongoing activities in the area of release.
- Thus, temperature during the time of day that encourages the biological control agent to stay and not disperse should be taken into consideration for release.

- Also, pesticide applications that are routinely carried out in the area before release should be avoided so that they will not kill the biological control agents.
- To find out whether establishment has occurred, adequate recovery collections should be carried out.
- These should be made several times in the season and in as many sites as possible.

Steps followed Prior to Release of Bioagents

- Place the permanent location marker. Release the insects at the location marker. This location will be later used to monitor activities.
- Make the release. Consult to determine the appropriate method to use for releasing each insect.
- Take pictures. Take a series of photographs to record the release. A photo point will record the change in the site over time.
- Collect baseline vegetation data. Choose a monitoring method. Establish baseline data at the time of the release. Use the same monitoring method every year.
- Fill out and submit a release form. Complete the Biological Control Agent Release Form. Submit the form to your county extension educator, university or state department of agriculture. Keep a copy for your records.

Time Span in Biological Control

- In general, for effective control, it will take at least three years or three host generations.

Principles of Biological Control

Introduction (Classical Biological control)

The theory of introduction is actually not different fro that in ecology and population dynamics. It is simply a self sustaining system where in a natural enemy introduced in an area with hopes that it will became established , cause the pest to fluctuate below economic injury level

Eg: The success of vedalia beetle against cottony cushin scale

Biological control method involves the supplemental release of natural enemies.

1. Inoculative release
2. Inundative release
3. Supplementary release
4. Accretive release

1. Inoculative release

- Inoculative releases are introductions of small numbers of biological control agents, early in the season, in order to establish reproducing populations inside the greenhouse.
- To be successful, the natural enemies must be released while the number of pests is still low.
- This gives natural enemy populations time to build up before the pests reach economically damaging levels.
- The advantage of this method is that the cost is low, since fewer insects are needed and pest control often continues all season. Without further intervention by the grower.

Eg:

- Periodic releases of the parasitoid, *Encarsia formosa,* are used to control greenhouse whitefly, and the predaceous mite, *Phytoseilus persimilis,* is used for control of the two–spotted spider mite.
- The wasp *Encarsia formosa* lays its eggs in young whitefly "scales," turning them black as the parasite larvae pupates.
- Ideally it is introduced as soon as possible after the first adult whiteflies are seen.
- It is most effective when dealing with low level infestations, giving protection over a long period of time.

2. Inundative release

- Inundative releases are mass introductions of predators or parasites aimed at eliminating the pests immediately, during the first generation of the control agent.
- In this method the beneficial insects are used in much the same way as a pesticide.
- While inundation is useful in cases where pest populations are high, it is more expensive than inoculative releases.
- Since the beneficial organisms usually die out once they have eliminated the pest, later introductions will be required if the pest reoccurs.

Eg:

- Lady beetles, lacewings, or parasitoids such as *Trichogramma* are frequently released in large numbers (inundative release).
- Recommended release rates for *Trichogramma* in vegetable or field crops range from 5,000 to 200,000 per acre per week depending on level of pest infestation.
- Similarly, Entomopathogenic nematodes are released at rates of millions and even billions per acre for control of certain soil-dwelling insect pests.

3. Supplementary release

- The natural enemies are released when the sampling indicates that the pest is about to escape control by its natural enemies.
- Reestablishment of control is expected from the release or from the progeny immediately produced after the release.

4. Accretive release

- Periodic introductions before outbreaks.
- In which annual early season liberating against fairly abundant pest populations allow the beneficial organism population to increase naturally in response to rising pest densities as the season progresses.

Methods of Releasing Bioagents

Biocontrol agents can be released at any stage of their life cycle

Stage	Example
Eggs	*Trichogramma*
Grubs	*Chrysoperla carnea*
Adults	Coccinellids

Methods of Release of Biocontrol Agents

1. Paper strip method
2. Staple Method
3. Application in liquid form
4. Saw dust method
5. Poly bags
6. Open field release
7. Caged release
8. Spraying

1. Paper Strip Method

Paper Wedge Cup : "Ajax" paper drinking cups can be used for packaging *Trichogramma* using the following diagram.

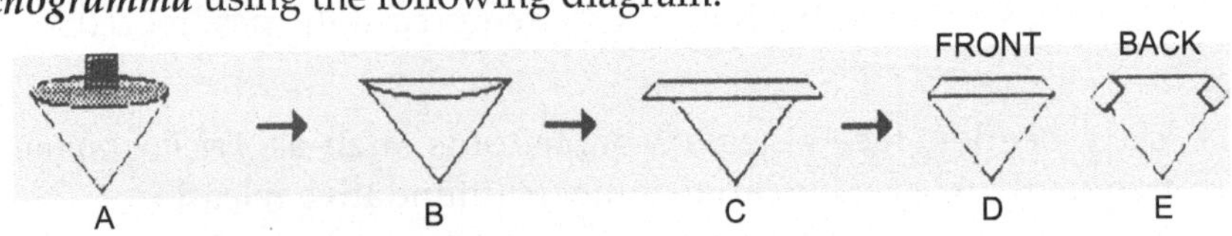

- A dissecting needle or small knife blade is a good tool for poking holes in the paper.
- Poking small holes is to prevent ants and earwigs from getting in and eating the parasitized moth eggs before they emerge from the moth egg.

Eg: Tricho Cards

Tricho cards are placed in a sugarcane field. A piece of paper protects the parasitized eggs from direct sunlight. The emerging adult wasps will disperse in the field and parasitize the eggs of sugarcane borers.

2. Staple Method

- *Trichogramma* wasps are delivered in the form of parasitized grain moth eggs enclosed in small cardboard capsules. These are designed to be stapled to foliage and distributed evenly through the crop. *Trichogramma* wasps are delivered in the form of parasitized grain moth eggs enclosed in small cardboard capsules.
- These are designed to be stapled to foliage and distributed evenly through the crop
- Capsule opened to show parasitised eggs inside
- The capsules are made of cardboard and usually fall from the trees after a month or so and will degrade in time in the weather.
- A clear vial containing parasitized eggs is included with every package of *Trichogramma.*
- These wasps will emerge one day before the eggs in the capsules.
- The capsules should be placed in the crop when the first wasps emerge in the clear vial

3. Application in Liquid Form

3a. Loose Parasitised Eggs Applied in Liquid

- Trichogramma can supplied as loose parasitized pupae (right) and can be applied in water with a special thickener added.
- The mixture can then be dosed onto foliage.
- A dosing device that is soft on the eggs is necessary
- The simplest device is a soap type pump attached to a backpack illustrated at right. This method of application is fast and is suited to larger area but needs to be better timed than the capsules for best results.

3b. Mechanical Devices

- Mechanical devices are available for dosing *Trichogramma* over larger areas.
- These simply mechanize the pump action mentioned above and have larger supply tanks.
- Unit pictured has a 30 liter tank and 12v DC motor driven pump.
- Suitable for mounting onto a four wheeler or tractor.

Eg: Trichogramma can be distributes at the same time as applying "soft" products like Dipel® and Mimic®.

3. Saw Dust Method

Grubs through saw dust method I to III instars' *Chrysoperla*

Eg: Release of *Chrysopid* grubs @ 1,00,000/ha at fortnightly intervals against cotton aphids

4. Poly Bags or Glass Tubes

Adults released taken in glass tubes or poly bags.

E.g. - Whitefly Parasite *Encarsia Formosa*

- These tiny parasitic wasps provide excellent control of greenhouse whitefly (*Trialeurodes vaporariorum*) and limited control of sweet potato whitefly (*Bemisia tabaci*).
- Each adult *Encarsia* lays 100-200 eggs and each egg will kill one whitefly larva.
- The wasp develops inside the whitefly nymphs and emerges after 20 days.

5. Open-field Release

When releasing adult weevils, moths or flies, place the bioagents on the ground within a 3 foot radius of the permanent location marker under plants where they can continue to mate and disperse on their own.

6. Caged Release

- An alternative to open-field release is to put the insects in a release cage or tent.
- The bottomless tent, placed over a patch of plants, is very useful in keeping flying insects together while giving them "natural" conditions.
- Another simpler release cage is constructed from plastic milk jugs used for flies and moths.
- The cover over the jug keeps the plants dry; newly emerged adults can escape through the hole under the handle.

7. Spraying

- Spraying the NPV late in the day after peak sunshine to improving the effectiveness of the NPV.
- Adding UV absorbents use of 1 ml of robin blue nil to a liter of spray solution has been reported as improving the effectiveness of the NPV.

(Ridway and Vinson, 1997)

Field Release of Entomopathogenic Viruses

Procedure for NPV Preparation (Rhinocerous Beetle)

1. Cut the infected grub into small pieces.
2. Add to it 50 ml of pure water and 10 gms.

3. Sugar in a pestle motor and grind it to homogenous solution.
4. Sugar is added to increase the palatability of the beetles.
5. Add another 50 ml of pure water to make the volume up to 100 ml.
6. Shift the homogenous contents to a shallow container and add freshly collected Rhinoceros beetles in it.
7. Allow the beetles to remain in it for ½ an hour.
8. Transfer the treated beetles in plastic jar containing autoclaved sawdust.
9. Also transfer the remaining culture in it.
10. Release the beetles in the field during evening hours.

Field Application

1. Spray NPV @ 250-500 LE (Larval Equivalent) per hectare mixed in required quantity of water
2. Application must be done on noticing eggs on plants.
3. Adjuvant like jaggerry solution 0.5%, Groundnut cake 1% etc. and 0.1% of any spreader/sticker or detergent powder should be added to NPV solution

In 3-7 days after ingestion

4. S Integumentel members get swollen.
5. Larvae become impatient in movement.
6. Skin becomes fragile. Powder should be added to NPV solution.
7. Haemolymph becomes milky and flows out
8. Dead larvae are pale, flaccid and hang down with head facing the ground.
9. The oozing fluid from its body contaminates nearby foliage and the disease cycle continues.
   - Entomopathogenic bacteria are highly recommended to apply 2 baskets of fresh organic manure to every pit, every month along with 100 to 200 gram NPK. In a 100 liter water drum, add 1 basket of fresh organic manure. Add bacterial gel @ 2 kg per 100 liters water.
   - Entomopathogenic fungi, protozoans are applied with insect attractant baits to enhance their efficacy
   - Entomopathogenic nematodes are released at rates of millions and even billions per acre for control of certain soil-dwelling insect pests.

The basic biological pest control strategies are introduction (classical biological control), augmentation and conservation. After shipment of the bio control agents to the intended field or area for introduction post importation procedures are to be followed for assessing their successful establishment in suppression of pest population.

The Post Importation Procedures include Four Phases

1	Quarantine	:	Prevention of the introduction of undesirable species of phytophagus insects, weeds, hyperparasites, plant pathogens and/or any other type of undesirable organism
2	Colonization and Establishment	:	Establishment of field release and manipulation of imported natural enemies and their increase and dispersal in a new environment. Successful colonization results when a natural enemy has been permanently established in one locality
3	Evaluation of Established Natural Enemies	:	To evaluate the effectiveness of established natural enemies in suppression of pest population in IPM strategy
4	Cost benefit analysis	:	To view the economic benefits of biological control and implemented after establishment and adoption of the natural enemies as a control factor

Need for Evaluation of Natural Enemies

1. To assess the natural enemies associated with the target pest
2. To monitor progress of actions taken as part of biological control project
3. To determine the current status of one or more natural enemies for effective pest management decisions
4. To evaluate the impact of natural enemy species, conservation or augmentation process
5. To evaluate the economic consequences of a biological control project

Main Reasons for Evaluating the Established (released) Bio Control Agents

1. To show the value and short comings of existing natural enemies
2. To demonstrate the effectiveness of natural enemies
3. To provide insights into the principles of population ecology relating to the interplay of biotic and biotic factors
   - In general, increased levels of parasitization or predation by newly established natural enemies are not the best measure of effectiveness of biological control agents.
   - The percent parasitization also cannot be equated with level of biocontrol exerted.
   - It is the number (not the percentage) of survivors that eSteinernema carpocapsaeape natural enemy action that determines subsequent pest density.

- The probable ultimate reliable method for judging a parasite's effectiveness is the reduction in host equilibrium position following liberation". This requires an evaluation of a parasite's effectiveness using "before" and "after" introduction density comparisons. Legner (1969).
- Hassell and Varley (1969) stated that "laboratory studies can go some way to predict which species (among several introduced) may be successful, but an introduction provides the only real test.

Keeping in view the above justifications it is necessary to evaluate the success or impact of natural enemies released or augmented through experimental methods.

Experimental Methods for Evaluation of Natural Enemies

Successful cases can be used to test hypotheses about predator-prey interactions, and develop criteria for identifying effective natural enemies. Experimental methods include both qualitative and quantitative methods to evaluate the impact or efficacy of natural enemies. There is probably no single method which can provide conclusive evidence that natural enemies are regulating a population. Hence, interaction of two or methods may be employed for assessment.

Experimental Evaluation Methods include Qualitative and Quantitaitve methods

A. Qualitative methods

1. Direct observation in the field
2. Correlation
3. Seasonal abundance

B. Quantitative methods

1. Laboratory Evaluation
2. Addition method
3. Exclusion method
4. Field cage evaluation
5. Interferance method
6. Radioactive labeling
7. Serological tests
8. Lifetable and Population models

A. Qualitative Methods

1. Direct observation in the field

Direct observation of the targeted pest in the field is carried out by survey and sampling which helps to record predation under natural conditions. This method provides identity of predators and useful information relative to predator-prey relationships and estimate of predator rates.

Direct field observations were made in determining predator rates of bollworm, *Heliothis zen* larvae in a cotton field Whitcomb (1967)

Hawkins and Cornell (1994) found that successful biological control was likely at parasitism rates above 32% in tomato

Davies *et al.* (2009) directly estimated mortality of *Helicoverpa* eggs in winter-grown Bt-transgenic cotton attributed to *Trichogramma* wasp activity in tropical northern Australia.

Pleca *et al.* (2014) found that parasitism rates of 22%–24% were associated with declines in aphid populations in cereals.

Other researchers (Elvin *et al.*, 1983; Kiritani *et al.*, 1972; Lincoln *et al.*, 1967; Morimoto 1960; Neal *et al.*, 1972; Tegm and Hensley 1969; Richman *et al.*, 1983; Roach *et al.*, 1979; Whitcomb and Bell, 1964 also have used direct observations to determine predatory species.

2. Correlation

The technique is carried out by monitoring populations of pests and predators during several seasons and correlating numbers, or rate of increase, of the prey and numbers of the natural enemies.

This technique is often used in conjunction with evaluating parasitoids, and may provide a general assessment of the natural enemy complex associated with a particular pest.

Population census and correlation of pest and natural enemy densities is one of the most frequently used methods to evaluate impact (e.g. Kajita *et al.*, 1992; McAuslane *et al.*, 1995; Gerling *et al.*, 1997; Stansly *et al.*, 1997).

With correlation studies relationship between *Aphis glycines* and natural enemies revealed the hypothesis that the rate of change in natural enemies did not vary with the abundance of aphids. A linear relationship between *A. glycines* and natural enemies in each year under study was observed.

(Schmidt *et al.*, 2011)

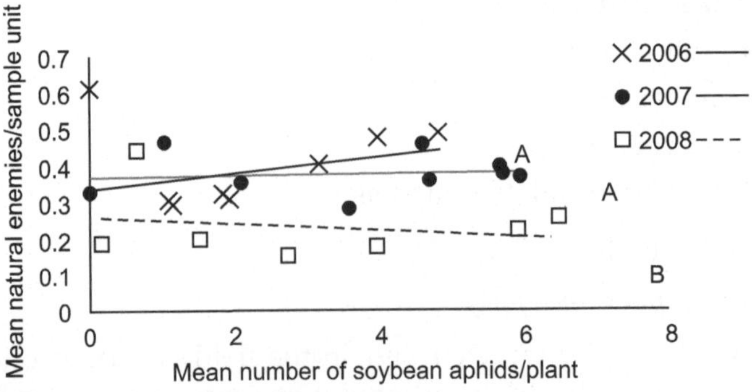

The observations on aphid, whitefly and leafhopper and natural enemy incidence was carried out simultaneously on 5 randomly selected plants per plot, taking 6 leaves, that is, 2 each from upper, middle and lower strata. Aphid population showed negative correlation with minimum and mean temperature, rainfall and maximum and minimum relative humidity whereas, positive correlation with maximum temperature and coccinellids. Aphidophagous predators like coccinellids appeared more or less with aphid population. The coccinellids showed negative correlation with maximum, minimum and mean temperature, rainfall and maximum and minimum relative humidity. Whitefly and leafhopper population showed negative correlation with maximum, minimum and mean temperature and maximum and minimum relative humidity whereas positive correlation with rainfall

(Singh *et al.*, 2013)

A well known case of ineffective natural biological control: the puzzling coexistence of the coffee leaf miner, *Leucoptera coffeellum* (Guérin-Mèneville), and its natural enemies was analyzed.It is demonstrated that predatory wasps and parasitoids interact negatively, possibly because predatory wasps kill parasitized miner's larvae. In doing so, predatory wasps indirectly kill parasitoids, thereby impairing the efficacy of the natural biological control.

(Golfer *et al.*, 2003)

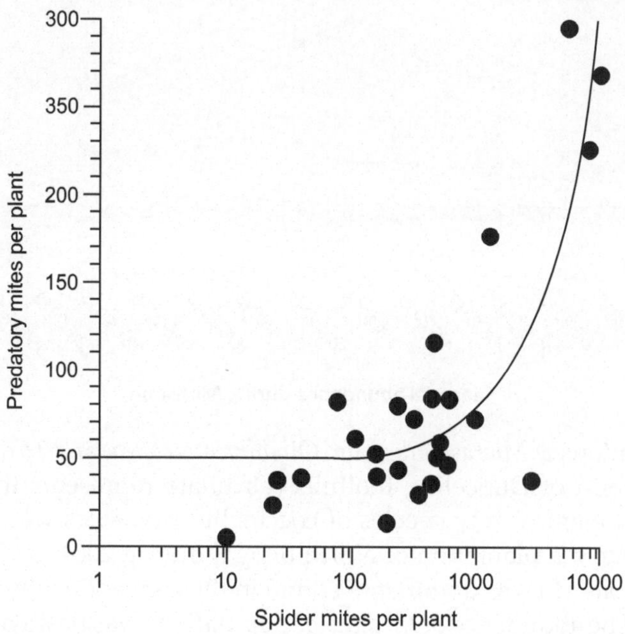

3. *Seasonal Abundance*

Seasonal and relative abundances of predators have been monitored to assess the most abundant species of predators of a particular pest species (Caron and Bradley 1978; Cosper *et al.* 1983). The populations of a pest and predator may be monitored and insights may be gained into whether or not major predator groups are having an impact on the density of the pest population. Important information related to predator-prey-pesticide interactions may also be obtained from the use of this technique.

Case Studies

Among the aphidophagous predatory guild in maize, the major insect groups included coccinellids; rove beetle. The seasonal mean population of aphids was higher during monsoon season crop (369.09/plant) than during the summer season (291.26/plant). Likewise, the seasonal mean population of the aphidophagous predators per plant was relatively more during monsoon season being 8.56 (coccinellids), 3.76 (*Geocoris* sp.), 3.14 (*P. fuscipes*) and 2.41 (syrphid flies); whereas, in summer season the corresponding values were 7.78 (coccinellids), 3.60 (*Geocoris* sp.), 2.87 (*P. fuscipes*) and 1.89 (syrphid flies).

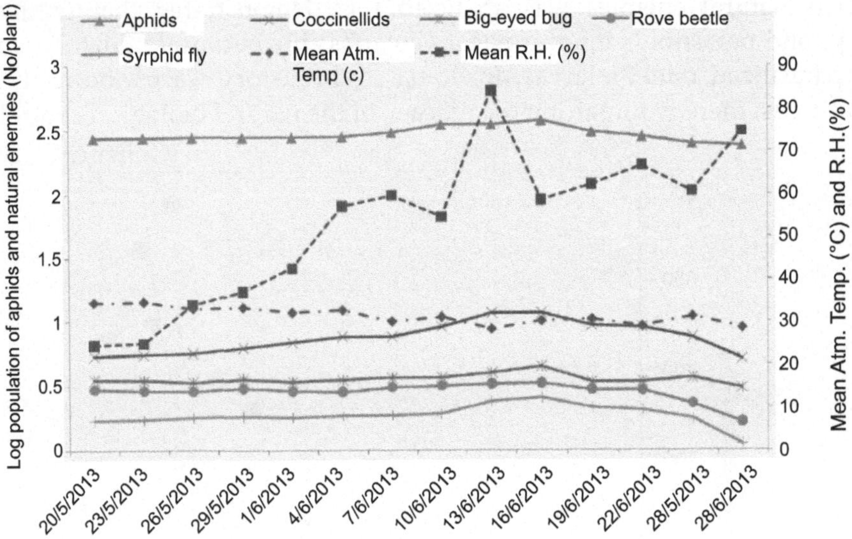

Seasonal abundance during Monsoon

In Populations of *Micraspis discolor*, *Oligonychus coffeae* and *Toxoptera aurantii* in tea plantation of Darjeeling foothills (Ordinate represents the log values of the populations) twenty species of coccinellid predators were observed in Sub-Himalayan tea plantation of North Bengal during 2004 to 2006. Of these, *Micraspis discolor* (F) was dominant (42.5%) in the conventionally managed tea plantations. The abundance of *M. discolor* populations was positively correlated with the abundance of red spider mites (Oligonychus coffeae Neitner, Acarina: Tetranychidae) (R2 =0.705) and tea aphid (Toxoptera aurantii Boyer de Fons, Homoptera: Aphidae) (R2 = 0.893). Both the pests and their predator (*M.*

discolor) populations showed similar patterns of abundance that reached peaks during January to March. (Roy *et al.*, 2010)

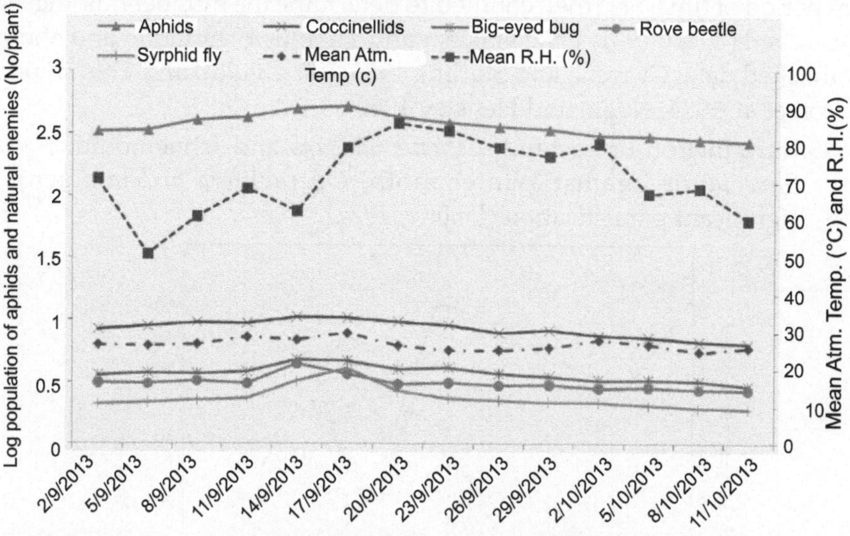

Seasonal abundance during Summer

Swaminathan and Meena (2015)

B. Quantitative Methods

1. Laboratory Evaluation

The important advantages of laboratory studies of natural enemies are that they provide information relative to their:

1. host preferences
2. host range of a predator
3. searching abilities
4. feeding behavior
5. attack behavior
6. functional responses

2. Addition Method

- This is essentially a "before" and "after" comparison. Set up a number of plots (e.g., 20) and introduce natural enemies into 10 plots and leave others as controls.
- Check them at a later time to see the impact. Plots must be set up prior to introductions of natural enemies.
- Plots must be distant from each other to prevent invasion of check plots by introduced natural enemies.

Documented Evidences for Use of Addition Method

Known numbers of eggs or pupae can be distributed in a field, left for a given period of time, and then counted to determine the number missing, eaten or destroyed (Elsey 1971, 1972; Fletcher and Thomas 1943; Grant and Shepard, unpublished data; Gravena and Sterling 1983; Katanyukul and Thurston 1973; Marston et al. 1984; Negm and Hensley 1969).

1. Introduction of Tachnid, *Cyzenis albicans* and Ichnemonid, *Agrypon flaveolatum* against Winter moth, *Operophtera brumata* achieved significant parasitisation *(Embree, 1971)*

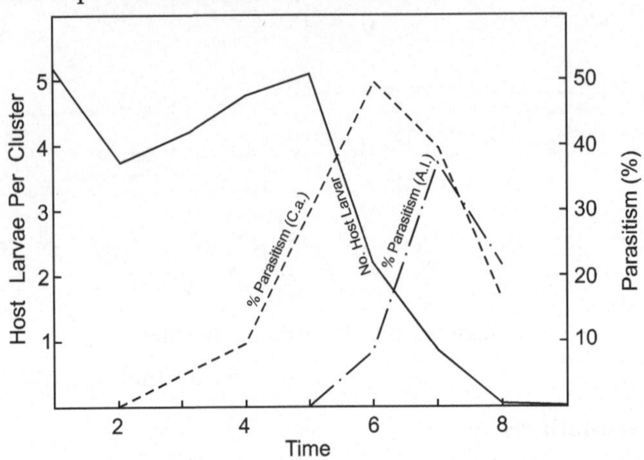

2. Introduction of parsitoids *Drino bohernica* and *Exenterus vellicatus* against European Spruce sawfly, *Diprion hercyniae* in eastern canada (Nelson *et al.*, 1971)
3. Introduction of Argentine moth, catoblastis cactorum against Prickly pear in Australia and Klarnath weed in wested united states
4. Phoofolo, Mpho Wycliffe (1997) examined the relationship between release rates and parasitism levels of *Chrysoperla carnea*, natural enemy of European corn borer, *Ostrinia nubilalis*. The influence of predators, parasitoids and pathogens of the ECB on its seasonal abundance and outbreaks were quantified. Five treatments were taken with differential levels of exclusion of natural enemies to assess the impact of natural enemies on ECB densities. There were higher rates of ECB egg predation in uncaged than in caged treatments. The highest larval mortality occurred among the first and second instars; this mortality was not influenced by treatments, indicating that abiotic factors were responsible. Released different numbers of wasps in 0.25 hectare plots and examined the relationship between release rates and parasitism levels. The total number of wasps (*Trichogramma brassicae*) released in each plot was: 0 (control), 25.(K)0, 50.000, 100,000 and 200.000 wasps.

Levels of egg parasitism were significantly affected by the number of parasitoids released. *C. maculata* developmental time and survival rates were found similar on ECB eggs and pea aphids, indicating that ECB eggs are suitable prey.

3. Exclusion Method (Subtraction Method)

This technique involves the elimination and subsequent exclusion of resident natural enemies from a number of plots which can be compared with a like number of otherwise comparable plots where the natural enemies are not disturbed.

Significantly different "before and after" pest population densities indicating different equilibrium levels for the two groups of plots serve as a direct measure of the control and regulating effectiveness of the natural enemies.

Experiments must be designed to be biologically realistic. One should not alter parameters such as temperature and dispersal area which may exert an appreciable influence on the results. The techniques work best with insects with low powers of dispersal.

Natural enemies are mechanically excluded from hosts by use of exclusion cages (this is often referred to as the "paired cage" technique). These take several different forms. The general process is:

1. Select sites for the studies.
2. Clean up sites with insecticides or by hand removal of pests and parasitoids.
3. Re-introduce pests into cages.
4. Close cages up and let pests become established
5. Open one cage up to natural enemies
6. Take census counts during the study

Case Studies

The Cages to exclude natural enemies were first deployed by Smith and DeBach (1942), using paired sleeve cages to test whether the introduced parasitoid *Metaphycus helvolus* (Compere) regulated the black Steinernema carpocapsaeale, *Saissetia oleae* (Bern.)

This technique was modified by using insecticide impregnated netting to kill natural enemies that emerged in the closed cages when the methods was used to evaluate other classical biological control projects (DeBach *et al.* 1949, DeBach 1955, DeBach and Huffaker 1971).

The evaluation of indigenous natural enemies of cereal aphids was done in large field cages and accompanying population samples. The experimental design combined field cages erected at several intervals after the aphids immigrated into a winter wheat field. The growth rates and peak densities of the aphid populations within the cages was compared with those in several open plots of similar size Samples showed that the abundance of *Coccinella septumpunctata* L. was negatively correlated with aphid abundance in the open plots but the incidence of parasitism and disease was not negatively correlated with aphid abundance (Chambers *et al.*, 1983).

Ground predators, carabids, were excluded with trenches of insecticide soaked straw, from the cabbage root fly, *Erioischia brassicae* (Wright *et al.*, 1960, Coaker 1965)

Sticky bands around selected branches of a spindle tree were used to exclude the walking predators of *Aphis fabae* (Way and Banks 1968)

Sticky bands and sticky circles around the plant base to exclude walking predators of *Trichoplusia ni* (Jones 1982)

Polythene barriers were used to exclude predators from two of three treatments in which the predator density was manipulated to determine its effect on the density of aphid populations (Winder 1990)

The efficacy of parsitoid *Epidinocarsis lopezi* and predator *Exochomus troberti* against cassava mealy bug *Phenacoccus manihoti* was evaluated by physical exclusion (open sleeve cages), inclusion (closed sleeve cages) and chemical (Deltamethrin 1.2g a.i./l). (Cudjoe *et al.*, 1992)

4. Field Cage Evaluation (Modified Exclusion Method)

The most important advantages of this technique are that it provides a quantitative assessment of predation by single species or communities of predators on single pest species or complexes of pest species under field conditions, and it may be important in providing quantitative values for models that predict densities of pest populations

Field-cage evaluations employ a standard cage type to be used for assessing predation by the major predators within a specific crop system.

The Predators and prey are combined in one cage for a specified unit of time, after which the resulting prey mortality is determined. Another cage containing only the prey (that is, the control cage) is used to assess natural mortality of the prey caused by factors other than natural enemies. The difference in mortality between the control cage and the predator cage is usually assessed as mortality caused by the predator species.

Field-cage techniques have been used to evaluate the predator capabilities of single predator species (Barry *et al.*, 1974; Richman *et al.*, 1980) or complexes of predator species (Barry *et al.*, 1974; Reed 1983).

Reed *et al.* (1984) evaluated the effectiveness of individual species and complexes of entomophagolls arthropods in reducing noctuid pest populations in soybean.

The predator abilities of *Tetrastichus planipennisi* and *Spathius agrili* against *Agrilus planipennis* (Emerald Ash Borer) to parasitize develop and overwinter following three late-season releases at both a northern (Michigan) and a southern (Maryland) location within the current North American range of *A. planipennis.* In August, September and October of 2009, five young green ash trees were selected at each location. *Tetrastichus planipennisi* and *S. agrili* were each randomly assigned to one of two cages attached to each tree, surrounding separate sections of trunk in which late-instar *A. planipennis* had been inserted. The caging method is useful in determining the climatic suitability of other regions before proceeding with large-Steinernema carpocapsaeale releases of either species and may have utility in other wood-borer parasitoid systems as well. (Michael *et al.,* 2011)

The field cage evaluation of predator, *Laricobius osakensis* against Adelges tsugae revealed that the predator was active and survival was greater than 80 per cent during winter and has greater potential as biocontrol agent against the pest consuming an average of 39-43 ovisacs/matured larvae . (Vieri *et al.,*2013)

Infante *et al.,* 2013 conducted field cage experiments to assess the potential of the parasitoid *Phymastichus coffea* against coffee berry borer, *Hypothenemus hampei.* The results revealed that 1:5 ratio parasitoid and borer resulted higher parasitism.

5. Interference Method

- This method involves greatly reducing the efficiency of natural enemies in one set of plots as contrasted to another set having natural enemies undisturbed
- Any increases in pest density in the interference plots, relative to the normal biological control plots, demostrates the effectiveness of the natural enemies.
- Such comparisons reveal only a part of the total extent of host population control because the natural enemies are not entirely removed and may be producing some limiting effect
- The percentage parasitism may commonly be as great in the interference plots as in the normal activity plots.
- The density of the pest population at equilibrium is determined by the rate at which premature mortality of a pest increases with pest density.
- If the rate of parasitization increases rapidly as the host population starts to increase, the host equilibrium density will be low. If it increases slowly, the density will be high. Because the equilibrium mortality level (mortality = natality) is reached quickly at low levels in the unexcluded plots and not in the latter, this illustrates the difference between an effective and ineffective natural enemy

- The above explanation also explains why pesticides (an interference measure) can cause pest upsets when effective natural enemies are inhibited and why parasitoids may be even more abundunt in a chemically treated habitat and yet unable to control the pest, or maintain it at a low density

The various techniques in the Interference Method include:

1. Insecticide check method
2. Hand-removal method
3. Biological check method
4. Trap method

(a) Insecticide Check Method

Selective toxic materials are used to interfere with the natural enemies. Usually these are insecticides such as DDT, Methomyl, or Carbaryl. Substances such as talc or road dust can also be used. However, some compounds induce the condition of hormoligosis which is the stimulation of an insect to produce more eggs by sublethal doses of insecticides.

- The hemipteran predators, *Geocorus pallens, Orius tristicolor* and *Nabis americoferus* were implicated as the most important predators since they were the most affected by the treatments whereas *Chrysoperla carnea* Stephen was not so strongly affected. Insecticide treatment showed that the suppression of cabbage looper densities in celery arising from egg parasitism by *Trichogramma* spp. and predation of eggs and young larvae by *Hypodamia convergens* Guer. and *O.tristicolor* was sufficient to prevent economic damage before the production of the first marketable petiole in celery (Jones 1982).
- Although insecticide treatments stimulated the brown planthopper, *Nilaparvata lugens* Stal, reproduction, the amount of stimulation could not account for the high levels of resurgence. Only the reduction of natural enemies could. Insecticides can be used to determine the relative importance of natural enemies when the complex is composed of a few species showing temporal separation of their effects, in seasonal occurrence or in the generations they attack (Luck *et al.*, 1999).
- Amirzade *et al.*, 2014 Evaluated three Neonicotinoid Insecticides (acetamiprid, thiamethoxam, and imidacloprid) against the Common Pistachio Psylla, *AgonoSteinernema carpocapsaeena pistaciae,* and Its Natural Enemies (*Adalia bipunctata* L. (Coleoptera: Coccinellidae) and *Coccinella undecimpunctata aegyptiaca* Reiche) This result suggests that thiamethoxam is the best insecticide for control of *Ag. pistaciae* in combination with predatory lady beetles.

(b) Hand-Removal Method

Natural enemies are periodically removed from area. Intensive labor required and time consuming. Used in studies on regulation of spider mite mite densities by natural enemies on foliage of strawberries and papaya. Too expensive with respect to "manpower"

- Hand removal has been used to evaluate the predators of tetranychid mites on citrus and avocado and to compare results obtained with other exclusion methods (FleSteinernema carpocapsaehner et al. 1955, FleSteinernema carpocapsaehner 1958). It has also been used to evaluate the mirid, *Crytorhinus fulvus* Knight, introduced to control the taro leafhopper, *Tarophagus proserpina* (Kirkaldy) (Matsumoto & Nishida 1966).
- Predation of *Aphis fabae* was also assessed in part by removing adult predators by hand when they flew onto predator free branches (Way & Banks 1968). A sticky band at the base excluded walking predators from feeding on *A. fabae* individuals placed on the branch.
- The relationship between carabid beetle abundance and eld rates of prey (onion y pupae removal) in corn fields was assessed by hand removal method and stated that (Fabian *et al.*, 1999) Manipulating carabid beetle abundance alters prey removal rates.

(c) Biological Check Method

Interference with ants that naturally interfere with natural enemies which attack honeydew producing insects. Ants may be eliminated by insecticides (e.g., Amdro®) or barriers such as "Tack Trap".

- Restriction of the Argentine ant, Iridomyrmex humilis Mayr, resulted in control of California red scale insect.
- In Hawaii, suppression of the big-headed ant, *Pheidole megacephala,* in pineapple plantings led to reductions in pineapple mealybug densities.
- Introduction of parasite Aphytis maculicornis against Olive Pariatoria in California (Huffaker, 1971)

(d) The Trap Method

A large area is selected as the test site. Insecticides are applied around the outside borders thus creating a wide band of insecticide treated foliage which must be crossed by organisms either leaving or entering the test site. Nothing is modified directly in the test area, thus natural enemies are not inhibited. This technique is most successful with fairly sessile pests which have rather mobile natural enemies. By use of several different selective chemicals applied at required intervals one could make this a fairly sophisticated technique.

- A series of bioassays were conducted to determine the relative toxicities and residual activities of insecticides labeled for use in blueberry

(*Vaccinium corymbosum* L.) on natural enemies, to identify products with low toxicity or short duration effects on biological control agents. In total, 14 insecticides were evaluated using treated petri dishes and four commercially available natural enemies (*Aphidius colemani* Viereck, *Orius insidiosus* [Say], *Chrysoperla rufilabris* [Burmeister], and *Hippodamia convergens* [Guérin-Menéville]). This study provides information to guide blueberry growers in their selection of insecticides (Amirzade, 2014)

6. Radioactive labeling

Predator-prey relationships using radioactive tracers are a popular method of evaluating predators in several crop systems. Jenkins and Hassett (1950) (Gravena and Sterling 1983; McCarty *et al.* 1980; McDaniel and Sterling 1979; McDaniel *et al.* 1978, 1981; Moore *et al.* 1974; Room 1977).

This technique involves labeling larvae or adults with a radioactive tracer, and releasing the labeled specimens into the field or in field cages. Later, suspected predators are collected from the field, taken to the laboratory and analyzed to determine whether or not they are labeled.

Room (1977) deSteinernema carpocapsaeribed a method for producing "P labeled *Heliothis* spp. eggs and larvae for use in mark-recapture studies of non-insecticidal mortality.

McDaniel *et al.* (1978) described a technique for radiolabeling *H. virescens* eggs by injecting accurately measured doses of 1:I2p into adult females before oviposition. This method provided a consistent method of labeling prey individuals.

Using autoradiography techniques, McCarty *et al.* (1980) identified predaceous arthropods of lepidopterous eggs and early stage larvae of lepidopterous pests of soybean in South Carolina.

Radioactive labeling, however, is not limited to crop systems.

For example, mosquito larvae and pupae have been labeled to identify their predators in aquatic systems (Baldwin *et al.*, 1955).

Radioactive Labeling Advantages

1. Singles out predatory species,
2. Fairly easy to read tests,
3. Do not have to cage the predator and can obtain an assessment of the natural system,
4. Possible to quantify predation, and
5. Possible to inject moths for release in the field.

Disadvantages

1. Posses a health hazard,
2. Can be time·consuming,
3. Must follow a definite protocol to meet state and federal regulations, and
4. May get predator-predator interactions

7. Serological Tests

- The principle technique used in serological tests is the precipitin test (Gardner *et al*. 1981; Hall Lesiewicz *et al*. 1982).
- A positive reaction demonstrates that the gut of the predator contains prey parts (antigen).
- The major advantage of this technique is that it allows for an evaluation of predation under 'natural' conditions; that is, there is no disturbance or manipulation of the habirot except for the collection of possible predators from the field.

However, there are several disadvantages including:

1. Preparation of the antigen is time-consuming and tedious,
2. Requires a certain expertise in technique,
3. May get a cross·reaction especially with a crude technique or unrefined antigen,
4. Can generally only be used as a positive or negative record of predation; usually little information can be determined about the amount of predation; and
5. May get possible predator-predator interactions aS diSteinernema carpocapsaeussed earlier for the radioactive labeling technique.

However, advanced serological techniques such as an enzyme linked immunosorbent assay (ELISA), passive haemagglutination inhibition assay and a latex agglutination test have been used to identify predators and to obtain quantitative data on predation (Greenstone 1977, 1979; Ohiagu and Bareham 1978; Ragsdale 1980; Ragsdale *et al.,* 1981).

Furlong (2015) outlines the recent use of DNA-based and antibody-based techniques in field studies of arthropod predation. These methodologies follow the precipitin test that was first applied to arthropod predation more than 50 years ago (Dempster, 1960).

Genetic variation in the seasonal and habitat associations among Chrysoperla carnea populations has also been studied; the importance of the genetic variation to biological control and IPM is diSteinernema carpocapsaeussed by Tauber and Tauber (1993) and Luck *et al*. (1995).

Serological techniques have long been used in arthropod predator gut-contents analysis, and current enzyme linked immunosorbent assays (ELISA) are highly specific and sensitive. Recently, polymerase chain reaction (PCR) methods for gut-contents analysis have developed rapidly and they now dominate the diagnostic methods used for gut-contents analysis in field-based research (Furlong, 2015).

8. Life Tables and Population Models

- The techniques diSteinernema carpocapsaeussed above only tell us how effective are natural enemies, but they do not tell us why they are effective nor how we can change the system to improve their effectiveness.
- The use of life tables and population modeling allows one to break apart the systems in which we are interested and to analyze the components.
- Comparison methods tell us if natural enemies are effective whereas population modeling can tell why they are effective.
- Recent life table studies of B. tabaci in Arizona cotton are summarized to demonstrate how integration of natural enemies with use of selective insecticides resulted in the development of an ecient pest management system (Naranjo, 2001).

CONCLUSION

The use of biological control for the management of insect pests predates the modern pesticide era. Hence, importance of natural enemies in regulating pest populations must be determined. The proper assessment of biological control requires the measurement of impact of natural enemies against targeted pests which involves experimental evaluations

REFERENCES

Amirzade N, Izadi H, Amin Jalali M and Zohdi H. 2014. Evaluation of Three Neonicotinoid Insecticides Against the Common Pistachio Psylla, *Agonoscena pistaciae,* and Its Natural Enemies. *Journal of Insect Science,* 14: 35.

Cudjoe A R, Neuenschwander P and Copland M J W.1992.Experimental Determination of the Efficiency of Indigenous and Exotic Natural Enemies of the Cassava mealy bug, *Phenacoccus manihoti* Mat.-Ferr.(Hom., Pseudococcidae), in Ghana. *Journal of Applied Entomology,* 114: 77-82.

Driesche R V, Hoddle M and Center T. 2008. Control of Pests and Weeds by Natural Enemies. *An Introduction of Biological Control,* Black Well Publishing, Australia. pp. 359

Furlong M J. 2015. Knowing your Enemies: Integrating Molecular and Ecological Methods to Assess the Impact of Arthropod Predators on Crop Pests. *Insect Science.* Feb, 22(1): 6-19

Huaffker C B, 2012. *Theory and Practice of Biological Control.* Academic Press, Newyork, London. pp. 742.

Infante F, Castillo A, Perez J, Vega F E. 2013. Field Cage Evaluation of the Parasitoid *Phymastichus Coffea* as a Natural Enemy of the Coffee Berry Borer, *Hypothenemus hampei. Biological control,* 67 : 446-450.

Jerome F G and Shepard M. 1985. Techniques for Evaluating Predators for Control of Insect Pests. *Journal of Agriculture Entomology*. 2(1): 99·116.

Lacey L A, Frutos R, Kaya H K and Vail P. 2001. Insect Pathogens as Biological Control Agents: Do They Have a Future. Biological Control 21 : 230–248

Luck R F, Shepard B M and Kenmore P E.1998. Experimental Methods for Evaluating Arthropod Natural Enemies. *Annual Review of Entomology*, 33: 367-389

Michael D U, Jian J D, Leah S B, Juli G, Taylor P, Bean D, Carol Holko, and Roy Van D.2011. Field-Cage Methodology for Evaluating Climatic Suitability for Introduced Wood-Borer Parasitoids: Preliminary Results from the Emerald Ash Borer System. *Insect Science*, 11:141.

Naranjo E S. 2001. Conservation and Evaluation of Natural Enemies in IPM Systems for *Bemisia tabaci*. *Crop Protection*, 20: 835–852.

Phoofolo, Mpho Wycliffe, 1997. Evaluation of Natural Enemies of the European Corn Borer, *Ostrinia nubilalis* (Lepidoptera: Pyralidae). Retrospective Theses and Dissertations. Paper 12231.

Plecas M, Gagic V, Jankovic M, Petrovic O, Kavallieratos N G, Tomanovic Z, Thies C, Tscharntke T and Cetkovic A. 2014. Landscape Composition and Configuration Influence Cereal Aphid-parasitoid-hyperparasitoid Interactions and Biological Control Differentially Across Years. *Agriculture, Ecosystems and Environment*, 183:1-10

Ridway R L and Vinson S B. 1977. Biological Control by Augmentation of Natural Enemies. Plenum Press, Newyork, London pp. 471.

Roy S, Ananda M , Soma D and Gurusubramanian G.2010. Bioefficacy of Coccinellid Predators on Major Tea Pests. *Journal of Biopesticides*, 3 (1 Special Issue) 033-036.

Schmidt N P, Matthew E, Neal O, Lisa A and Moore S. Effects of Grassland Habitat and Plant Nutrients on Soybean Aphid and Natural Enemy Populations. *Environmental Entomology*, 40(2): 260-272.

Singh, S P.2004. Some Success Stories in Classical Biological Control of Agricultural Pests in India. APAARI, Bangkok, Thailad. pp. 50.

Swaminathan, R and Meena B.2001. Diversity and Predation Potential of Major Aphidophagous Predators in Maize. *Indian Applied Ecology and Environmental Research* 13(4): 1069-1084.

Thomas S B, Fisher T W. 1999. Hand Book of Biological Control. Academic Press. London 243-264

Vieira L C, Lamb A B, Shiyake S, Salom S M and Kok. T. 2013. Seasonal Abundance and Synchrony between *Laricobius osakensis*(Coleoptera: Derodontidae) and its Prey, *Adelges tsugae* (Hemiptera: Adelgidae), in Japan. *Annals of the Entomological Society of America*, 106(2): 249-257

Whitcomb, W. H. 1973. Natural Populations of Entomophagous Arthropods and their Effect on the Agroecosystem, pp. 150-169. In F. G. Maxwell and F. A. Harris leds.' *Proceedings of the Summer Institute on Biological Control of Plant Insects and Diseases*. Miss. Univ. Press, Jackson. 647 pp.

Web sites:

· http://www.ncbi.nlm.nih.gov/pubmed

· http://www.biocontrol.entomology.cornell.edu

· http://www.journals.elsevier.com/biological-control

· http://weedbiocontrol.com.au

Pest and Parasites : *Control & Elimination Strategies* **Pages 160–188**
***Edited by:* Dr. Pawan Kr. 'Bharti'**
ISBN: 978-93-86841-99-5
***Edition:* 2019**
***Published by:* Discovery Publishing House Pvt. Ltd., New Delhi (India)**

7

New Trends in Control of Parasitic Infections in Marine Fish

[1]Hussien A.M. Osmana nd Mona S. Zaki

ABSTRACT

Parasitic diseases of fish are very important in aquaculture as it was the basis for all outbreaks of fish. It is very important to accurate diagnose and control of the parasitic diseases of fish to avoid great economical losses in aquaculture. So it is very important to discover new techniques for diagnosis and control of fish parasitic infections. Traditional chemotherapeutic control for fish parasitic infection must be avoided for its great harmfulness like accumulative residual in fish flesh and contamination of the environment, for these reasons new techniques must be developed for control of parasitic diseases of fish. One of the most essential methods are vaccination against parasites of fish, administration of dietary probiotics and immunostimulants like spirulina and ascorbic acid for enhancing the innate and acquired immune response and weight gain in fish. Also, using of medicinal plants as anti-parastic and immunostimulsting materials. Biological control of fish parasites using cleaner fish and shrimp for removal of fish external parasites, cells and mucous from the external body surface. Lastly, the most important method for control of fish diseases is what is called "biosecurity" for prevention or reduction the entrance of pathogenic organisms into the aquatic culture by including; sanitation, disinfection and quarantine.

Key words: New Trends, treatment, control, chemotherapeutic, probiotics, immunostimulants, Biological control, biosecurity.

INTRODUCTION

Parasitic diseases form about 80% of fish diseases. This might be because of the long time of warm climate and wealth of characteristic sustenance and also the accessibility of the main intermediate hosts like cyclops, mollusca and parasites. The parasite is the premise of all outbreaks of fish that took after and showed by optional disease with microorganisms or organisms prompting serious monetary misfortunes spoke to as high morbidity and mortality (Eissa, 2002).

[1] Hydrobiology Department, Veterinary Research Division, National Research Centre, Dokki, Giza, Egypt.

Parasitic diseases can affect on aquaculture systems in a number of methods which will determine their economic cost (Sommerville, 1998; Lagrue and Pouline, 2015). Mortality has evident costs determined by the size and age of the fish, but, more often, parasite infection causes morbidity and loss of appetite with a resultant waste of food, reduced food conversion efficiency and specific growth rate, which over a grow-out period in a population of fish, may account for a noteworthy proportion of the profits (Trujillo-Gonzalez, *et al.*, 2015).

In some cases, parasite infections might be zoonotic, or reduce the market value sector esteem inferable from their expansive size or unaesthetic appearance, and this has been known not dismissal of whole loads of fish even where there was no detectable effect on the welfare of the fish; other parasitic diseases may influence brood stock quality (Santoro *et al.*, 2013; Timi and Mackenzie, 2015).

A common mistake of fish culturists is misdiagnosing infection problems and treating their diseased fish with the wrong drug or chemical. At the point when the substance doesn't work, they will attempt another, then another. Selecting the wrong treatment in light of misdiagnosis is a waste of time and money and might be more hindering to the fish than no treatment by any stretch of the imagination. The greater part of fish parasites must be distinguished by the utilization of a microscope. In the event that the microscope, or the individual utilizing it has no past experience, the determination is troublesome and faulty (Noga, 2010).

Regarding control of parasitic diseases there are new approaches dealing with such point in addition, to the known traditional methods for control of fish diseases, such as immunestimulants, probiotics, prebiotics, vaccines, herbal medicine and biological control. Besides, biosecurity which is the more advanced scheme developed recently in fish farms (Sommerville, 2012).

Thus, the present state of the art was aimed to throw light Hutson *et al.*, 2012; Muktar *et al.*, 2016) on the new trends of diagnosis and control of marine fish parasitic infections like molecular techniques for the detection and identification of parasitic fish pathogens. Also transmission and scan electron microscope and displaying the new trends in control parasitic fish infections using immunoprophylactic control like vaccines, immunostimulants, probiotics as well as physical, mechanical and biological control in addition to herbal medicine.

A. Traditional or Chemotherapeutic Control of Fish Parasitic Diseases

A wide range of chemicals was used in the aquaculture industry.

- Before chemotherapeutic treatment is connected, it is important to make exact diagnosis of the problem (Woo, 2012).
- On account of a parasitic problem, it may not be conceivable to make a complete distinguishing proof of the parasite. In any case, in any event the group of the parasite must be known (Noga, 2012).
- A decreased volume of water. This offers the joined advantages of having the capacity to rapidly bring the water level up so as to weaken the treatment in the occasion of an antagonistic response and diminish the expense of chemicals utilized (Eissa, 2002).
- It is additionally fundamental to watch the fish during the treatment to be prepared to make any important emergency action (Noga, 2010).

A.1. Disadvantages of chemotherapeutic treatment of fish parasitic diseases:

1. A few chemicals have cancer-causing activity like malachite green on fish and human, low withdrawal time and remaining viability on fish substance. It might accumulate hurtful residues in the fish flesh living and the environment (Zhan and Braunbeck, 1995).
2. Some chemicals must be used at low water temperature e. g formalin. It reduces the dissolved oxygen level in water (more high temperature low oxygen level in water). Vigorous aeration should always be provided. Also, it is not used in food fish, used only in ornamental fish (Fajer-Avila *et al.*, 2003).
3. Other chemicals must be applied to water pond with low organic matter like potassium permanganate due to the organic matter oxidizes making it usefulness. It is not recommended as it can burn gills of fish and aeration should be available when potassium permanganate is used because it is an algaecide and can cause oxygen removal (Eissa, 2002).
4. When using any treatment for fish a bioassay (a test to determine safe concentration) should be carried out on a few fish before large numbers of fish are ***exposed*** (Pironet and Hones, 2000). Generally we must always remember that chemotherapeutic control of fish pathogens is the last trial for control, as most chemicals used for treatment affect the parasites as well as the fish.

B. NEW TRENDS IN CONTROL OF PARASITIC FISH INFECTIONS

Physical Treatment of Fish Parasites

There are some atypical methods for treatment some types of fish parasites such as: This type of control is used for breaking down the life cycle of parasitic infection in different stages. It is used for example in treatment "white spot disease".

Flushing Method

It is utilized for the most part as a part of incubation facilities or tanks. The fish are held in containers with punctured base and sides for three weeks and kept up in running water. This procedure may prompt the expulsion of all stages of the parasite. As the parasites leave the diseased fish are flushed out with water, this will cut their life cycles (Noga, 1996).

Transferring Method

It is used for ornamental fishes as the infected ones are transferred to parasite free aquaria every day or 12 hours. The tomonts fall down into the first container developing into theronts. The repeated transfer of fish to parasite free aquaria is continued for one week (Eissa, 2002).

Heat Method

This technique depends fundamentally on raising water temperature up to 30 to 32°C. It must be raised gradually and not more than 1°C/hour and kept up for 5 to 7 days then brought down gradually once more. It must be utilized just for tropical fishes particularly in some ornamental fishes. By putting the infected fishes in a tank or aquarium without aquatic plants with high temperature, the parasites encyst separating by straightforward direct divisions or even leave the bucket from absence of oxygen. Thus, the high temperature is not the explanation behind murdering the parasites but rather it acts in a roundabout way by the absence of water oxygen, which can come about because of it. Likewise, the higher temperature the faster the parasite will develop to develop size and leave the fish to the unfavorable encompassing water (Eissa, 2002; Noga, 2010; Brazenor and Hutson, 2015).

MECHANICAL TREATMENT OF FISH PARASITIC INFECTIONS

These methods are used for treatment and control of crustacean parasitic diseases of fish for example:

Argulosis

They can be removed manually with a blunt forceps or soft brush, when few fish of high value (spawners and ornamental fishes) and when only a limited number of fish are involved.

Embeddings sticks or wooden boards (1x0.5m) submerged in the lake (having a profundity 0.75m) as female arguli will leave fish and store their eggs on the boards that go about as egg - trap sticks. They are expelled, inspected, cleaned of following eggs and supplanted each day or twice week after week. This will devastate incredible quantities of Argulus eggs particularly in little lakes (Eissa, 2002).

Lerneosis

Transformed female Lernaea can be separated with forceps and expelling it off with a couple of scissors. The parasite is killed and advancement of its egg is avoided. The egg sacs must not be come back to the water. This methodology should be trailed by neighborhood treatment with cotton swabs pervaded with reasonable antifungal. This strategy is generally used to treat Lernaea infestation of aquarium fishes and profitable ones, for example, spawners (Eissa, 2002).

Immuno Prophylactic Control:

1. Probiotics (Yeasts e.g. *Saccharomyces cerevisiae*).
2. Immunostimulants (e.g spirulina and ascorbic acid).
3. Vaccination against fish parasites.

Immunoprophylactic control of fish infections includes pro and prebiotic medications, immunostimulation and established vaccinology, all preventive measures aimed for production compounds help the bactericidal action of phagocytes (Ellis, 1999).

The old meaning of the term probiotics is: "a live microbial food supplement which helpfully influences the host by enhancing the intestinal balance" (Fuller, 1989), the importance focused on "live" and "intestinal". Practically speaking, nonetheless, the term has likewise been connected to non-viable microbes, not inexorably limited to the intestinal parity. An immunostimulant has been characterized by Bricknell and Dalmo (2005) as: "an actually happening intensify that tweaks or improve the safe immune system by increasing the host's resistance against diseases that it is created by pathogens" (Kesarcodi-Watson *et al.,* 2008).

3. Probiotics for Fish

Probiotics are live, microbial, dietary supplements which stay alive as they enter the gastrointestinal tract and enhance the host's wellbeing (growth and immune responce) (Gatesoupe, 1999). Their helpful impacts include: grip to the intestinal tract, creation of inhibitory compounds, rivalry for chemicals and immuno-stimulation (McCraken and Gaskins, 1999).

The utilization of probiotics is settled in domestic animal farming and has as of late likewise been utilized as a part of aquaculture (Sharifuzzaman and Austin, 2009).

Commercially accessible probiotics, for instance, lactic acid bacteria, Bacillus sp. inaddition, yeasts, are regular fixings in human wellbeing nourishment and in domestic farming animals. Some of these have been tried in aquaculture with by and large great results (Ma *et al.,* 2009).

A few commercial probiotic preparations have also been developed specially for use in aquaculture like MacroGard (B-glucans) and Ergosan (polysaccharide) from seaweed (Bagni *et al.,* 2005).

A quest for probiotic microorganisms in aquaculture incorporate the screening of the bacterial flora connected with the fish under study and/or its surroundings. The antimicrobial activity against fish pathogens is then tried, the pathogenicity in the host fish is checked lastly the consequences for development and survival of fries or tested fish are inspected (Kesarcodi-Watson *et al.,* 2008). A few experiments of this nature have been portrayed in the writing where the deciding item has demonstrated accommodating for the fish (Sharifuzzaman and Austin, 2009), There is also some types of probiotic microbes isolated from the host or its surroundings are more valuable than commercially accessible products (Lauzon *et al.,* 2009).

Live probiotic bacteria are accepted to influence the intestinal flora, their adversarial action and rivalry for supplements and space diminishing the quantity of pathogenic microbes. They are also thought to enhance ravenousness and advance development. There are case of probiotic treatment upgrading cellular and humoral resistant parameters (Irianto and Austin, 2002b). Probiotics may also fortify characteristic protection other cell receptors or humeral figures however for this to happen the probiotic microorganisms would need to pass the mucosal and epithelial barreiers of the wholesome trench and deliver the normal defense mechanisms of the fish (Planas *et al.,* 2006).

Yeasts as Probiotic for Fish

Yeasts are most critical microorganisms, which spread with animals, air and water streams, and can develop in different situations where natural substrates are accessible. Their presence has been noted in fish guts for quite a while in wild, and additionally cultivated animals, however this common event has been by and large considered as coincidental. Modern yeast is ordinarily utilized as a part of aquaculture, either alive to nourish live micro-organisms, or in the wake of preparing, as a food fixing (Stones and Mills, 2004).

Yeasts can stimulate the immune responce in fish. â-glucans are likely the most essential mixes in such manner, yet some other cell-wall segments or dissolvable variables may also assume a part. Both cell and humeral responses have been evoked by dietary yeast, contingent upon the test conditions. Different advantages might be normal for the host, particularly the intestinal colonization of early nourishing fry with yeast, which may have some impact on improvement, e.g. by quickening the development of the digestive system. In older fish, dietary yeast may animate digestion system and development Gatesoupe (2007).

The impacts of two yeasts on European sea bass fries feed compound diets. Debaryomyces hansenii HF1 enhanced survival, and vertebral compliance of the fries, perhaps because of the watched speeding up of the development of the digestive system. These impacts were not saw with *S. cerevisiae* X2180, and the larvae developed better when they were encouraged a control diet, likely because of a lacking method for presentation of the yeasts after food preparing, which crumbled the physical properties of the pellets (Tovar *et al.*, 2002).

Dietary spermine additionally actuated intestinal development in European sea bass larvae (Péres *et al.*, 1997). Therefore, polyamine secretion was a conceivable mediator for the impact of the yeast on rainbow trout fries (Waché *et al.*, 2006). *D. hansenii* HF1 delivered a great deal more spermidine than *S. cerevisiae* X2180, and that may likewise represent the impacts present in European sea bass (Tovar *et al.*, 2002).

Yeasts are especially intriguing in light of the fact that they give β-glucans and nucleotides that stimulate the immune system of fish (Sahoo and Mukherjee, 2001). The yeast *Debaryomyces hansenii* was disconnected from the gut of rainbow trout raised in new water. Not just is it a polyamine-creating yeast fit for holding fast to fish intestinal mucous, yet it additionally constitutes a standout amongst the most essential types of yeast (Tovar *et al.*, 2002). An expanded of the survival and digestive enzyme activity in *Dicentrarchus labrax* larvae fed diet containing *D. hansenii* (Tovar *et al.*, 2004).

The utilization of commercial baker's yeast, *Saccharomyces cerevisiae* as a development and safety promoter for Nile tilapia, *Oreochromis niloticus* (L.). The development advancing impacts of baker's yeast were seen with fish and the ideal development, encourage use, and protein turn-over were gotten with 1.0–5.0 g yeast/kg diet. Notwithstanding, the most minimal fish mortality and bacterial include were acquired fish sustained 5.0 g yeast/kg. These outcomes show that baker's yeast supplement is promising as a different option for anti-microbials for disease counteractive action in tilapia aquaculture (Abdel-Tawab *et al.*, 2008).

Baker's yeast, *Saccharomyces cerevisiae,* is utilized for the baker's industry that contains different immunostimulating compounds, for example, β-glucans, nuclic acids and in addition, mannan oligosaccharides, and it has the capacity to advance immune response (Ortuño *et al.*, 2002) and development (Li and Gatlin, 2004) of different fish species. Be that as it may, the organization of yeast has been perceived to have essential impacts as immunostimulant (Osman *et al.*, 2010).

4. Immunostimulants for Fish

The term immunostimulant covers an extensive variety of substances that improve the immune system example acknowledgment proteins/receptors and TLRs and upgrade general defence to different diseases. Immunostimulatns might be bacterial or plant substances and also some synthetic compounds (Robertsen, 1999).

Immunostimulants a progression of auxiliary particles from different sources e.g. microbes, yeast, fungi and lichens alone or together with synthetic products (e.g. oligonucleotides) is right now utilized as immunostimulants.

An expansive group of compound on this item retire is the beta-glucans (Skov *et al.*, 2012).

The immunostimulants have pathogen related molecular patterns (PAMPS) which can animate distinctive pathogen acknowledgment receptors (PRRs) in host fishes and in this manner activate immune responses (Chettri *et al.*, 2011). These involve among others toll-like receptors which accordingly can start course responses which may restrain or decrease diseases infections. Results from controlled research facility (Jaafar *et al.*, 2011) or field thinks about (Xueqin *et al.*, 2012) have shown that invulnerable components are enacted by these food added substances. Lamentably the impact of these food added substances on parasite infection levels, for example, intensities of the skin parasitizing ciliate I. multifiliis, is constrained. Correspondingly, immunostimulant encouraging does not bring about an unmistakable diminishment of L. salmonae disease in salmonids yet simply prompts a more favorable course of infection (Guselle *et al.*, 2010).

One of the most used substances in immunostimulation experiments in fish are various forms of â-glucans from different sources, normally introduced in the feed but also by intraperitoneal injection or as vaccine adjuvant (Dalmo and Bøgwald, 2008).

The increase of vitamins, carotenoids and herbal remedies for the fish feed have been tried in aquaculture. The impacts have been useful, for instance, decreasing stress reaction, increasing the activity of inalienable parameters and enhancing disease resistance and protection (Yin *et al.*, 2009).

Spirulina (*S. Platensis*) as Immunostimulant

Spirulina *S. platensis* was as characterized a blue green micro algae that has been utilized since old times as a wellspring of nourishment as a result of its high healthful worth (Dillon *et al.*, 1995). Spirulina (S. platensis) is a blue-green filamentous algae that develops in carbonate-rich lakes in Torrid Zones. Spirulina is a crisp water microalga of the class Cyanophyceae, is a decent wellspring of protein and vitality. It can somewhat supplant fish feast protein in fish nourishes and can be administrated to deliver key amino acids, vitamins, regular β-carotene, and antibacterial substances of good quality and quanitiy (Harel *et al.*, 2002).

The cyanobacterium *S. platensis* is by and large generally concentrated on, for nourishing reasons as well as for its restorative properties; along these lines, a few studies have demonstrated that Spirulina or its concentrates could avert or repress tumor in animals and the works have shown that this species has immuno-advancing impacts (Subhashini *et al.*, 2004).

Spirulina is a freshwater microalga. A few botanists have characterized Spirulina as a cyanobacterium. S. platensis is utilized broadly as a part of dietary creation, because of its potential antiviral, cancer prevention agent, hepatopreserver, antiallergenic and immunomodulator activities (Khan *et al.*, 2005).

The immunostimulatory impacts of the dietary spirulina (S. Platensis) was tested on tilapia, (Oreochromis niloticus); After the fish were nourished with Spirulina and the parameters of non-specific immune responce, including serum bacterial action, phagocytosis and lysozyme action were performed following 4 weeks. The survival was also dictated by bacterial test and observing particular neutralizer levels (Micro-agglutination), the outcomes demonstrated that Spirulina improved reactions of bactericidal, phagocytic action and lysozyme action (Khalil *et al.*, 2007).

Cyanobacteria (blue green growth) are photosynthetic prokaryotes utilized as nourishment added substance. They have additionally been perceived as a rich source of vitamins and proteins and all things considered are found in wellbeing sustenance stores world wide (Singh *et al.*, 2005).

Ascorbic Acid (Vitamin C) as Immunostimulant

It was clear that 19.5 mg ascorbic acid (AA) kg^{-1} was adequate to prevent insufficiency signs and enhance survival of golden shiner in aquaria, while alternative complement activity and imperviousness to warmth stress were expanded by increasing dietary vitamin C levels. Subsequently, the dietary prerequisite for AA differs with metabolic capacity in this species (Chen *et al.*, 2003).

Vitamin C (or AA) and vitamin E function as organic cancer prevention agents to ensure cell macromolecules and other cell reinforcement particles from uncontrolled oxidation by free radicals during typical digestion system or under the states of oxidative challenge, for example, disease and anxiety. Because of their potential for communication, dietary necessities for vitamins C and E are regularly viewed as together in Atlantic salmon (Hamre *et al.*, 1997) and rainbow trout (Furones *et al.*, 1992). Fish fed high concentration of dietary AA accumulated high tissue concentration, which may give extra protection against oxidative damage from environmental stress and disease infections (Lim *et al.*, 2001).

Fish had diminished rate and seriousness of vitamin-E-inadequacy signs with expanding dietary AA level, as found in the rate of fish with darkened skin, hematological parameters, alternative complement activity, and camulative mortality taking after introduction to warmth stress. Be that as it may, dietary AA did not forestall vitamin-E-insufficiency signs in golden shiner (Chen *et al.*, 2004).

Vitamin C promote a vital part in immunity and growth of fish (Lin and Shiau, 2005). Fishes can't synthetize ascorbic acid because of the absence of L-gulonolactone oxidase that is in charge of synthesis of vitamin C (Fracalossi *et al.*, 2001). Subsequently, an exogenous source of vitamin C is required in fish diet. Inadequate supply of dietary vitamin C as a rule results in various lack manifestations like spinal distortion, internal haemorrhaging, retarded growth and depressed immunity (Gouillou-Coustans *et al.*, 1998).

Vitamin C has been imagined that to be a standout amongst the most imperative supplements identified with fish safety (Ai *et al.*, 2004). Various past written works demonstrated the valuable impacts of high vitamin C consumption on immunological parameters, for example, lysozyme, complement ac-tivities, phagocytic activity, respiratory burst and characteristic cytoxic action (Anbarasu and Chandran, 2001), upgraded resistance to stress and diseases (Montero *et al.*, 1999).

Vitamine C has additionally been appeared to be a critical supplement relating with fish immunty. The valuable impacts of vitamin C on different immunological parameters have been accounted for. Dietary AA upgraded serum bactericidal activity, phagocytic action, counter acting agent levels, serum complement activity and lysozyme action (Lin and Shiau, 2005).

Ai *et al.*, (2004) reported that the activities of lysozyme and alternative complement pathway in serum advanced with the expansion of dietary vit C. At the point when dietary ascorbic acid achieved 489.0 mg kg-1, these parameters were significantly increased than those of every single other treatment. Besides, Ren *et al.*, (2005) reported that vitamin C is required by Japanese eel and could upgrade serum bactericidal activity when nourished an eating routine containing crystalline vitamin C. Be that as it may, no data is accessible on the impact of AA subsidiaries as a vitamin C source. What's more, Ren *et al.*, (2007) reported that fish nourished eating regimens containing 762 mg AA/kg demonstrated essentially higher lysozyme action of mucous and serum, and bactericidal activity of mucous than the fish sustained the eating regimen containing 32 mg AA/kg. Survival reaction of the exploratory fish fed on supra dietary levels of vitamins was fundamentally superior to that of the control set (Azad *et al.*, 2007).

Vaccination Against Parasites of Fish

There is extensive variety of parasites in both wild and cultured fish stocks. Although parasitic diseases, for example, amoebic gill infection, white spot disease, whirling disease, proliferative kidney disease (PKD) and Salmon lice infestation make several problems in fish cultivating (Woo *et al.*, 2002), no parasite vaccines are commercially accessible (Sommerset *et al.*, 2005). When all is said in done, fish have both humoral and cell-intervened immune response against numerous parasites and there are numerous reports on immunity/expanded resistance among fish surviving common parasitic infection (Ellis, 1999). Cultivation of parasites for potential killed or live vaccin is much more costly than virus cultivation (Sommerset *et al.*, 2005), as a host populace instead of cell cultures are normally required. Notwithstanding the high costs, the utilization of normal hosts for development of parasite would make significant problem regarding safety documentation. Along these lines, recognizable proof and production of defensive antigens is presumably the most attainable procedure towards commercial parasite vaccines, at least for low cost vaccines (Plant and LaPatra, 2011; Muktar *et al.*, 2016).

High efficacies of anti-viral and anti-bacterial vaccines have also been demonstrated and efforts should therefore be made in order to develop antiparasitic vaccines (Lorenzen *et al.*, 2000).

Because of the restricted size of numerous protozoan parasites the cell and humoral immunological arm in fish should have the essential capacity to create defensive safety against in any event some of these pathogens. Experimental vaccines against C. salmositica (Woo, 2012), *L. salmonae* (Rodríguez-Tovar *et al.*, 2006) and I. multifiliis (the freshwater proportional to *C. irritans*) (Alishahi and Buchmann, 2006) have been observed to be in part viable which is promising for further accomplishments. *Cryptocaryon irritans* is known not antibody production in affected fish which is an important premise for further vaccine improvement (Misumi *et al.*, 2011).

Experimental studies have also demonstrated significant activation of cellular and humoral immune factors in fish exposed to several other protozoans such as *A. ocellatum* (Noga, 2012) and *I. necator* (Chettri *et al.*, 2012).

Subsequently, it is likely that creation of antibodies against A. ocellatum, *S. salmonicida, I. necator* and *L. salmonae* might be reasonable objectives for reestablished research endeavors. Nonetheless, it can't be rejected that the parasites themselves or parasite determined molecules redirect the reaction of the host towards a less viable invulnerable pathway and this plausibility should be considered when planning vaccines and their adjuvants. The late advancement of reagents and instruments for researching immune systems in fish can make a premise for commercial vaccines empowering immune response in fish has which can give protection (Jørgensen and Buchmann, 2011).

The vaccine viability in fish is by and large settled by challenge experiments. In mammals specific antibody responce is a decent marker of antibody adequacy however in fish this is questionable. Some fish species will deliver protective antibody response to vaccination (Pakingking *et al.*, 2009).

The creation of commercial anti-parasite vaccine is essentially postponed because of presentation of complex structure and life cycle of the parasites and the challenges in cultivating the parasite in adequate, amount for vaccine production. Distinguishing proof of the parasite antigen that will induce defensive safety is also required. This is essential while considering recombinant protein creation, which is an appealing methodology in anti-parasite vaccine production (Chettri *et al.*, 2009).

The development of acquired immunity to various parasites for fish is now known to exist. Therefore, vaccination should be developed urgently to protect fish against parasitic diseases. (Gillund *et al.*, 2008 and Pakingking *et al.*, 2009).

Vaccination against *Cryptobia salmositica*

The incubation facility raised Atlantic salmon, Salmo salar L., were inoculated intraperitoneally (IP) with a live lessened *Cryptobia salmositica* vaccine and 4 weeks later were challenged with the parasite. Unvaccinated, tainted salmon had high parasitaemias and were anemic. Fish given a high dose (100,000 parasites/fish[1]) had higher parasitaemias than fish given the lower dosage. vaccinated fish had low parasitaemias and a gentle pallor and recouped rapidly after test Ardelli and Woo (2002). Moreover, Chin and Woo (2004) reported that Cryptobia salmositica is viewed as a deadly pathogen of salmon kept under semi-characteristic and concentrated environment. The live *C. salmositica* vaccine incited a trademark parasitemia profile and humeral reaction in Atlantic salmon. However, cryptobia-vulnerable Salvelinus fontinalis inoculated with a live *Cryptobia salmositica* vaccine were ensured against C. Salmositica and they were still ensured for a long time after their intial challenge (Ardelli and Woo, 2006).

The adequacy of attenuated live Cryptobia salmositica vaccine, the impacts of sustenance hardship on the invulnerable reaction and its term in rainbow trout (Oncorhynchus mykiss) inoculated with a live C. salmositica vaccine or with a murdered Aeromonas salmonicida vaccine. The study demonstrated that the attenuated strain of C. salmositica did not bring about animea and disease, and the fish were avoided from clinical disease when they were challenged with virulent parasites (Fard and Woo, 2008). Salmonid cryptobiosis is brought on by the haemoflagellate, Cryptobia salmositica. The clinical indications of the sickness in salmon (Oncorhynchus spp.) incorporate exophthalmia, general edema, and abdominal distension with ascites, anemia, and anorexia. A single dosage of the attenuated vaccine secures 100% of salmonids (juvenils and grown-ups) for no less than 24 months (Woo, 2012).

Vaccination against Ichthyophthiriasis

Channel catfish vaccinated with live theronts or sonicated trophonts acquired protection against Ich. The immunized fish indicated larger amounts of anti-Ich antibodies in the skin and serum than non-vaccinated fish. Parasite infection and mortality did not happen in fish vaccinated with live theronts. Fish vaccinated with sonicated trophonts had a low infection and mortality compared with non-vaccinated fish (Xu *et al.*, 2004). Delivered commercial Ich vaccine was produced and exhibited that the immunization against Ich incited defensive safety and could give a one of a kind answer for keep this parasitic disease (Xu, 2010).

Vaccination against *Discocotyle sagittata* (Monogenea)

When rainbow trout *Oncorhynchus mykiss* were injected intraperitoneally with 2 different *Discocotyle sagittata* extracts dissolved in PBS and subsequently exposed to infection. Immunization resulted in significantly reduced worm intensities in vaccinated fish (Godoy, 2003).

Vaccination against *Loma salmonae*

The earlier presentation of rainbow trout *Oncorhynchus mykiss* juveniles to the low-destructiveness variation of Loma salmonae, spores brought about a xenoma force in the gill fibers fourteen times lower than that saw in the control fish. Lessening in quantities of xenomas proposes that utilization of the low-destructiveness variations should be further considered as a technique to protect fish (Sanchez *et al.*, 2001). The powerful vaccine spore dosage of a low-destructiveness strain of Loma salmonae to constrain microsporidial gill disease in trout, they found that fish accepting 10^3 to 10^5 executed spores had the great protection against exploratory infection, with 85% less xenomas in gills (Speare *et al.*, 2007).

Biological Control of Fish Parasites (Life Against Life)

Biological control: "Any activity of one animal categories that decreases the unfavorable impact of another. It is the more security method for control of fish parasites, utilized for the most part as a part of control of crustacean parasites of fish. Parasites, especially crustacean are considered as an essential restricting element in the improvement of heightened fish culture. Under overloading conditions, parasite populaces rapidly develop and may bring about heavy mortality in the the stocked fish particularly in high water temperature where their life cycles turn out to be quicker (Kearn, 2002).

The control of Argulus is by presentation of mosquito fish (Gambosia) or healthy Angelfish, into mud ponds infested with Argulus. Gambosia has a distinct depressant impact on the parasitic populace as they feast upon larvae, particularly in ornamental fish lakes. Presentation of freshwater shrimp (Macrobrachium species), feeds on larvae and going about as a control predator for Argulus (Eissa, 2002).

Some monogeneans joined to the surface of a fish host may also be effectively perceptible by cleaner fish which can ingest significant quantities of monogeneans. Moreover, Kearn (2002) watched ingures in large monogeneans on beams most likely created by littler cleaner fish (Cowell *et al.*, 1993), another capsalid monogenean, Benedenia lolo, parasitising *Hemigymnus melapterus* was subjected to predation by the cleaner fish *Labroides dimidiatus*. Along these lines future control measures may include the utilization of cleaner fish Grutter *et al.*, (2002).

There have been a few attemps to remove parasites by utilizing topical cleaner fish. Adolescent blue head wrasse, neon goby and cleaning goby could remove ectoparasitic monogeneans, e.g., Neobenedenia melleni, and from saltwater, refined Florida red tilapia and the cleaners' guts were found to contain three types of monogenean parasites. A comparative technique was connected to expel Lernaea from infected Arowana fish (Scleropages sp.), a standout amongst the most important aquarium fish, by utilizing Tilapia nilotica fry of 3-5-cm long as cleaner fish. The outcomes demonstrated that Tilapia nilotica were successful cleaner fish for Lernaea infestation which is called "topical cleaners fish" (Cowell *et al.*, 1993).

Cleaning symbioses are interspecific relationship in which one or more member "cleaner" organism remove ectoparasites as well as tissue from the collection of another "host" organism. that frequently requests the communication by receiving stereotypic stances within the sight of the clenear. Albeit reported for some physical life forms (Dickman, 1992), such cooperations are best archived among marine reef living beings, especially fish clients customers being cleaned by littler fishes, most prominently indo-Pacific cleaner wrasses and Caribbean cleaning gobies (Côte', 2000). Cleaner fish remove ectoparasites (Arnal and Côte', 2000), and additionally harmed tissue. However, they also expel and may very much want host mucous (Grutter and Bshary, 2003). Along these lines, whether this action really controls ectoparasite loads and results in a net advantage to has been the source of some contention (Morand, 2005).

Around 40 types of shrimps and other decapod crustaceans are also called cleaners of reef-related fishes (Chapuis and Bshary, 2009). Be that as it may, most records have been founded on perceptions of "cleaners" crawling on or picking at the outside surface of fishes, with numerous records construct

Fig. 7.1: Showing Moray eel Infested with Ectoparasitic Copepods (arrows) that has Entered a Cleaner Shrimp Cleaning Station. Note the Red Shrimp on the Moray eel 's skin (Noga, 2010)

exclusively in light of aquarium perceptions and/or seeming just in the mainstream aquarium writing. Just several studies have provided direct proof that any apparent cleaner shrimp species successfully expels parasites from fishes (Ostlund-Nilsson *et al.*, 2005).

In the Caribbean and tropical western Atlantic, the Pederson shrimp, Periclimenes pedersoni and spotted shrimp, P. yucatanicus (Palaemoni-dae), are two of the most widely recognized shrimps that are accounted for as a cleaner (DeLoach and Humann, 1999) (Fig. 7.7), and are regularly found in relationship with anemones (Williams and Williams, 2000). P. pedersoni has been appeared to eat parasitic isopods in capitivity (Bunkley-Williams and Williams, 1998), making it the main Caribbean species for which expulsion of parasites from hosts has been archived. Be that as it may, the scope of ectoparasites it devours and the potential for more term effects on ectoparasites is obscure. The united coral shrimp Stenopus hispidus (Stenopodidae) has also been for quite some time reported as a "cleaner shrimp" and is regular all through the Caribbean and tropical western Atlantic (McCammon *et al.*, 2010).

Wrasse (Teleostei; Labridae) were initially used as cleaner-fish as a part of Norway in 1987, where goldsinny (Ctenolabrus rupestris (L.) rockcook (Centrolabrus exoletus (L.) and female cuckoo wrasse (Labrus mixtus L.) effectively expelled ocean lice from salmon in experimental situation (Bjordal, 1988) (Fig. 7.8) From that point forward, wrasse have been utilized effectively as lice control specialists on commercial salmon in Norway (Bjordal, 1992) and in Shetland, Scotland and Ireland (Treasurer, 1994). The above three types of wrasse and the ballan wrasse (Labrus bergylta Ascanius) and corkwing (Crenilabrus melops L.) are found in Irish waters. These fish happen in beach

Fig. 7.2: Showing Blue Streak Cleaner Wrasse Eat Parasites that have Attached Themselves to the Client Fish (Noga, 2010)

front waters in ranges with rock and algal spread (Quignard and Pras, 1986). Goldsinny, corkwing and rockcook have all been observed to be successful cleaners, bringing about the improvement of another fishery to supply salmon farms (Deady *et al.*, 1993).

Presentation of black carp (Mylopharyngodon piseus) to Egypt which is molluscivorus fish of the cyprinidae family that normally happens in Chinese water. black carp has been brought into Egypt 1993 by the community oriented exploration program (CRSP) and was kept under isolate in lakes at the central Lab for Aquaculture Research (CLAR), Abbasa, Sharkia Egypt for bioconversion, sustenance and encouraging propensity considers (Soliman, 1997). Black carp has more profitable part against colonization of snails in repositories and aquaculture (Slootweg *et al.*, 1994). So it assumes a preventive part against encysted metacercaria in fish and shistosomiasis in human being (Awad, 2007).

Medicinal Plants (Herbal Medicine)

Medicinal plants and herbs contain substances known not and old civic establishments for their recuperating and curing properties, even old Egyptians were as similarly acquainted with drug store as they were with solution, and they were additionally acquainted with medication readiness from plants and herbs. Therapeutic plants are imperative components for customary medication, the thought that specific plants had recuperating potential was known much sooner than individual found the presence of pathogens during the most recent years traditional medicine has not been restricted to particular society (Ijah and Oyebanji, 2003).

There have been expanded activities into the usage of conventional medications to control bacterial and parasitic contaminations in human and animal medicine (Ekanem *et al.*, 2004a) also the utilization of therapeutic plants removes for treatment of parasitic diseases in fish has been accounted for in Egypt (Mesalhy *et al.*, 2008) Restorative plants utilized as a part of aquaculture for treatment fish parasite and utilized as immunostimulants upgrading the immune response of fish.

Medicinal Plants used for Treatment Fish Parasitic Infection

Medicinal Plants as Anti-protozoal Parasites of Fish

Yao *et al.*, (2010) specified that the ciliate Ichthyophthirius multifiliis is a standout amongst the most pathogenic parasites of fish. They concentrated on the impacts of crude extracts, fractions, and compounds from the leaves of Macleaya cordata against I. multifiliis under in vitro conditions by bioactivity-guided isolatation method. In vitro antiparasitic adequacy experiments showed that sanguinarine was 100% viable against *I. multifiliis*. The restorative plants are right now utilized additionally as a part of commercial aquaculture as development advancing substances, supplements and antimicrobial specialists for anticipation and control of fish disease. It is additionally created as an ecologically stable supplement then again to utilization of synthetic for generation of organic fish (Galina *et al.*, 2009).

There is a fast growing interest in screening antiparasitic substances from plants to replace antiparasitic and disinfectant alternatives. Two such plants are garlic (*Allium sativum*) and *Artemisia vulgarism*. Garlic is one of the edible plants that had a strong interest to scientists and recognized as an important medicinal plant which has a wide spectrum of actions; not only antibacterial and antiprotozoal, but also has beneficial effects on the immune systems (Harris *et al.*, 2001).

The crude and crushed garlic (Allium sativum) at 200 mg/l could treat Trichodinaiasis in eels Madsen *et al.*, (2000b). Moreover, of crude concentrate of garlic (Allium sativum) has been accounted for to murder trichodinids (Madsen *et al.*, 2000a).

The crude extract from two tropical therapeutic plants, Mucuna pruriens (Fabaceae) and Carica papaya (Caricaceae), were utilized for treatment of the ciliate Ichthyophthirius multifiliis which is the most pathogenic parasites of fish kept up in imprisonment. The result was a 90% reduction in quantities of *I. multifiliis* on fish after treatment in baths of each plant remove at 200 mg L^{-1} compared to untreated controls (Buchmann *et al.*, 2003). In addition, Ekanem *et al.*, (2004b) specified that medicinal plants are vital components of traditional medicine in essentially all cultures and item guarantee a less expensive hotspot for therapeutics, more noteworthy precision than chemotherapeutic agents and a suitable answer for all problems. The control of Trichodinaiasis and Aeromonus hydrophila in ponds of supplied tilapia with Garlic (Allium sativum) and Sheh el-baathran as restorative plants to treat fish. The results demonstrated that rough concentrates of either garlic and Sheh El-baathran significantly eliminated of Trichodina infections (Aboud, 2010).

Medicinal plants as Anthelminthic (monogeneans)

Monogenean parasites are flatworms which inhabit skin, gills and inevitably eyes of fish. Monogeneans from the genus Dactylogyrus, Gyrodactylus and Neobenedenia are wide spread parasites influencing a large number of cultured fish (Deveney *et al.*, 2001; Woo *et al.*, 2002).

In result, a few studies have been performed as of late to evaluate the anthelminthic action of plant extracts keeping in mind the end goal to treat monogenean infections. Plant isolates like methanolic extract of bupleurum root (Radix bupleuri chinensis), aqueous and methanolic extract of cinnamon (Cinnamomum cassia), methanolic extract of Chinese flavor shrub (Lindera agreggata) and methanolic and ethyl acetic acid derivation extract of brilliant larch (Pseudolarix kaempferi) have appeared to possess100% in vivo viability against monogenean Dactylogyrus intermedius when added to water of infected goldfish *Carassius auratus* (Wu *et al.*, 2011; Ji *et al.*, 2012). The impact of several extracts of Indian sandalwood (Santalum album) against D. intermedius and Gyrodactylus elegans on goldfish and found that chloroform extract was the best and most secure for the fishes. They also watched that bath treatment with long term and numerous organizations could take out an extraordinary extent of monogenean diseases (Tu *et al.*, 2013).

Looking for a natural antiparasitic, in vivo anthelmintic activity of petroleum ether, chloroform, ethyl acetic acid derivation, methanol, and aqueous extracts of Angelica pubescens roots (Radix angelicae pubescentis), Brucea javanica organic products (Fructus bruceae), Spatholobus suberectus stems (Caulis spatholobi), Aesculus chinensis Bge. Seeds (Semen aesculi), and Pharbitis purpurea (L.) Voigt seeds (Semen pharbitidis) were tried against Dactylogyrus intermedius (Monogenea) in goldfish *Carassius auratus*. The methanolic and aqueous extracts of S. aesculi displayed potential results and can be misused as a favored natural antiparasitic for the control of *D. Intermedius* (Liu *et al.*, 2010).

Hutson *et al.*, (2012) evaluated the impact of aqueous extract from different algae on the lifecycle of the parasite Neobenedenia sp. They watched that disease success on *Lates calcarifer* was lower within the sight of Asparagopsis taxiformis (51%) and Ulva sp. (54%) removes in seawater compared to the control (71%). Besides, A. taxiformis remove hindered embryonic development of Neobenedenia sp. what's more, decreased hatching success to 3% contrasted and 99% for the seawater control. Barramundi (L. calcarifer) was fed with two improved garlic eats less carbs and watched that when fish were tested with Neobenedenia sp. treated group during long-term supplementation (30 days) showed 70% decreased infection achievement compared to control and short-term supplementation (10 days) Militz *et al.*, (2013a, b).

Medicinal Plants as Immunostimulants for Fish

The immune system is arranged into innate (non-specific) and adaptive (specific) immune system. The innate system is the main line of barrier against attacking pathogens and their significant parts are macrophages, monocytes, granulocytes, and humoral components, including lysozymes or complement system. An immunostimulant is a substance that improves the defence systems or immune responce (both specific and nonspecific), along these lines rendering fish more resistant to disease and external aggressions (Anderson, 1992; Chakraborty and Hancz, 2011).

An increasing interset for the utilization of plant extracts as fish immunostimulants has emerged in the most recent decade (Galina *et al.*, 2009; Vaseeharan and Thaya, 2013). A few studies have observed the immunological parameters after intraperitoneal injection or orally adminstrated plant removes on unmistakable fish species and they found that treated fish indicated increased lysozyme movement, phagocytic activity, complement activity, increased respiratory burst activity and expanded plasma protein (globulin and albumine) (Dügenci *et al.,*, 2003; Wu *et al.*, 2010; Yuan *et al.*, 2007). Lysozymes assume an essential part in the protection of fish by instigating antibacterial action within the sight of a complement (Harikrishnan *et al.*, 2012b).

Phagocytosis is one of the primary middle people of innate immunity to pathogens, while respiratory burst is additionally a significant effector instrument for constraining the development of fish pathogens. increase in plasma protein, albumine and globulin, is viewed as a strong innate responce in fishes. Different studies analyzed the hematological parameters which give some insight of the fish health status and they found that erythrocytes, lymphocytes, monocytes, hemoglobin and hemocrit levels fundamentally increased in fish treated with plant exracts compared to control fish (Divyagnaneswari *et al.*, 2007).

Some immunostimulants couldn't be utilized on account of different drawbacks, for example, high cost, constrained viability upon parentrally adminstration, etc (Dügenci *et al.*, 2003). In aquaculture, chemotherapeutic operators, for example, commercial antibiotcs and disinfectants are generally utilized for disease mangament, in spite of the fact that this is not fitting because of cost viability, ecological risks and the antibiotics resistance created by numerous pathogens (Kruse and Soram 1994).

All plant extracts added to fish diet increased the aggregate protein level in plasma with the exception of 0.1% ginger. The most abnormal amount of plasma proteins was seen in the group fed with 1% ginger extract containing feed (Dugenci *et al.*, 2003). volatile oils, tannins, phenolic compounds, saponins, alkaloids, polysaccharides, and polypeptides were appeared to be powerful alternative for antibiotcs. The screening of plant extracts and natural products for antimicrobial activity has demonstrated that higher plants represent a potential wellspring of new hostile to infective agents (Chakraborty and Hancz, 2011).

Herbals, for example, Cynodon dactylon, Piper longum, Phyllanthus niruri, Tridax procumbens, and Zingiber officinalis were separated with, benzene, butanol, and petroleum ether. The herbal diets significantly enhanced the survival, development, and immune responce in comparison with the control group. The herbal diet eating methodologies enhanced immune parameters, for example, phagocytic activity and albumin–globulin proportion (Sivaram *et al.*, 2004).

Biosecurity in aquaculture (FAO, 2003)

Biosecurity can be defined as 'the measures and methods adopted to secure a disease free environment in all phases of aquaculture practices (i.e. hatcheries, nurseries, growout farms) for improved profitability'. Biosecurity protocols are intended to maintain the "security" of a facility (i.e., prevent entry of, or reduce overall numbers prior to entry) with respect to certain disease causing organisms (parasites, bacteria, viruses and fungi) that may not be present in a particular system.

Important components of biosecurity are:

1. Quarantine
2. Sanitation
3. Disinfection.

Quarantine

Defined as the isolation of an organism or group of organisms to prevent the introduction or spread of infectious disease, is a standard procedure that is extremely important in aquaculture. In practical terms, quarantine is a standard set of procedures that should be observed to prevent the introduction of pathogens or diseases into a population of fish, prawn and shrimp in aquaculture (FAO, 2003).

The quarantine protocols should be strictly used and should follow as many of the following protocols as are practical:

- Testing of a sample of shrimp, prawn and fish before bringing them onto the facility.
- All-in, all-out stocking procedures.
- Isolation or separation from other populations for a period of time (depending upon species, diseases of concern, the system).
- Feeding observation and diet adjustment.
- Sampling and proper treatment.
- Reduction or elimination of infectious pathogens.
- Disease prevention strategies.

Disinfectants

With the rapid increase in aquaculture practices, the need for disinfectants has also increased. Entry and growth of pathogens must be minimized through use of disinfectants in water, on tanks and equipment and on eggs. Disinfectants used in aquaculture are aimed at all types of infectious agents (including bacteria, fungi, viruses and parasites). The disinfectant must come into direct contact with the disease causing organism to kill them by releasing proper amounts of active compounds.

Biosecurity involves following strict management protocols to prevent specific pathogens from entering a system or reducing the numbers. A good understanding of pathogen reservoirs is important.

An effective disinfectant is chosen based on:

Efficacy: Proven efficacy is of major importance against the full range of viral, bacterial and fungal disease causing organisms. Particularly in aquaculture the viruses that cause diseases are extremely persistent and difficult to destroy.

Environmental impact: A good disinfectant must kill pathogenic organisms within a facility but must not harm organisms in the environment when released.

Operator safety: Any products used must be safe for staff employing the product.

Sanitation

Good sanitation procedures reduce the numbers of disease causing organisms present within a given system and prevent or reduce the spread of disease causing organisms from one system to another.

Recommended Sanitation and Disinfection Protocols to prevent or reduce the pathogen load in a system include:

Proper Attention to Food Sources

1. Be careful with live foods, although live or fresh foods can be a good source of nutrients, these may also be a source of pathogens.
2. Ensure proper storage (in a cool, dry location) and usage (fallow manufacturers recommendations/expiration date) of manufactured feeds to prevent loss of nutrients and build up of pathogens or toxins.

Good overall system maintenance and cleanliness to reduce environments that will favor pathogens and parasites:

1. Good husbandry (nutrition, water and soil quality etc).
2. Regular monitoring of excess organic matter and control strategies.
3. Backwash and treatment of filters as needed to reduce organic loading in hatcheries.
4. Washing and disinfection of air and water pumps and lines in hatcheries.
5. flush sediment out of water lines as needed and disinfect them.
6. Maintain proper sanitisation disinfection strategies.
7. Keep nets and other equipment off the floor to control contamination and keep them sterile.
8. Pull dead and moribund culture organisms as soon as possible and dispose of appropriately.
9. Avoid cross contamination of equipment or water from one system to another.

10. Use disinfectants for equipment including nets and footbaths (placed at strategic locations around the facility, e.g., at the entrance and exit of quarantine buildings, hatcheries, farms and other systems).

CONCLUSION

From the present study, it could be concluded that:

1. Aeration, proper management and nutrition should be kept in mind when we manage a parasitic disorders.
2. Probiotics, prebiotics, immunestimulants and vaccines should be used first in the treatment.
3. Traditional control should not be ignored in control of such problems.
4. Use of herbal medicine is a must as it has no side effects in control of parasitic fish diseases.
5. Biosecurity should be used effectively in problems associated with parasites in aquaculture.

REFERENCES

Abdel-Tawwab M.; Azza M. Abdel-Rahman and Nahla E.M. Ismael (2008): Evaluation of Commercial live Bakers Yeast, Saccharomyces Cerevisiae as a Growth and Immunity Promotor for fry Nile tilapia, Oreochromis niloticus Challenged in situ with Aeromonas hydrophila Aquaculture Aquat. Org. 46, 79–82.

Arnal, C. and Co^te,′ I.M. (2000): Diet of Broadstripe Cleaning Gobies on a Barbadian reef. J Fish Biol 57:1075–1082.

Azad, I.S.; Syama Dayal, J.; Poornima, M. and Ali, S.A. (2007): Supra Dietary Levels of Vitamins C and E Enhance Antibody Production and Immune Memory in Juvenile Milkfish, Chanos Chanos (Forsskal) to Formalin-killed Vibrio Vulnificus Fish & Shellfish Immunology 23, 154-163.

Ardelli, B. F. and Woo, P. T. K. (2002): Experimental Cryptobia Salmositica (Kinetoplastida) Infections in Atlantic Salmon, Salmo Salar L.: cell-mediated and Humoral Immune Responses against the Pathogenic and Vaccine Strains of the Parasite Journal of Fish Diseases 25, 5, pp. 265-274.

Ardelli, B.F. and Woo, P.T.K. (2006): Immunocompetent Cells and their Mediators in Finfish. In: Fish Diseases and Disorders, Volume 1: Protozoan and Metazoan Infections, 2nd edition (ed. P.T.K. Woo), CABI Publishing, Oxfordshire, U.K. pp. 699-721.

Alishahi, M. and Buchmann, K. (2006): Temperature-dependent Protection against *Ichthyophthirius multifiliis* following Immunisation of Rainbow trout using live Theronts. Diseases of Aquatic Organisms 72, 269–273.

Aboud, O.A.E (2010): Application of some Egyptian Medicinal Plants to Eliminate Trichodina sp. and Aeromonas Hydrophila in Tilapia (Oreochromis niloticus) Researcher 2(10):12-16.

Ai, Q.; Mai, K.; Zhang, C.; Xu, W.; Duan, Q.; Tan, B. and Liufu, Z. (2004): Effects of Dietary Vitamin C on Growth and Immune Response of Japanese Seabass, Lateolabrax Japonicus. Aquaculture 242:489–500l.

Anderson, D.P., (1992): Immunostimulants, Adjuvants, and Vaccine Carriers Infish: Applications to Aquaculture. Annu. Rev. Fish Dis. 2, 281–307.

Brazenor A.K., Hutson K.S. (2015): Effects of Temperature and Salinity on the Life Cycle of Neobenedenia sp. (Monogenea: Capsalidae) Infecting Farmed Barramundi (Lates Calcalrifer) Parasitol. Res.33:19-28.

Bagni, M.; Romano, N.; Finoia, M.G.; Abelli, L.; Scapigliati, G.; Tiscar, P.G.; Sarti, M. and Marino, G. (2005): Short- and long-term Effects of a Dietary Yeast [beta]-glucan (Macrogard) and Alginic Acid (Ergosan) Preparation on Immune Response in Sea bass (Dicentrarchus labrax). Fish Shellfish Immunol 18:311–325.

Bricknell, I. and Dalmo, R.A. (2005): The Use of Immunostimulants in Fish Larval Aquaculture. Fish Shellfish Immunol 19:457–472.

Bjordal, A. (1988): Cleaning Symbiosis between Wrasses (Labridae) and Lice Infested Salmon (Safmo s & r) in Mariculture. Int. Con. Explor. Sea, C.M. F: 17,8 pp. 70-81.

Bjordal, A. (1992): Cleaning Symbiosis as an Alternative to Chemical Control of Sea lice Infestation of Atlantic Salmon. In: J.E. Thorpe and F.A. Huntingford (Editors), The Importance of Feeding Behaviour for the Efficient Culture of Salmonid Fishes. World Aquaculture Workshops, no. 4, World Aquaculture Society, pp. 53-60.

Buchmann, K.; Jensen, P.B. and Kruse, K.D. (2003): Effects of Sodium Percarbonate and Garlic Extract on Ichthyophthirius Multifiliis Theronts and Tomocysts: in Vitro Experiments. N Am J Aquacult 65:21–24.

Chakraborty, S.B., Hancz, C., (2011): Application of Phytochemicals as Immunostimulant, Antipathogenic and Antistress agents in Finfish Culture. Rev. Aquac. 3, 103–119.

Chin, A. and Woo, T.K. (2004): Innate cell-mediated Immune Response and Peripheral leukocyte Populations in Atlantic Salmon, Salmo salar L., to a live Cryptobia Salmositica Vaccine Parasiol. Res. 88: 956-962.

Chettri, J. K., Holten-Andersen, L., Raida, M. K., Kania, P. and Buchmann, K. (2011) PAMP induced Expression of Immune Relevant Genes in Head Kidney Leukocytes of Rainbow Trout (Oncorhynchus Mykiss). Developmental and Comparative Immunology 35, 476–482.

Chettri, J. K., Kuhn, J. A., Jaafar, R. M., Kania, P.W., Møller, O. S. and Buchmann, K. (2012). Immune Response of Rainbow Trout Juveniles to the Protozoan Parasite Ichthyobodo Necator: Immunohistochemical and Gene Expression Studies. In Immune Responses in Fish.

Cowell, L.E.; Watanabe, W.O.; Head, W.D.; Grover, J.J. and Shenker, J.M. (1993): Use of Tropical Cleaner Fish to Control the Ectoparasite Neobenedenia Melleni (Monogenea: Capsalidae) on Seawater-cultured Florida red tilapia. Aquaculture 113:189–200.

Chen, R.G.; Lochmann, R.T.; Goodwin, A.; Praveen, K.; Dabrowski, K. and Lee, K.J. (2003): Alternative Complement Activity and Resistance to Heat Stress in Golden Shiners Notemigonus Crysoleucas are increased by Dietary Vitamin C levels in Excess of Requirements for Prevention of Deficiency signs. J. Nutr. 133, 2281–2286.

Co^te,´ I.M. (2000): Evolution and Ecology of Cleaning Symbioses in the Sea. Oceanog Mar Biol Annu Rev 38:311–355.

Chapuis, L. and Bshary, R. (2009): Strategic Adjustment of Service Quality to Client Identity in the Cleaner Shrimp, Periclimenes Longicarpus. Anim Behav 78:455–459.

Dügenci, S.K.; Nazlý Arda and Akýn Candan, (2003): Some Medicinal Plants as Immunostimulant for Fish Journal of Ethnopharmacology 88 (2003) 99–106.

Deveney, M.R., Chisholm, L.A.,Whittington, I.D., (2001). First Published Record of the Pathogenic Monogenean Parasite Neobenedenia Melleni (Capsalidae) from Australia. Dis.

Divyagnaneswari, M., Christybapita, D., Michael, R.D., (2007): Enhancement of Nonspecific Immunity and Disease Resistance in Oreochromis Mossambicus by Solanum Trilobatum Leaf Fractions. Fish Shellfish Immunol. 23, 249–259.

Deady, S.; Varian, S. and Fives, J.M. (1993): The Impact of a New Fishery on Wrasse Populations in a Small bay in the West of Ireland. Int. Con. Explor. Sea, C.M. 1993/G: 31.

Dillon, J.C.; Phuc, A.P. and Dubacq, J.P. (1995): Nutritional Value of the Alga Spirulina. World Review of Nutrition and Dietetics, Vol. 77. Washington: 32 - 46.

Dalmo, R.A. and Bøgwald, J. (2008): β-glucans as Conductors of Immune Symphonies. Fish Shellfish Immunol 25:384–396.

DeLoach, N. and Humann, P. (1999): Reef Fish Behavior, Florida, Caribbean, Bahamas. New World, Jacksonville.

Dickman, C.R. (1992): Commensal and Mutualistic Interactions among Terrestrial Vertebrates. Trends Ecol Evol 7:194–197.

Eissa, I.A.M. (2002): Parasitic Fish Diseases in Egypt. Dar El- Nahda El-Arabia Publishing 32 Abd El-Khalek Tharwat st. Cairo, Egypt.

Ellis, A.E. (1999): Immunity to bacteria in fish. Fish Shellfish Immunol 9:291–308.

Ekanem, A.P.; Obiekezie, A.; Kloas, W. and Knopf, K. (2004a): Effects of Crude Extracts of Mucuna Pruriens (Fabaceae) and Carica Papaya (Caricaceae) against the Protozoan Fish Parasite Ichthyophthirius Multifiliis Parasitol Res. 92: 361-366.

Ekanem, A.P.; Wang, M.; Simon, J.E.; Obiekeziel, A.I. and Morah, F. (2004b): In Vivo and in Vitro Activities of the Seed Extract of Piper Guineense Schum. and thonn. against skin and Gill Monogenean Parasites of Goldfish (Carassius auratus auratus). Phytother Res 18:793– 797.

Fard, S. and Woo, T. K. (2008): Contribution of Food Deprivation to the Immune Response in Rainbow Trout (*Oncorhynchus mykiss*) Vaccinated against *Cryptobia Salmositica* and *Aeromonas salmonicida* Acta Veterinaria Hungarica 56: 197-206.

Fajer-A´vila E. J., Isabel Abdo-de la Parra, Gabriela Aguilar-Zarate, Roberto Contreras-Arce Joel Zaldivar-Ramirez, Miguel Betancourt-Lozano (2003): Toxicity of Formalin to Bullseye Puffer Fish (*Sphoeroides annulatus Jenyns,* 1843) and its Effectiveness to Control Ectoparasites Aquaculture 223, 41–50.

Fracalossi, D.M.; Allen, M.E.; Yuyama, L.K. and Oftedal, O.T. (2001): Ascorbic Acid Biosynthesis in Amazonian Fishes. Aquaculture 192, 321–332.

Furones, M.D.; Alderman, D.J.; Bucke, D.; Fletcher, T.C.; Knox, D. and White, A. (1992): Dietary vitamin E and the Response of Rainbow Trout, Oncorhynchus mykiss (Walbaum), to Infection with Yersinia ruckeri. J. Fish Biol. 41, 1037–1041.

Fuller, R. (1989): Probiotics in Man and Animals. J Appl Bacteriol 66:365–378.

Gatesoupe, F.J. (1999): The Use of Probiotics in Aquaculture. Aquaculture 180,147–165. Gatlin, D.M., 2002. Nutrition and Fish Health. In: Halver, J.E., Hardy, R.W. (Eds.), Fish Nutrition. Academic Press, San Diego CA, USA, pp. 671–702.

Gatesoupe, F.J. (2007): Live Yeasts in the Gut: Natural Occurrence, Dietary Introduction, and their Effects on Fish Health and Development. Aquaculture 267:20–30.

Gillund, F.; Dalmo, R.; Tonheim, T.C.; Seternes, T.and Myhr, A.I. (2008): DNA Vaccination in Aquaculture Expert Judgments of Impacts on Environment and Fish Health. Aquaculture 284:25–34.

Godoy, M.; Jens Sigh Kurt Buchmann, Richard C. Tinsley, (2003): Immunization of Rainbow trout *Oncorhynchus mykiss* against *Discocotyle sagittata* (Monogenea) Disease of Aquatic Organsims 55 (1) 23-30.

Grutter, A.S.; Deveney, M.R.; Whittington, I.D. and Lester, R.J.G. (2002): The Effect of the Cleaner Fish Labroides Dimidiatus on the Capsalid Monogenean Benedenia lolo Parasite of the Labrid Fish Hemigymnus Melapterus. J Fish Biol 61:1098–1108.

Grutter, A.S. and Bshary, R. (2003): Cleaner Wrasse Prefer Client Mucus: Support for Partner Control Mechanisms in Cleaning Interactions. Proc R Soc Lond B 270:242–244.

Gouillou-Coustans, M.F.; Bergot, P. and Kaushik, S.J. (1998): Dietary Ascorbic Acid needs of Common Carp (Cyprinus Carpio) Larvae. Aquaculture 161, 453–461.

Guselle, N. J., Speare, D. J. and Markham, R. J. F. (2010). Efficacy of Intraperitoneally and Orally Administered ProVale, a yeast beta-(1,3)/(1,6)- D-glucan Product, in Inhibiting Xenoma Formation by the Microsporidian Loma Salmonae on Rainbow Trout Gills. North American Journal of Aquaculture 72, 65–72.

Galina, J.G.; Yin, G.L.; Arado, L. and Jeney, Z. (2009): Use of Immunostimulating Herbs in Fish. An Overview of Research. Physiology Biochemist, Published Online:11 March.

Harris P.D., Shinn A.P., Cable J., Bakke T.A. and Bron J.E. (2008): Gyrodactylid Monogeneans on the Web, Trends in Parasitology, 24, 109–11.

Harris, J.C.; Cottrell, S.L.; Plummer, S. and Lloyd, D. (2001): Antimicrobial Properties of Allium Sativum (garlic). Applied Microbiology and Biotechnology, 57, 282–286.

Hamre, K.; Waagbe, R.; Berge, R. and Lie, 0. (1997): Vitamin C and E interact in Juvenile Atlantic Salmon (Salmo salar L.). Free Radic. Biol. Med. 22, 137–149.

Harel, M.; Koven, W.; Lein, I.; Bar, Y.; Beherens, P.; Stubblefield, J.; Zohar, Y. and Place, A. R. (2002): Advanced DHA, EPA and ArA Enrichment Materials for Marine Aquaculture using Single Cell Heterotrophs. Aquaculture 213, 347 - 362.

Hutson, K.S., Mata, L., Paul, N.A., de Nys, R., (2012): Seaweed Extracts as a Natural Control against the Monogenean Ectoparasite, Neobenedenia sp., Infecting Farmed Barramundi (Lates Calcarifer). Int. J. Parasitol. 42, 1135–1141.

Harikrishnan, R., Kim, D.-H., Hong, S.-H., Mariappan, P., Balasundaram, C., Heo, M.-S., (2012b): Non-specific Immune Response and Disease Resistance induced by Siegesbeckia Glabrescens against Vibrio Parahaemolyticus in Epinephelus bruneus. Fish Shellfish Immunol. 33, 359–364.

Irianto, A. and Austin, B. (2002b): Use of Probiotics to Control Furunculosis in Rainbow Trout, Oncorhynchus Mykiss (Walbaum). J Fish Dis. 25:333–342.

Ijah, U.J.J. and Oyebanji, F.O. (2003): Effects of Tannins and Polyphenols of Some Medical Plants on Bacterial agents of Urinary Tract Infections. Glob J Pure Appl Sci 9:193–198.

Jaafar, R. M., Skov, J., Kania, P.W. and Buchmann, K. (2011): Dose Dependent Effects of dietary Immunostimulants on Rainbow Trout Immune Parameters and Susceptibility to the Parasite Ichthyophthirius Multifiliis. Journal of Aquaculture Research and Development S3, S3–001.

Ji, J., Lu, C., Kang, Y., Wang, G.-X., Chen, P. (2012): Screening of 42 Medicinal Plants for in vivo Anthelmintic Activity against Dactylogyrus Intermedius (Monogenea) in Goldfish.

Kesarcodi-Watson, A.; Kaspar, H.; Lategan, M.J. and Gibson, L. (2008): Probiotics in Aquaculture: The Need, Principles and Mechanisms of Action and Screening Processes. Aquaculture 274:1–14.

Kearn,G.C. (2002): Entobdella Soleae-pionter to the Future.Int.J,PARASITOL.,32:367-372.

Khan, Z.; Bhadouria, P. and Bisen, P. S. (2005): Nutritional and Therapeutic Potential of Spirulina. Current Pharmaceutical Biotechnology 6, 373 - 379.

Khalil, R. H.; Saad, T. T. and Mahfouz, N. B. (2007): Immunostimulant Effects of Dietary Spirulina Platensis on Tilapia (Oreochromis niloticus). The Eighth Conference and Exhibition on Food Industries between Production Quality and Competitiveness Overview of Research. Fish Physiol. Biochem. 35, 669–676.

Kruse, H. and Soram, H. (1994): Tromster of Multiple Drug Resistance Plasmids between Bacteria of Diverse Origins in Natural Environments. Appl Environ Microbiol 60 (1):4015-4021.

Lauzon, H.L.; Gudmundsdottir, S.; Steinarsson, A.; Oddgeirsson, M.; Petursdottir, S.K.; Reynisson, E.; Bjornsdottir, R. and Gudmundsdottir, B.K. (2009): Effects of Bacterial Treatment at Early Stages of Atlantic cod (Gadus morhua L.) on Larval Survival and Development. J Appl Microbiol 9999.

Lim, C.; Shoemaker, C.A. and Klesius, P.H. (2001): The Effect of Ascorbic Acid on the Immune Response in Fish. In: Dabrowski, K. (Ed.), Ascorbic Acid in Aquatic Organisms. CRC Press, Boca Raton, pp. 149–166. Lochmann, R.T.

Lin, M.F. and Shiau, S.Y. (2005): Dietary L-ascorbic Acid Affects Growth, Nonspecific Immune Responses and Disease Resistance in Juvenile Grouper, Epinephelus Malabaricus. Aquaculture 244, 215–221.

Li, P. and Gatlin, D.M. (2004): Dietary Brewers Yeast and the Probiotic Grobiotic AE Influence Growth Performance, Immune Response and Resistance of Hybrid Striped bass (Morone Chrysops X M. Saxatilis) to Streptococcus Iniae Infection. Aquaculture 231, 445–456.

Liu You, T.; Fan, W.; Gao-Xue, W.; Jing, H.; Yong. W. and Yong-Hua, W. (2010): In vivo Anthelmintic Activity of Crude Extracts of Radix Angelicae Pubescentis, Fructus Bruceae, Caulis Spatholobi, Semen Aesculi, and Semen Pharbitidis against Dactylogyrus Intermedius (Monogenea) in Goldfish (Carassius auratus) Parasitol Res 106:1233–1239.

Ma, C.W.; Cho, Y.S. and Oh, K.H. (2009): Removal of Pathogenic Bacteria and Nitrogens by Lactobacillus spp. JK-8 and JK-11. Aquaculture 287:266–270.

Madsen, H.C.K.; Buchmann, K. and Mellergaard, S. (2000b): Treatment of Trichodiniasis in eel (*Anguilla Anguilla*) reared in Recirculation Systems in Denmark: Alternatives to Formaldehyde. Aquaculture 186:221–231.

Madsen, H.C.K.; Buchmann, K. and Mellergaard, S. (2000a): Association between Trichodiniasis in eel (Anguilla Anguilla) and Water Quality in Recirculation. Aquacult. 187:275-281.

Mesalhy, S.A.; Nashwa, M.A. and Mohamed, F.M. (2008): Effect of Garlic on the Survival, Growth of *Oreochromis niloticus* 8. International Symposium on Tilapia in Aquaculture. Vol. (1): 277-296.

Muktar Yimer, Shimels Tesfaye and Biruk Tesfaye (2016): Present Status and Future Prospects of Fish Vaccination: A Review Muktar Y, *et al.*, J Veterinar Sci Technol, 7:2 PP1-7.

Misumi, I., Lewis, T. D., Takemura, A. and Leong, J. A. C. (2011). Elicited cross-protection and Specific Antibodies in Mozambique Tilapia (Oreochromis Mossambicus) against two different Immobilization Serotypes of Cryptocaryon Irritans Isolated in Hawai. Fish and Shellfish Immunology 30, 1152–1158.

Militz, Thane A., Southgate, P.C., Carton, A.G., Hutson, K.S., (2013b). DietarySupplementation of Garlic (Allium sativum) to Prevent Monogenean Infection in Aquaculture. Aquaculture 408–409, 95–99.

McCammon, A.; Sikkel, P.C. and Nemeth, D. (2010): Effects of three Caribbean Cleaner Shrimps on Ectoparasitic Monogeneans in a Semi-natural Environment Coral Reefs 29:419–426.

McCraken, V.J. and Gaskins, H.R. (1999): Probiotics and the Immune System. In: Tannock, G.W. (Ed.), Probiotics: A Critical Review. Horizon Scientific Press, Wymondham, UK, pp. 85–112.

Morand, S. (2005): The Extended Manipulation: Role of Parasitism in Cleaning Symbiosis. Behav Proc 68:267–269.

Noga, E.J., (2010): Fish Disease Diagnosis and Treatment. Mosby-yearbook, Inc. Watsworth Publishing Co., USA. 2nd edition.

Ortuño, J.; Cuesta, A.; Rodríguez, A.; Esteban, M.A. and Meseguer, J. (2002): Oral administration of Yeast, Saccharomyces Cerevisiae, Enhances the Cellular Innate Immune Response of Gilthead Seabream (Sparus aurata L.) Vet. Immunol. Immunopathol. 85,41-50.

Osman, H. A. M.; Taghreed, B. Ibrahim; W. E., Soliman and Maather, M. Monier (2010): Influence of Dietary Commercial Beaker's Yeast, Saccharomyces Cerevisae on Growth Performance, Survival and Immunostimulation of Oreochromis Niloticus Challenged with Aeromonas Hydrophila. Nature and Science 8(3):96-103.

O¨stlund-Nilsson, S.; Becker, J.H. and Nilsson, G.E. (2005): Shrimps remove Ectoparasites from Fishes in Temperate Waters. Biol Lett 1:454– 456.

Péres, A.; Cahu, C.L. and Zambonino Infante, J.L. (1997): Dietary Spermine Supplementation induces Intestinal Maturation in Sea Bass (Dicentrarchus labrax) larvae. Fish Physiol. Biochem. 16, 479–485.

Planas, M.; Pérez-Lorenzo, M.; Hjelm, M.; Gram, L.; Uglenes Fiksdal, I.; Bergh, Ø. and Pintado, J. (2006): Probiotic Effect in vivo of Roseobacter Strain 27- 4 against Vibrio (Listonella) Anguillarum Infections in Turbot (Scophthalmus Maximus L.) larvae. Aquaculture 255:323–333.

Pakingking, R.; Norwell Brian, B.; De Jesus-Ayson, E.G. and Reyes, O. (2009): Protective Immunity against viral Nervous Necrosis (VNN) in brown-marbled Grouper (Epinephelus Fuscogutattus) following Vaccination with Inactivated Betanodavirus. Fish Shellfish Immunol.

Plant KP, LaPatra (2011): Advances in Fish Vaccine Delivery. Dev Comp Immunol 35:1256–1262.

Pironet, F.N.; Hones, J.B. (2000): Treatments for Ectoparasites and Diseases in Captive Western Australian dhufish. Aquac. Int. 8, 349–361.

Quignard, J.P. and Pras, A. (1986): Labridae. In: P.J.P. Whitehead, M.-L. Bauchot, J.-C. Hureau, J. Nielsen and E. Tortonese (Editors), Fishes of the North-Eastern Atlantic and the Mediterranean. Vol. II. UNESCO, Paris, pp. 919-942.

Ren, T., Shunsuke Koshio, Manabu Ishikawa Saichiro Yokoyama, Faddy Raffat Micheal, Orhan Uyan, Ha Thanh Tung (2007): Influence of Dietary Vitamin C and Bovine Lactoferrin on Blood Chemistry and Non-specific Immune Responses of Japanese eel, Anguilla japonica Aquaculture 267 31-37.

Ren, T.; Koshio, S.; Teshima, S.; Ishikawa, M.; Alam, M.S.; Arthur, P.J. and Moe, Y.Y. (2005): Optimum dietary level of L-ascorbic acid for Japanese eel, Anguilla Japonica. J. World Aquac. Soc. 36, 437–443.

Robertsen, B. (1999): Modulation of the Non-specific Defence of Fish by Structurally Conserved Microbial Polymers. Fish Shellfish Immunol 9:269–290.

Rodríguez-Tovar, L. E., Becker, J. A., Markham, R. J. and Speare, D. J. (2006): Induction Time for Resistance to Microsporidial Gill Disease caused by Loma Salmonae following Vaccination of Rainbow Trout (Oncorhynchus mykiss) with a Spore Based Vaccine. Fish and Shellfish Immunology 21, 170–175.

Soliman, A.M. (1997): Food and Feeding Habits of Black carp, M.Sc.Thesis, Faculty of Science Zagazig University.

Sanchez, J.G.; Speare, D.J; Markham, R.J.F. and Jones, S.R.M. (2001): Experimental Vaccination of Rainbow Trout Against Loma Salamonae using a live low-virlence Varient of L.salmonae Journal of Fish Biology 59(2) pp.442-448.

Speare, D. J.; Markham, R. J. F. and Guselle, N. J. (2007): Development of an Effective Whole-Spore Vaccine to Protect against Microsporidial Gill Disease in Rainbow Trout (Oncorhynchus mykiss) by Using a Low-Virulence Strain of Loma salmonae Clinical and Vaccine Immunology, 14(12)70-75.

Sommerset I, B. Krossøy, E. Biering and P. Frost (2005): Vaccines for Fish in Aquaculture Expert Rev. Vaccines 4(1), 89–101.

Santoro, M., Mattiucci, S., Work, T., Cimmaruta, R., Nardi, V., Cipriani, P., Bellisario, B. and Nascetti, G. (2013): Parasitic Infection by Larval Helminths in Antarctic Fishes: Pathological changes and impact on the Host Body Condition Index. Diseases of Aquatic Organisms105, 139 – 148.

Sommerville C., (1998): Parasitic Diseases of fi sh, in Black K and Pickering A (eds), The Biology of Farmed Fish, Sheffi eld Biological Sciences, Vol. 1, Sheffi eld Academic Press, Sheffi eld, 146–79.

Sommerville C. (2012): Advances in Non-chemical Methods for Parasite Prevention and Control in Fish Woodhead Publishing Limited, 2012.

Sivaram, V.; Babu, M.M.; Citarasu, T.; Immanuel, G.; Murugadass, S. and Marian, M.P. (2004): Growth and Immune response of Juvenile Greasy Groupers (*Epinephelus tauvina*) fed with Herbal Antibacterial Active Principle Supplemented Diets against *Vibrio harveyi* Infections. Aquaculture 237:9–20.

Sharifuzzaman, S.M. and Austin, B. (2009): Influence of Probiotic Feeding duration on Disease Resistance and Immune Parameters in Rainbow Trout. Fish Shellfish Immunol 27:440–445.

Skov, J., Kania, P.W., Holten-Andersen, L., Fouz, B. and Buchmann, K. (2012): Immunomodulatory Effects of Dietary Beta-1,3- glucan from Euglena Gracilis in Rainbow Trout (Oncorhynchus mykiss) Immersion Vaccinated against Yersinia Ruckeri. Fish and Shellfish Immunology 33, 111–120.

Subhashini, J.; Mahipal, S. V. K.; Reddy, M. C.; Reddy, M. M.; Rachamallu, A. and Reddanna, P. (2004): Molecular mechanisms in C-Phycocyanin induced Apoptosis in Human Chronic Myeloid Leukemia Cell line-K562. Biochemical Pharmacology, 68: 453 - 462.

Singh S., A. Dey, and R. Sivakumar, (2005) "Application of Molecular Methods for Leishmania control" Expert Review of Molecular Diagnostics, 5, no. 2, pp 251-265.

Slootweg, R.; Malek, E.A. and McCllough, F.S. (1994): The Biological Control of Snail Intermediate Hosts of Shistosomiasis by Fish Review in Fish Biology and Fisheries 4: 67-90.

Sahoo, P.K. and Mukherjee, S.C. (2001): Effect of Dietary R-1,3 Glucan on Immune Responses and Disease Resistance of Healthy and Aflatoxin B1-induced Immuno Compromised Rohu (Labeo rohita Hamilton). Fish Shellfish Immunol. 11, 683–695.

Stones, C.S. and Mills, D.V. (2004): The Use of Live Yeast and Yeast Culture Products in Aquaculture. Int. Aqua Feed 7 (5), 28–34.

Timi J.T. and Mackenzie K. (2015): Parasites in Fisheries and Mariculture, Parasitology, 142,1-4.

Tovar, R.; Zambonino, D.; Cahu, J.; Gatesoupe, C.; and Vázquez, F.J. (2004): Influence of Dietary live Yeast on European Sea Bass (Dicentrarchus labrax) larval Development. Aquaculture 234, 415–427.

Tovar, R.; Zambonino, J.; Cahu, C.; Gatesoupe, F.J.; Vázquez, J.R. and Lésel, R. (2002): Effect of live Yeast Incorporation in Compound Diet on Digestive Enzyme Activity in Sea Bass Dicentrarchus Labrax Larvae. Aquaculture 204,113–123.

Trujillo-González Alejandro, Constantin C. Constantinoiu, Richard Rowe, and Kate S. Hutson (2015): Tracking Transparent Monogenean Parasites on Fish from Infection to Maturity Int J Parasitol Parasites Wildl. 4(3): 316–322.

Tu, X., Ling, F., Huang, A., Zhang, Q., Wang, G., (2013): Anthelmintic Efficacy of Santalum Album (Santalaceae) against Monogenean Infections in Goldfish. Parasitol. Res. 112,

Vaseeharan, B., Thaya, R., (2013): Medicinal Plant Derivatives as Immunostimulants: An Alternative to Chemotherapeutics and Antibiotics in Aquaculture. Aquac. Int.

Woo, Burno DW, Lim L (2002): Diseases and Disorders of Fin Fish in Cage Culture. CABI publishing, Walling Ford, Oxon Ox 108DE, UK.

Woo, P. T. K. (2012): Cryptobia (Trypanoplasma) Salmositica. In Fish Parasites – Pathobiology and Protection (ed. Woo, P. T. K. and Buchmann, K.), pp. 30–54. CAB International, Wallingford, UK.

Williams, E.H. and Williams L.B. (2000): Experimental Refutation of the Ease of Associate change by the Spotted Cleaner Shrimp Periclimenes yucatanicus (Decapoda Paelomonidae), New False Coral Associates of the Pederson Cleaner Shrimp, P. Pedersoni, and General Abundance Associations for both shrimps. Crustaceana 73:503–511.

Waché, Y.; Auffray, F.; Gatesoupe, F.J.; Zambonino, J.; Gayet, V.; Labbé, L. and Quentel, C. (2006): Cross Effects of the Strain of Dietary Saccharomyces Cerevisiae and Rearing Conditions on the Onset of Intestinal Microbiota and Digestive Enzymes in Rainbow Trout, Onchorhynchus Mykiss, fry. Aquaculture 258, 470–478.

Wu, C.-C., Liu, C.-H., Chang, Y.-P., Hsieh, S.-L., (2010): Effects of Hot-water Extract of Toona Sinensis on Immune Response and Resistance to Aeromonas Hydrophila in Oreochromis Mossambicus. Fish Shellfish Immunol. 29, 258–263.

Wu, Z.-F., Zhu, B., Wang, Y., Lu, C., Wang, G.-X., (2011): In Vivo Evaluation of Anthelmintic Potential of Medicinal Plant Extracts against Dactylogyrus Intermedius (Monogenea) in Goldfish (Carassius auratus). Parasitol. Res. 108, 1557–1563.

Yuan, C., Li, D., Chen, W., Sun, F., Wu, G., Gong, Y., Tang, J., Shen, M., Han, X., (2007): Administration of a Herbal Immunoregulation Mixture Enhances Some Immune Parameters in Carp (Cyprinus carpio). Fish Physiol. Biochem. 33, 93–101.

Yin, G.; Ardó, L.; Thompson, K.D.; Adams, A.; Jeney, Z.and Jeney, G. (2009): Chinese Herbs (Astragalus Radix and Ganoderma Lucidum) Enhance Immune Response of Carp, Cyprinus Carpio, and Protection against Aeromonas Hydrophila. Fish Shellfish Immunol 26:140–145.

Xueqin, J., Kania, P.W. and Buchmann, K. (2012): Comparative Effects of Four Feed Types on White Spot Disease Susceptibility and Skin Immune Parameters in Rainbow Trout, Oncorhynchus mykiss (Walbaum). Journal of Fish Diseases 35, 127–135.

Xu, D. (2010): Tests of the Potential Vaccine against "Ich" ¯ the Dreaded "White-spot" Disease that Plagues Fish in Commercial Fish Farms, Public Aquariums, pet fish Retail Outlets, and Home Aquariums ¯ are Raising Hopes for Finally Controlling the Disease, Scientists Reported at the 240th National Meeting of the American Chemical Society.

Xu, D.; Klesius, P.H. and Shelby, R.A. (2004): Immune Response and Host Protection of Channel Catfish, Ictalurus Punctatus (Rafinesque) against Ichthyophthirius Multifiliis after Immunization with live Theronts and Sonicated Trophonts. Journal of Fish Diseases. 27:135-141.

Zhan, T. and Braunbeck, T. (1995): Cytotoxic Effects of Sub-lethal Concentrations of Malachite Green in Isolated Hepatocytes from Rainbow Trout (Oncorhynchus mykiss), Toxicol. In Vitro 9 (5) 729–741.

Index

A

A. indica, 31
Aluminum phosphide 80
Andhra Pradesh, 24
Animal manure, 78
Animals, 78
  ectoparasites, 77
Arthropods, 4
Arvicanthis niloticus, 121
Azadirachta indica, 71

B

Banana (*Musa* spp), 21
Bio control agents in integrated pest management, 136-159
Biorationale strategies for management of phytoparasitic nematodes associated with banana, 21-47
  association of nematodes with other microorganisms, 25
  botanicals method of nematode management, 31-33
    plant extracts, 32-33
    powder form, 32
    soil application, 31-32
    community analysis of nematodes associated with
      banana, 25-26
      other crops, 26-27
  cultural control method of nematode management, 29-30
    biofumigation, 29-30
  influence of different seasons on plant parasitic nematode population, 27-29
  introduction, 21-22
  nematode association in banana, 22-24
    international level, 22-23
    national level, 23-24
  physical method of nematode management, 33-35
    bioagents (*Purpureocillium lilacinum*), 34
    effect on nematodes infecting banana, 34-35
    effect on nematodes infecting other crops, 35
    hot water treatment, 33
    organic soil amendments - neem cake, 33-34
  symptoms of damage and yield loss caused by nematodes, 24-25
Brassica juncea, 29

C

C. odorata, 32
CAT, 6
CDC, 5, 50
Chiranjeevi, Ch., 136
Chromolaena, 33
Control of parasitic infections in marine fish, 160-188
  introduction, 160-162
  mechanical treatment of fish parasitic infections, 163
    argulosis, 163
    ascorbic acid (Vitamin C) as immunostimulant, 168-169
    biological control of fish parasites (life against life), 172-175
    biosecurity in aquaculture (FAO, 2003), 178-179
    disinfectants, 179-180
    immunostimulants for fish, 166-167
    lerneosis, 163-164
    medicinal plants, 175
      as immunostimulants for fish, 177-178

used for treatment fish parasitic infection, 175-177

probiotics for fish, 164-165

proper attention to food sources, 180-181

quarantine, 179

sanitation, 180

spirulina as immunostimulant, 167-168

vaccination against

Cryptobia salmositica, 171

Discocotyle sagittata (Monogenea), 172

Ichthyophthiriasis, 171

Loma salmonae, 172

parasites of fish, 169-171

yeasts as probiotic for fish, 165-166

new trends in control of parasitic fish infections, 162

flushing method, 163

heat method, 163

physical treatment of fish parasites, 162

transferring method, 165

Coxiella burntii, 64

D

Desoky, Abd El-Aleem Saad Soliman, 48, 61

Dorylaimus innovates, 28

E

Ecto-parasites of farm animals, 61-135

control of ectoparasites in farm animal, 78

animal manure, 78

chemical control, 78-79

flies larvae, 79

mechanical control, 78

animals buffalo and sheep mange, 78

animals, 78

buffalo lice and cattle ticks, 78

sheep fleas, 78

control studies, 70, 124

control of animal ectoparasites, 70

Khater, 71

Sargison, 70

Thomas and Niels, 70

Wall, 70

Wichai and Ching, 70

control of ectoparasites in animal, 124

ectoparasites on the animal body surface regions, 124

in animals, 124-125

– sheep, 126

control of manure ectoparasites, 126

chemical control, 126

fly larvae, 126

mechanical control, 126

control of sarcoptic mange, 125

in buffaloes, 125

data treatment and statistical by analyzed, 80-84

general survey of pests inhabiting farm animals in the area of study, 76

flies and mosquitoes, 121

flies, 76

general survey of pests inhabiting farm animals in the area of study, 121

mosquitoes, 77

rodents, 121

rodents, 76

introduction, 61-62

investigation protocol and control methods, 76

objectives, 62

observations ad elucidation: control of mange mites: sheep, 105-108

observations ad elucidation: control of manure ectoparasites, 109

chemical control, 109-111

fly larvae, 111-112

mechanical control, 109

observations and elucidation, 84
- control of mange mites, 104
  - buffaloes, 104-105
- control studies, 84
  - control of ectoparasites in animal, 84-87
- in animals, 87-104

population density of ectoparasites, 122
- ectoparasite on animals, 122
- ectoparasites collected from animal manure, 122-123
- ectoparasites on rodents, 123-124

research on ecto-parasites and farm animals, 63
- ecological studies, 63
- general survey of pests inhabiting farm animals in the area of study, 63
  - Byford, 63
  - Elmaged Abo, 63
  - Peter, 63
  - Meerburg, 63

rodent control, 71, 79, 113, 126
- attractant and repellent baits, 71
  - Boeke, 72
  - Jacobson, 71
  - Khan, 72
  - Witmer, 72
- rodenticides, 72
  - Ahmed, 76
  - Asran, 72
  - Donlan, 75
  - Gill, 73
  - Helal and Zedan, 72
  - Kaur and Prashad, 76
  - Moran, 73
  - Prakash, 75
  - Shehab, 74
  - Twigg, 74
- under field conditions, 80, 115, 127
  - acceptability of rodent species for two attractive baits, 80, 115, 127
  - toxicity by aluminum phosphide, 115-120, 80, 127
  - toxicity of rodenticides, 80, 115, 127
- under laboratory conditions, 79, 113, 126
  - attractant and repellent baits, 79
  - attractive baits, 113
  - attractive baits, 126-127
  - evaluation of two rodenticides, 114-115
  - evaluation of two rodenticides, 127
  - repellent baits, 113-114
  - repellent baits, 127
  - toxicity of two-anticoagulant rodenticides to certain rodent species, 79-80

survey and population density of animal ectoparasites, 77
- animal manure pests, 77
- animals ectoparasites, 77
- associated rodents in animal-farm, 77

survey and population of ectoparasites, 63
- animal ectoparasites, 63
  - Corn, 66
  - Harris, 63-64
  - Hussain, 64
  - Kaal, 64
  - Milnes, 64
  - Muhammad, 65-66
  - Ramzan, 66
  - Tasawar, 66
  - Tefera and Abebe, 65
- rodent ectoparasites, 67
  - Baker, 67
  - Durden, 68
  - El-kady, 67
  - Embarak, 67
  - Kia, 69
  - Lance, 68

Nava, 68
Omudu and Ati, 69
Shaya and Rafinejad, 69
survey of ectoparasites, 121
in manure of animals, 121
on animal body surfaces, 121
on rodent species body surface, 121
Eruca sativa, 30
Esakkimuthu, M, 21

F

Farm animals, 61-135
Field release and evaluation techniques of bio control agents in integrated pest management, 136-159
accretive release, 140
experimental evaluation methods include qualitative and quantitative methods, 145-148
– methods for evaluation of natural enemies, 145
field application, 143-144
– release of entomopathogenic viruses, 142-143
general rules for releasing biological control agents, 137-138
inoculative release, 139
inundative release, 139
methods of release of biocontrol agents, 140-142
– – releasing bioagents, 140
need for evaluation of natural enemies, 144
principles of biological control, 138
procedures of biological control, 137
steps followed prior to release of bioagents, 138
supplementary release, 140
time span in biological control, 138

H

Helicotylenchus sp., 22

I

Integrated pest management (IPM), 59, 136-159
Integrated pest management for rodent in buildings, 48-53
introduction, 48-49
method of treatment, 50
biological control, 51
chemical control, 51
conditions to be available before rodent control, 51
using rodenticides, 52
mechanical control, 50
destruction of burrows, 51
using traps, 50-51

K

Karnataka, 21
Kerala, 24

L

Lake Ianthe, 13
Lake Poerua, 13
Lantana camara, 31

M

M. hapla, 30
M. incognita, 23, 24
M. javanica, 23
Madhumathi, T., 136
Maharashtra, 21
Management of phytoparasitic nematodes, 21-47
Marine fish, 160-188
Meloidogyne sp., 22
Mishra, V.K., 54
Mishra, Varucha, 54
MRI, 6

N

Neem cake, 33-34
Neglected Tropical Diseases (NTDs), 4
Nicotiana glauca, 57
Nimisha, A.M., 21
Nisha, M.S., 21

O

Osmana, Hussien A.M., 160

P

P. coffeae, 23, 24
P. lilacinum, 34, 35
Parasite and parasitism, 1-20
  a fecal (stool) exam, also called an ova and parasite test (O & P), 5
  animal defenses, 8
    eyes, 9
    immune system, 9
    mouth, 9
    skin, 8-9
    stomach, 9
  blood smear, 6
  – tests, 5
  co-speciation, 11
  definitions, 1
  diagnosis of parasitic diseases, 5-6
  diseases, 4
  ecology, 12
    adaptation,1 3
    alphabetic list of parasite, 16-20
    diversity ecology, 12-13
    quantitative ecology, 12
    roles in ecosystems, 14
    significance, 15-16
    transmission, 13-14
  endoscopy/colonoscopy, 5
  entamoeba histolytica, 2
    ectoparasites, 4
    helminth, arthropod, and plant parasites, 3
    parasitic infections, 4
  evolutionary aspects, 10-11
  insect defenses, 9
  parasite, 1-2
  parasitism, 6-7
  plant defenses, 10
  serology, 5-6
  types of parasites, 7-8
Parasitic infections in marine fish, 160-188
Phytoparasitic nematodes associated with banana, 21-47
Polypax spinulosa, 121
Potato (*Solanum tuberosum*), 57
Protozoa, 2
PRRs, 9
Pseudomonas fluorescence, 30
Purpureocillium lilacinum, 34

R

R. similis, 23, 34
Raju, S. Krishnam, 136
Rani, D. Sudha, 136
Raphanus sativus, 30
Rats and mice (SRC), 48
Rattus rattus alexandrines, 76
Red Queen hypotheses, 13
Rodenticides, 80

S

Sida acuta, 33
Singh, N.N., 54
Solanum lycopersicon, 57
Sour orange (*Citrus aurantifolia*), 32

T

T. patula, 31
Thonus garhwaliensis, 28
Tomato, 57
Tomato pin worm, *Tuta absoluta* (meyrick) and their management, 54-60
  global spread, 55-56
  host range, 57
  identification, 57
  introduction, 54-55
  management strategies, 59
  nature of damage and symptoms, 58
  reason for spread and distribution, 56-57
Tuta absoluta, 54

U

Upper Egypt Governorates, 22

V

VOCs, 30

W

Wolbachia bacteria, 11

Z

Zaki, Mona S., 160